Therapeutic Recreation in the Community: An Inclusive Approach

2nd Edition

Marcia Jean Carter
&
Stephen P. LeConey

Sagamore Publishing, Inc.
Champaign, Illinois

Book and cover design: Michelle R. Dressen

ISBN: 1-57167-513-2
Printed in the United States.
Library of Congress Catalog Card Number: 2004101734

Sagamore Publishing
804 N. Neil Street
Champaign, IL 61820
www.sagamorepub.com

10 9 8 7 6 5 4 3 2 1

TABLE OF CONTENTS

PREFACE

The second edition of Therapeutic Recreation in the Community: An Inclusive Approach reflects the changing and evolving nature of recreation and health care services. A number of social, economic, and political directives and technological advancements have fostered recreation in the community for all individuals. Due in part to a rising awareness of disability rights, concern for controlling escalating health care costs, and legislation that promotes accessible options, professionals are designing supports and services that embrace opportunities for individuals to be fully included in recreation experiences. Thus our intention is to provide and overview of the process and procedures professionals use to design programs to fully incorporate individuals with disabilities in community recreation. The revised edition is designed for professionals in recreation, therapeutic recreation, and related health and human service professions who provide recreation programs and services to all community residents. The text is useful to students enrolled in introductory course work in recreation, therapeutic recreation, and courses with a focus of inclusive recreation.

The features that make this text useful to professionals and students include (1) illustrations and resource materials presently used in public agencies to effect inclusion, (2) application of the APIE process (assessment, planning, implementation, and evaluation) to the development of inclusive service options, (3) content and strategies for training professionals to accommodate persons with disabilities in recreation, (4) review of participant needs and implications for managing these needs during inclusion experiences, and (5) management and leadership recommendations to facilitate reasonable accommodations during program planning and delivery. The text is comprised of an introduction that overviews the directives and advancements resulting in inclusion. This is followed by six chapters: The first four chapters present elements from the APIE process and the use of the APIE process to develop inclusive programs; chapters five and six focus on participant needs and how to manage and motivate participants during inclusive experiences. The final section is a case study that uses the forms presented in the text to apply the APIE process. Figures within the text are field-based documents and resources that may be replicated by professionals to use during their agency programs and while training professionals. Illustrations represent the spectrum of staffing patterns and organizations found in the public sector.

The interpretations and implications of legislation and court actions are ongoing. Every situation like every individual is unique. Each is assessed to identify the most effective accommodation. The authors encourage an initial positive response to requests for accommodation. This is followed by application of the best practices reviewed throughout the text to present reasonable support, assistance, and accommodations during inclusion programs. Application of this approach prevents undue economic, administrative, or programmatic burden on the agency yet assures all participants options in community recreation.

ACKNOWLEDGMENTS

To the professionals and participants who have and who will share in the benefits of inclusive programming we extend our appreciation and encouragement.

We are also appreciative to those who have shared their expertise and resources:

Cincinnati Recreation Commission, Cincinnati, Ohio
City of Boulder Parks and Recreation, EXPAND, Boulder, Colorado
City of Fort Collins Recreation Programs and Services for People with Disabilities, ARO, Ft. Collins, Colorado
City of St. Petersburg, Therapeutic Recreation, St. Petersburg, Florida
City of Reno, Parks, Recreation, and Community Services
Fairfax County Community and Recreation Services, Therapeutic Recreation Services, Fairfax County, Maryland
Fox Valley Special Recreation Association, North Aurora, Illinois
Howard County Recreation and Parks, Columbia, Maryland
Maryland-National Capital Park and Planning Commission, Prince George's County, Maryland
Northern Suburban Special Recreation Association, Northbrook, Illinois
Therapeutic Recreation Division, Cincinnati Recreation Commission, Cincinnati, Ohio

Special consideration is given to our colleagues, friends, and families who have been with us in spirit and given their time and support to this project: John and Peg Carter, John, Nancy, Cory, Zachary, and Nathan Carter; and William and Lucia LeConey, Beth, Andrew and Sarah LeConey.

Marcia Jean Carter
Stephen P. LeConey

INTRODUCTION

Inclusion

The inclusive community recreation movement took root in the early 1980s (Anderson & Heyne, 2000). The catalyst promoting the inclusion of people with disabilities in community life is the Americans with Disabilities Act (ADA) (Devine & Kotowski, 1999). This law and other federal legislation require agencies to accommodate (unless it can be proven the accommodation is unreasonable) people with disabilities in leisure programs. "Inclusion refers to a philosophy that...takes a proactive approach to including all people in all programs and services" (Montgomery & Kazin, 2003, p. 1). ADA encourages the provision of programs and services in the most integrated setting. The word inclusion is "associated with the concept of integrating persons with disabilities into general services" (Montgomery & Kazin, 2003, p. 1).

The inclusion of people with disabilities in community life is perceived as beneficial for persons with and without disabilities (Devine & Wilhite, 2000). Participants with disabilities expand their leisure repertoires, acquire new leisure skills, experience feelings of success and increased self-confidence and develop friendships (Anderson & Heyne, 2000). Purported benefits realized by persons without disabilities include gaining an understanding about disabilities, altered attitudes toward persons with disabilities, appreciation for individual differences, and learning ways to interact with people with disabilities (Anderson & Heyne, 2000; Block & Conatser, 2002).

A number of challenges are found with agency readiness to make accommodations. Administrative and programmatic issues arise as agencies prepare to comply with key provisions of Title II of the ADA that states no qualified person with a disability shall, on the basis of a disability, be excluded from participation in or be denied the benefits of the service or program (Cincinnati Recreation Commission [CRC], n.d.). A primary intent of this publication is to present administrative and programmatic practices that facilitate inclusive experiences. The text is helpful to students becoming familiar with inclusion and professionals with and without recreation and therapeutic recreation experience working in agencies that offer inclusive programming. Administrators and direct service staff will find information and resources to use in management and delivery of services. With this publication, we hope all professionals will feel more comfortable developing a support system for inclusion.

Legislation

A number of social, economic, and political directives have fostered recreation in the community for all individuals. Due in part to a rising awareness of disability rights, concern for controlling escalating health care costs, and legislation that promotes options and accessibility, professionals are devoting resources to programs and services for all individuals. Legislation tends to formalize social, economic, and political initiatives. A number of laws, their reauthorizations and amendments, guide professionals as recreation services are delivered. These directives led to the development of supports and services that embrace diversity and opportunities for individuals to be fully included in recreation experiences.

A number of laws passed since the late 1960s form the basis for provision by public and private agencies of programs and services that are accessible, supportive, and accommodate alternative experiences with individuals with disabilities.

PL 90-480, the Architectural Barriers Act of 1968, amended twice since, requires any building or facility constructed in whole or part by public monies to be accessible and usable by persons with physical handicaps.

As early as 1954, the first Vocational Rehabilitation Act was passed to rehabilitate veterans with disabilities. The intent of the act was broadened, and earlier acts were strengthened with passage of the Rehabilitation Act of 1973, PL 93-112. One section, Section 502, created the Architectural and Transportation Barriers Compliance Board to ensure compliance with PL 90-480. Another section, Section 504, known as the discrimination section, required any programs or activities receiving federal money to allow participation by qualified handicapped individuals. Reauthorizations and amendments continue to promote the inclusion of recreation as a way of enhancing quality of life. These changes also support newer legislative pieces that promote natural supports and informed choices in all aspects of everyday life.

A number of laws affecting educational opportunities for children with disabilities included recreation and therapeutic recreation as related services (supportive services that assist children with disabilities to benefit from special education). As early as 1967, PL 90-170, Education for Handicapped Children Act, monies were made available to train recreation professionals to work with children in a variety of recreational settings. The Education for All Handicapped Children Act of 1975 (PL 94-142) extended educational rights to school-age children in the least restrictive environment, including recreation as a related service. When the law was amended in 1990, nomenclature was changed, and the law was entitled Individuals with Disabilities Education Act (IDEA) (PL 101-476) and the term therapeutic recreation was added to recreation (Smith, Austin, & Kennedy, 2001). A number of reauthorizations and amendments have extended the benefits of the law to younger children and their families including 1) planning for transitions into adult life, 2) development of community recreation skills, 3) use of assistive technology, and 4) the design of behavior support plans to support the individual education plan (IEP) (Lawson, Coyle, & Ashton-Shaeffer, 2001). Allowable (for funding) related services are assessment of leisure functioning, therapeutic recreation services, recreation programs in schools and community agencies, and leisure education (Ashton-Shaeffer, Johnson, & Bullock, 2000).

Commencing with legislation in 1963, PL 88-164 Mental Retardation Facilities and Community Mental Health Centers Construction Act, funding through grants became available to state agencies to provide individuals with developmental disabilities opportunities to be included in the community (Bullock & Mahon, 2000). Reauthorizations and amendments to the Developmental Disabilities Assistance and Bill of Rights Act of 1990, PL 101-496, promote self-determination, employment, and community inclusion with individuals with developmental disabilities and their families through culturally competent services and supports.

Assistive technology is a key to resources and opportunities in the community (Bullock & Mahon, 2000). PL 100-407, Technology-Related Assistance for Individuals with Disabilities Act of 1988, provided financial resources to states to establish statewide programs of technology-related assistance (devices that improve functional capabilities). Reauthorizations provide loans to persons who purchase assistive technology devices or services in order to make living more accessible and set up state-wide information and referral centers to support technology requests (Dattilo, 2002).

Americans with Disabilities Act (ADA) of 1990, PL 101-336, signed into law on July 26, 1990 is referred to as the civil rights act for individuals with disabilities (Dattilo, 2002). This law extended the mandates of earlier legislation (PL 90-480 and PL 93-112) on public access to the private sector. The intent of the law is to support equal opportunities in employment, government services, public transit, public accommodations, and telecommunications. Although the United States Supreme Court continually interprets the definition of disability, the initial law defined a person with a disability as one who has a physical or mental impairment that limits substantially one or more major life functions; has a record of such impairment; or is regarded as having the impairment (Dattilo, 2002). If an individual meets essential eligibility requirements to participate, with or without reasonable accommodations, the service, program, or activity is to be made available (Dattilo, 2002). Reasonable accommodations include changing rules, policies and practices; removing architectural, transportation, and communication barriers; and, providing auxiliary aids and services (Bullock & Mahon, 2000; Dattilo,

2002). If an adjustment like building an accessible entrance or paying for interpreters over an extended time period is too costly, disruptive, or would fundamentally alter the nature of the service, program, or activity, an agency may experience undue financial or administrative burdens and may seek alternative ways to provide the experience (Dattilo, 2002; Smith, et al., 2001). A number of standards interpreting the intent of this law have been developed. The Americans with Disabilities Act Accessibility Guidelines (ADAAG) for Buildings and Facilities further define physical accessibility criteria of the American National Standards Institute and the Uniform Federal Accessibility Standards. The U. S. Access Board (www.access-board.gov) prepared accessibility guidelines for recreation facilities, outdoor developed areas (golf courses, pools, amusement rides, for example) and playgrounds (www.cpsc.gov) (Hendy, 2001; McGovern, 2002; Thompson, Hudson & Bowers, 2002). Future legislation is likely to be impacted by ADA as legal interpretations continue to evolve.

A piece of legislation signed into law by President Clinton on August 21, 1996, the Health Insurance Portability and Accountability Act (HIPAA) guarantees the security and privacy of health information (Hellerstein, 1999). Henceforth professionals must be cautious about making health information individually identifiable: A name, address, employer, birth date, social security number or e-mail address (for example) are elements of a verbal, written, or electronic communication that might inadvertently disclose a person as having a particular health situation. Professionals must make a reasonable effort to use only the minimum necessary amount of protected health information in order to provide treatment. Consequently a discussion with a volunteer or in a public area about a participant's medications or diagnostic label is probably inappropriate; an exception might be to obtain or use information from the individual support or behavior plan in the provision of health care or behavioral intervention (since clarification of HIPAA regulations is ongoing, staff compliance with the standards is a recommended agency training topic). Collectively, legislation impacts programs and services by encouraging access, support and alternatives that embrace diversity while protecting the consumer from undue exposure. Professionals are challenged to remove participation barriers while protecting the privacy and confidentiality of the consumer.

Terminology

A number of terms have been used to describe concepts of mutual acceptance in the community. Normalization, mainstreaming, integration, and inclusion each at various times has described the advocacy effort to gain access to recreation, education, employment, and social experiences by individuals with disabilities. Inclusion suggests reciprocal relationships and an assessment and identification of supports and skills essential to successful engagement. Inclusion requires a demand response service system with the ability to provide accommodations and support anywhere at any time so all programs and services are fully accessible.

One professional organization adopted a position statement (NRPA, 1999) that embraces the benefits of inclusive leisure services and describes the concepts encompassed by this frame of reference: Key tenets are a right to leisure for all; enhancement in quality of life; support, assistance and accommodations; and barrier removal (see figure on page 6). The term inclusive leisure services refers to opportunities that include individuals with diverse experiences and skills (Dattilo, 2002). Support, assistance and accommodations recognize individual preferences and choices and occur naturally.

"The words used to talk about disabilities are constantly changing" (Getskow & Konczal, 1996, p. 43). Language tends to label, categorize, and shape our beliefs. Using terms like "disabled people" or "blind individual" tends to categorize people with disabilities as all being similar and emphasizes the negative "dis" rather than the positive "ability". People-first language places the person first, "person with a disability," so the individual is more important than the disability, "person who is blind" (Bullock & Mahon, 2000; Getskow & Konczal, 1996). People-first language is, therefore, ability-oriented and projects positive beliefs and attitudes (Dattilo, 2002). Sensitive terminology takes into consideration cultural preferences. Consequently, in some instances, as with individuals with hearing losses, persons may refer to themselves as being from the "deaf community". Terms may also reflect the nature of the setting; to illustrate, patients go to see doctors and are treated in hospitals while customers have memberships in private clubs. Word choices like "person confined to a wheelchair" vs. "person using a wheelchair" project images and describe our beliefs about human capacities. Appropriate terminology today may not be the preferred language of the future. Regardless, awareness and sensitivity are the first steps toward modeling appropriate examples.

NATIONAL RECREATION AND PARK ASSOCIATION POSITION STATEMENT ON INCLUSION

Adopted by the NRPA Board of Trustees as an NRPA Policy, October 24, 1999

Diversity is a cornerstone of our society and culture and thus should be celebrated. Including people with disabilities in the fabric of society strengthens the community and its individual members. The value of inclusive leisure experiences in enhancing the quality of life for all people, with and without disabilities, cannot be overstated. As we broaden our understanding and acceptance of differences among people through shared leisure experiences, we empower future generations to build a better place for all to live and thrive.

Inclusive leisure experiences encourage and enhance opportunities for people of varying abilities to participate and interact in life's activities together with dignity. It also provides an environment that promotes and fosters physical, social and psychological inclusion of people with diverse experiences and skill levels. Inclusion enhances individuals' potential for full and active participation in leisure activities and experiences. Additionally, the benefits of this participation may include:

- providing positive recreational experiences which contribute to the physical, mental, social, emotional, and spiritual growth and development of every individual;
- fostering peer and intergenerational relationships that allow one to share affection, support, companionship and assistance; and
- developing community support and encouraging attitudinal changes to reflect dignity, self-respect and involvement within the community.

Purpose

The purpose of the National Recreation and Park Association (NRPA) Position Statement on Inclusion is to encourage all providers of park, recreation, and leisure services to provide opportunities in settings where people of all abilities can recreate and interact together.

This document articulates a commitment to the leisure process and the desired outcomes. Accordingly, the NRPA Position Statement on Inclusion encompasses these broad concepts and beliefs:

Right to Leisure

- The pursuit of leisure is a condition necessary for human dignity and well-being.
- Leisure is a part of a healthy lifestyle and a productive life.
- Every individual is entitled to the opportunity to express unique interests and pursue, develop and improve talents and abilities.
- People are entitled to opportunities and services in the most inclusive setting.
- The right to choose from the full array of recreation opportunities offered in diverse settings and environments and requiring different levels of competency should be provided.

Quality of Life

- People grow and develop throughout the life span.
- Through leisure an individual gains an enhanced sense of competence and self-direction.
- A healthy leisure lifestyle can prevent ill-

ness and promote wellness.
- The social connection with one's peers plays a major role in his/her life satisfaction.
- The opportunity to choose is an important component in one's quality of life; individual choices will be respected.

Support, Assistance and Accommodations

- Inclusion is most effective when support, assistance and accommodations are provided.
- Support, assistance and accommodations can and should be responsive to people's needs and preferences.
- Support, assistance and accommodations should create a safe and fun environment, remove real and artificial barriers to participation, and maximize not only the independence but also the interdependence of the individual. People want to be self-sufficient.
- Support, assistance and accommodations may often vary and are typically individualized. Types of support, assistance and accommodations include, but are not limited to: qualified staff, adaptive equipment, alternative formats for printed or audio materials, trained volunteers, or flexibility in policies and program rules.

Barrier Removal

- Environments should be designed to encourage social interaction, "risk-taking," fun, choices and acceptance

that allow for personal accomplishment in a cooperative context.
- Physical barriers should be eliminated to facilitate full participation by individuals with disabilities.
- Attitudinal barriers in all existing and future recreation services should be removed or minimized through education and training of personnel (staff, volunteers, students, and/or community at-large).

The National Recreation and Park Association is dedicated to the four inclusion concepts of:

- *Right to Leisure* (for all individuals)
- *Quality of Life* (enhancements through leisure experiences)
- *Support, Assistance and Accommodations*
- *Barrier Removal*

in all park, recreation and leisure services. Properly fostered, inclusion will happen naturally. Over time, inclusion will occur with little effort and with the priceless reward of an enlightened community. Encouraged in the right way, inclusion is the right thing to plan for, implement and celebrate.

Therapeutic Recreation Process

"Delivering therapeutic recreation services in community settings has been particularly successful when the therapeutic recreation process is applied" (LeConey, Devine, Bunker, & Montgomery, 2000, p. 70). The therapeutic recreation process (TR process) of assessment, planning, implementation, and evaluation (APIE) is viewed as an accountability model to guide the design of programs and services that realize individual participant objectives (Peterson & Stumbo, 2000). The TR process is a systematic method of planning and delivering programs and services. Pre-determined outcomes are achieved through specific experiences identified prior to service delivery. The programs and services that best meet participant needs and enable participants to achieve predetermined outcomes are implemented. The use of this process allows professionals "to individualize within recreation programs designed specifically for people with disabilities and to systematically develop support plans for inclusive recreation programs" (LeConey, et al., 2000, p. 71).

The text is designed to aid in the planning of community recreation programs and services with all individuals. Successful components of recreation program design are assessment, planning, implementation, and evaluation (APIE). The implementation of the APIE process is useful to initiate or redevelop programs and services to achieve individual support plan outcomes.

The demand for community recreation services by individuals with disabilities has recently experienced an increase and is likely to continue (Devine & McGovern, 2001). Persons with and without professional preparation in therapeutic recreation and recreation are called upon to deliver accountable individualized programs and services. A second function of the text is to present resources helpful during professional development whether that be staff orientations, in-services, or through personal access (Internet, professional libraries).

The APIE process is the framework for the text content and organization. Consideration is given to the management of programs and services and delivery of programs or direct services. The initial section presents community and agency assessments and includes topics like reasonable accommodations, accessibility, financial resources, policies and procedures, quality service indicators, and risk management. Planning is the responsibility of properly prepared and trained professionals: Because staff and volunteers are integral to delivery of quality programs and services, the second section is devoted to personnel resources. Marketing and advocacy are essential requisites to program implementation and are addressed in the third section. Individualization of the APIE process occurs as direct services are planned, implemented, and evaluated; the next portion of the text. Closing sections consider participant characteristics and needs and strategies to motivate and manage consumers. These sections present information on how to apply the APIE process so programs and services accommodate consumer choices and abilities while addressing individual needs.

References

Anderson, L., & Heyne, L. (2000). A statewide needs assessment using focus groups: Perceived challenges and goals in providing inclusive recreation services in rural communities. *Journal of Park and Recreation Administration, 18*(4), 17-37.

Ashton-Shaeffer, C., Johnson, D. E., & Bullock, C. C. (2000). A survey of the current practice of recreation as a related service. *Therapeutic Recreation Journal, 34*(4), 323-334.

Block, M. E., & Conatser, P. (2002). Adapted aquatics and inclusion. *JOPERD, 73*(5), 31-34.

Bullock, C. C., & Mahon, M. J. (2000). *Introduction to recreation services for people with disabilities a person-centered approach* (2nd ed.). Champaign, IL: Sagamore Publishing.

Cincinnati Recreation Commission. (n.d.). *Understanding the ADA: Our responsibility to assure accessible programs.* (Available from Cincinnati Recreation Commission, Division of Therapeutic Recreation, 805 Central Avenue, Cincinnati, Ohio 45202).

Dattilo, J. (2002). *Inclusive leisure services responding to the rights of people with disabilities* (2nd ed.). State College, PA: Venture Publishing, Inc.

Devine, M. A., & Kotowski, L. (1999). Inclusive leisure services: Results of a national survey of park and recreation departments. *Journal of Park and Recreation Administration, 17*(4), 56-72.

Devine, M. A., & McGovern, J. (2001). Inclusion of individuals with disabilities in public park and recreation programs: Are agencies ready? *Journal of Park and Recreation Administration, 19*(4), 60-82.

Devine, M. A., & Wilhite, B. (2000). The meaning of disability: Implications for Inclusive leisure services for youth with and without disabilities. *Journal of Park and Recreation Administration, 18*(3), 35-52.

Getskow, V., & Konczal, D. (1996). *Kids with special needs information and activities to promote awareness and understanding.* Santa Barbara, CA: The Learning Works, Inc.

Hellerstein, D. (1999). HIPPA's impact. *Health Management Technology, 20*(3), 10-12, 14-15.

Hendy, T. (2001). The Americans With Disabilities Act insures the right of every child to play. *Parks & Recreation, 36*(4), 108-117.

Lawson, L. M., Coyle, C. P., & Ashton-Shaeffer, C. (2001). *Therapeutic recreation in special education and IDEA for the future.* Alexandria, VA: American Therapeutic Recreation Association.

LeConey, S., Devine, M. A., Bunker, H., & Montgomery, S. (2000). Utilizing the therapeutic recreation process in community settings: The case of Sue. *Parks & Recreation, 35*(5), 70-77.

McGovern, J. (2002). U.S. Access Board adopts recreation facility accessibility guidelines. *Parks & Recreation, 37*(6), 44-49.

Montgomery, S., & Kazin, A. (2003, March 17). Providing inclusive recreation opportunities: The Cincinnati model. *National Center on Accessibility.* Retrieved from http://www.ncaonline.org/research/inclusion.htm.

National Recreation and Park Association. (1999). *Position statement on inclusion.* Asburn, VA: The Association.

Peterson, C. A., & Stumbo, N. J. (2000). *Therapeutic recreation program design principles and procedures* (3rd ed.). Boston, MA: Allyn and Bacon.

Smith, R. W., Austin, D. R., & Kennedy, D. W. (2001). *Inclusive and special recreation opportunities for persons with disabilities* (4th ed.). Boston, MA: McGraw Hill Higher Education.

Thompson, D., Hudson, S. D., & Bowers, L. (2002). Play areas and the ADA providing access and opportunities for all children. *JOHPERD, 73*(2), 37-41.

CHAPTER 1

Defining the Service:
Assessing the Community and Agency

Each community is unique with regard to its leisure services, resources, and needs. This uniqueness is determined through assessment. Assessment through observation (time sampling), interview (door-to-door canvassing), and written response (paper-pencil checklists, questionnaires, or standardized instruments) identifies and gathers information about the community, agency, and individuals eligible to receive services. Assessment enables objective decisions about replacing current services, altering services, designing new services, or maintaining status quo. As a result of completing the assessment phase of planning, a service scope, plan of operation, and programmatic boundaries are determined.

Community assessments gather information on a number of features: economics, personnel, socio-cultural influences, demographics, geographic elements, standards, ordinances, laws, politics, protocols, trends, traditions, technology, transportation, networks, access, and advocacy. A systematic scan of all the forces impacting a community is an environmental scan or SWOT analysis (Wegner & Jarvi, 1999). Identification of strengths, weaknesses, opportunities, and threats provides basic information on the community's unique assets and participant needs. Information from this analysis is used to develop community master plans or strategic plans with vision, mission, and goal statements.

Community Services and Programs

Community involvement is essential to ensure satisfaction of residents' preferences while gaining commitment to support recreation and leisure with all participants. Awareness of the degree of programmatic, attitudinal, and physical accessibility within the community is assessed through a SWOT analysis. As a result of this analysis, program planners become aware of the supply and demand of supportive resources; opportunities and challenges to partner and network; priorities, expectations, standards governing service delivery; and, accessibility of features within the community. Most importantly, the potential users of leisure services are identified (Schleien, Ray, & Green, 1997).

Information on community services and programs is uncovered through visits to and collection of brochures from such places as the courthouse, library, schools, churches, human service agencies, government organizations, transportation centers, media centers, and other agencies offering leisure programs and services. On-line searches, review of newspapers, ordinances, legislation, council reports, census data, and land-use plans document past and present influences. Attendance during hearings, focus groups, or advocacy meetings helps the planner become familiar with community initiatives, growth patterns and trends, and precedents resulting from the community's history and traditions. The outcome of a community SWOT analysis is the identification of factors external to the agency that influence the delivery of agency recreation programs and services with all participants. Community information and resources helpful to a community-wide assessment are presented.

Community Information	Community Resources
Program supply and demand	Community directories, yellow pages, professional directories
Fiscal support	Community Chest, United Way, foundations, city budget, tax base, economic forecasts
Standards, trends, traditions	Governing codes, regulations, professional documents
Personnel resources	Talent pool from colleges, volunteer bureau, professional networks
Demography, geography	Climate data, census data, Chamber of Commerce, Visitor's Bureau, planning commissions
Political, legal, legislation	Party platforms, federal, state, local laws
Accessibility	ADAAG compliance, readiness survey
Transportation	Public, private, mass transit, usability, availability, and accessibility

Organizational Dynamics—Agency Assessment

A key to successful recreation programs and services with all individuals is adoption of an inclusive statement at the highest operating level (McGovern & Wetherald, 2001). The use of an inclusive mission statement like "provision of safe and enjoyable recreation for all participants" along with marketing strategies and collaboration with participants and parents/caregivers are recommended agency best practices (Klitzing, 2002; McGovern & Wetherald, 2001; Schleien, Germ, & McAvoy, 1996). Buy-in at the highest organizational level is promoted through an agency SWOT analysis. This process serves to assess the pulse of the agency while informing personnel within the agency of the rights of individuals with diverse interests. The structure and operation of the agency is assessed to ascertain the posture and commitment of the agency toward programs and services with all participants. Additionally, the resources available or needed to enhance or remodel offerings or create new services are determined. Gathering information is an ongoing process. Sources of information include annual reports, budget statements, personnel and operational manuals, charter and bylaws, board and committee minutes, and reports on programs and participants. Questions to consider during an agency SWOT analysis are organized into three convenient categories: administrative, program, staff.

Administrative:

- Does the agency mission statement promote the tenets of a professional position statement on inclusion?
- Is welcoming language evident in registration documents, advertising, program descriptions, and professional contacts?
- Has the governing board adopted an inclusion statement?
- What would be staff responses to an ADA awareness or readiness survey?
- Does the agency channel input from participants, caregivers, advocacy groups and consumer-oriented boards to appropriate personnel?
- What is the financial history and base of support? Are budgets sufficient to support successful inclusionary projects? Where are alternative funds available? Are sponsorships accessible?
- What are the agency policies with regard to participant confidentiality [interpretation of the Open Records Act, 1973; Freedom of Information Act (1958 amended 1974); and the Family Educational Rights and Privacy Act, 1976]?
- What agency policies govern sponsorships, partnerships, contracts, and scholarships?
- Does the environment promote social interaction and support or are there real or perceived architectural, transportation, policy and practice barriers?
- What are the agency policies on fees and charges?
- What are the agency policies on liability and standard of care?
- What are the agency policies that affect staffing matters like the use of part-time, contract, and volunteer staff?

Program:
- What programs and services are currently being offered and do they meet participant expectations and preferences?
- What is the physical condition of areas and facilities and the status of the ADAAG audit and/or renovation?
- Does scheduling of activities take into account transportation? What is the policy regarding agency-sponsored transportation?
- What is the condition and availability of program supplies and equipment? Are there available adaptive and assistive devices, technology, to augment communication and participation?
- Are available facilities physically, environmentally, and programmatically appropriate to diverse groups like individuals using wheelchairs, persons with visual or hearing impairments, and individuals with cognitive losses?
- Is there an ongoing assessment process and program monitoring and evaluation?
- What are the policies on program registration?
- What are the methods by which participants gain information on programs and services?
- What are the policies on health and safety? Are there protocols on dispensing medications, responding to emergencies and managing participant medication information? Do these practices comply with HIPAA?

Staff:
- Do professionals have experience, credentials, and opportunity for training regarding inclusive practices?
- Are staff given adequate administrative support and staff assistance?
- How are staff organized or what are the intra-relationships of staff among the units? Is staffing centralized or decentralized and is there a designated therapeutic recreation unit or person holding an administrative position that oversees the agency's inclusion efforts?
- What is the composition of the staff? Does this reflect the diversity of the community interests and needs?

As planners seek answers to these questions, a mission and business or strategic plan are developed. These documents become the benchmarks to assess the effectiveness and efficiency with which the agency embraces inclusive programs and services. A professional with expertise in therapeutic recreation, assessment, and strategic planning coordinates collection and analysis of information. During the process, agency employees and administrators become sensitized to the nature of "recreation with all persons" and the significance of their support as programs and services are developed to meet needs and preferences of all clientele.

Agency Statements and Planning Documents

An agency's mission states the reason for its existence and its service intent (O'Morrow & Carter, 1997). A mission statement that reflects services to people with disabilities commits the agency to support, assistance, accommodation, and barrier removal. Agency planning recognizes diverse interests and preferences while promoting reasonable accommodations. A mission statement is institutionalized at the highest organizational level by board policy. This policy states the agency vision, mission, goals and objectives, and describes action plans to include individuals with disabilities in programs and services. Policy statements articulate agency values or beliefs, service delivery model or philosophy, organizational structure, and steps or processes to implement inclusive services (Bullock & Mahon, 2000; O'Morrow & Carter, 1997; Schleien, et al., 1997).

Vision
After completing the SWOT analysis, the environment surrounding the delivery of programs and services is known to the planner. The next step in strategic planning is to draft a vision statement that describes where the agency would like to be or its preferred future with regard to satisfying the needs and preferences of all participants (Wegner & Jarvi, 1999). A shared vision focuses on results using welcoming language. A statement

maybe as brief as "The Recreation Department provides accessible programming and reasonable accommodations for persons of all abilities" (City of St. Petersburg, Therapeutic Recreation, 2003). A similar statement from the City of Boulder Parks and Recreation Department EXPAND program states: "Persons with disabilities have the right and should be given the opportunity to participate in recreation and leisure programs within their community" (Fitzgerald, 2003, p.1). Additional phrases in the vision statement may encourage individuals to make contact with the program or service in their respective neighborhood; acknowledge the intent of ADA; and, reference the desire to support and assist each person on an individual basis.

Mission

A mission statement is created from the vision statement, describes the values found in the vision statement, indicates the reason for the existence of programs, and states the concepts upon which programs are offered. For example, one mission statement outlines a purpose common to programs and services found in public, private, or non-profit agencies:

The mission of the Cincinnati Recreation Commission, Division of Therapeutic Recreation is to provide high-quality recreation and leisure experiences which contribute to the growth and development of individuals with disabilities. We provide these experiences through:

A. Support for inclusive participation in Recreation Commission programs and services. Assisting individuals with disabilities to participate in all programs and services provided by the Recreation Commission. Supporting inclusion through advocacy, training and coordination of services.

B. Developing and implementing therapeutic programs. In order to meet the needs of individuals with disabilities when inclusive options are not available, the Therapeutic Division may develop programs to supplement the programs/services offered by the Recreation Commission. (Cincinnati Recreation Commission, Division of Therapeutic Recreation, 2003).

The mission statement for ARO (Adaptive Recreation Opportunities) is also appropriate for various types of agencies: To provide community members with disabilities opportunities to participate in community recreation programs and services of their choice. We are advocates for health, fun and adventure (City of Fort Collins Recreation Programs and Services for People with Disabilities, n.d.).

Goals and Objectives

Goal statements are written to describe outcomes expressed in the mission statement. These are broad statements that lead to the development of measurable objectives. Goals and objectives are updated regularly and are written for the agency and each program or service delivered by the agency. Goals are derived from mission statements as illustrated by the City of Boulder EXPAND mission and goals (Fitzgerald, 2003):

To provide quality therapeutic recreation services which facilitate:
- The acquisition and improvement of recreation and leisure skills for people with disabilities, which enhance the development of physical and mental well being, as well as cognitive and social skills.
- Self-expression, creativity and playful behavior.
- Inclusive experiences that foster equal and harmonizing ties between people with and without disabilities.
- The education of the community and the education of city employees.
- Advocacy for the rights of individuals with disabilities within the community.
- New experiences and freedom of choice.

Objectives are statements that describe measurable outcomes and how the goal statements are to be realized. Each statement describes one outcome, the evaluation of which determines if goals are reached. Together goals and objectives are evaluation benchmarks that comprise the agency's quality improvement process. Objective statements are comprised of three segments: 1) action verbs that describe an observable and measurable outcome; 2) conditions or circumstances under which the outcome is to occur; and 3) performance level or criterion(a) that identifies whether the outcome is reached. This format is used with all objectives; individual support plans described in the Direct Services Chapter 4 illustrate how objectives are developed for programs and participants. An objective for an agency staff training might read: The agency will offer (action verb) three staff in-services on inclusionary practices (criterion) to administrators, direct service, and support personnel in the next FY (circumstances).

Action Plan

Goals and objectives lead to action plans that outline how the agency achieves its desired mission. To illustrate, the tasks undertaken to initiate or update the agency effort to integrate programs and services might include the following steps:

- Assess status of participant inclusion.
- Conduct ADA in-service for administrators.
- Assess awareness and sensitivity of agency personnel.
- Revise agency vision, mission, goals, objectives to reflect welcoming language and ADA compliance.
- Design agency training and education program.
- Revise budget to reflect reasonable accommodations.
- Develop transition plan to address physical accommodations.
- Revise registration and marketing procedures.
- Develop inclusion support process for direct services.
- Provide on-site technical support to individualize inclusion.
- Monitor, evaluate, and report inclusion outcomes.

Action plans are presented in PERT charts, networks, and system diagrams. These plans are developed, for example, during focus group meetings, retreats, in-services, and strategic planning meetings. Along with the vision, mission, goals and objectives, action plans are approved by the governing body. These documents guide policy-making, quality improvement efforts, budget decisions and interpret the agency's position on inclusion.

Financial Resources

A recognized barrier to inclusion is the cost of preparing for accommodations and providing supports and assistance (Devine & Kotowski, 1999; Schleien, et al., 1996). Lack of financial resources and staff constraints tend to be commonly faced challenges. Some barrier removal costs nothing, like flexibility in the application of policies (i.e., allowing a partner in the restroom or program area) or program rules (i.e., changing boundaries, numbers of players, or playing time). Others like training and hiring qualified staff and volunteers, purchasing adaptive equipment, modifying areas and facilities, and using alternative printed or audio materials to advertise programs and services do require additional financial expenditures. Some costs are directly related to the individual "seeking inclusion and the program being sought" (McGovern & Wetherald, 2001, p. 66). These expenses may not be known until the participant expresses an interest in the program or actually registers to take a lesson or complete a camp session, for example. Additional accommodation monies might include, but are not limited to: transportation, companions, interpreters, readers, program relocation or accessibility, retrofitting areas and facilities, marketing, research and development, assistive devices, participant assessment, personal services, home visits, collaboration, program fees and associated costs like appropriate apparel, use of consultants or inclusion specialists, and sensitivity or diversity awareness (Dattilo, 2002; Devine & Kotowski, 1999; Devine & McGovern, 2001).

A number of alternative funding sources might be accessed to finance accommodations: Yet, as noted in the next section, at times inclusion may result in undue economic burden; when this occurs, a number of factors are taken into account to ensure reasonable accommodations. Although the trend has been away from the use of property taxes to finance parks and recreation, taxation remains one option. Partnerships through formation of special districts or joint provision with schools offer avenues to maximize the use of existing resources while sharing expenses like staff training and the purchase of adaptive equipment. Collaboration with commercial agencies and vendors may result in cost reduction on equipment purchases and use (i.e., playground equipment or orthopedic and assistive devices) (Spencer, 2003). Advertising products of local vendors in agency brochures is one method of offsetting marketing costs associated with inclusion.

Additional user fees or a surcharge added to all registrations, entry fees, or special event tickets are options to generate operating funds. Individuals who donate to public agencies or entities that hold tax-exempt status under section 501 (c) (iii) of the Internal Revenue Code gain tax reductions: A parent or advisory group may seek this status, and as a result, receive monies to operate programs and services through contributions and grants. Donations like life insurance, gift annuities, bequests, and estates, also from individuals, may add physical resources to support program offerings. Business donations like product trial, public relations, and employee development add expertise and physical assistance that enhance services. Donation formats like gift catalogs, adopt-a-program, and check-off donations are used to supplement operating costs. Sponsorships may cover advertising fees, apparel, refreshments, interpreters, listening devices, and transportation. Finally, grants from public agencies and foundations (i.e., corporate, community and private) award monies to offset operating budgets and capital projects. A number of websites identify federal agencies, corporations, family, and community foundations that, upon acceptance of a proposal, contribute funds to research, training, program enhancement or start-up, and accessibility. These sites also offer tips on writing successful proposals. Several of these sites include:

The Foundation Center: www.fdncenter.org
Centers for Disease Control and Prevention: www.edc.org
National Institutes of Health: www.nih.gov/grants

United States Department of Education:
Office of Special Education and Rehabilitative Services: www.ed.gov/osers/funding
National Institute on Disability and Rehabilitation Research: www.ed.gov/osers/NIDRR/funding
Rehabilitation Services Administration: www.ed.gov/osers/RSA/funding

Professionals use a variety of forms and protocols to prepare proposals and budget requests on an ongoing basis. Accurate attendance records, documentation of staff and volunteers hours, recording of the monetary value of donations and in-kind services, and calculation of costs per participant or costs per program are examples of fiscal information important to administrators and potential funders. Professionals comfortable articulating outcomes and benefits to advocates are in a position to acquire external funding.

Reasonable Accommodations

The intent of ADA is to assure that all participants have equal access to programs and services in the most integrated setting. When a registrant with a disability seeks inclusive participation, an agency is required to make reasonable accommodations. If a participant meets essential eligibility requirements, with or without reasonable accommodations, the service or program is to be made available. "Essential eligibility means that a person either meets all of the typical requirements to be eligible for involvement in a particular activity or could meet the requirements with the provision of reasonable accommodations" (Bullock & Mahon, 2000, p. 108). Examples of the essential eligibility requirements include (Dattilo, 2002):

1. **The number of participants permitted to register or enroll in a program.** Program capacity is set according to size of the facility, number of available staff, resources like supplies and equipment, and site specific laws or regulations (i.e., room capacity or staff-to-participant ratio).

2. **Fees or charges associated with services.** Participants with disabilities are expected to pay the same associated fees like equipment rental, user fees, or instructor charges that participants without disabilities pay. Persons with disabilities are not to pay more to offset accommodation costs.

3. **Participants with reasonable accommodations are to abide by rules of conduct during programs.** Rules like staying with the group or in the program area, using equipment correctly, walking rather than running, and listening at appropriate times assure safe environments and allow all participants to enjoy and benefit from the experience. If participants display aggressive behavior, their experience may be modified only after making reasonable accommodations.

4. **Nature of the knowledge and skills to be demonstrated during participation and the chronological age of participants are considered.** Activity analysis determines the types and degree of skills required to successfully participate, and task analysis results in sequencing skills by degree of difficulty, refer to Direct Services Chapter 4. Assessment of participant skills identifies readiness to participate in various experiences at respective levels in a skill sequence. Professionals match participation requirements with participant competency levels to assure success and allow for continual skill development. Consequently, placing a beginner in an advanced class is inappropriate, whether or not a person has a disability. Likewise, having pre-school age

children mixed with junior high school age youth ignores growth and development patterns and places participants at risk for physical and emotional injury.

Reasonable accommodations are intended to enable the person with a disability to achieve the same benefits as those without disabilities participating in the program. ADA identifies five types of reasonable accommodations (Bullock & Mahon, 2000):

1. **Changes in policies, practices and procedures encompass how participants access or register for services, adaptations during specific activities, and adjustments to the setting in which the experience takes place.** To illustrate, a participant or caregiver might observe a program prior to making a decision to register the next time the program is offered. Leaders adapt equipment and allow additional substitutions or time-outs during activities. Adjustments to the setting may include changing the entry-exit way, relocating to a larger or smaller area, eliminating extraneous sounds (i.e., TV sets in fitness areas), or permitting participants to bring a leisure buddy, coach or assistive animal into the program area.

2. **Transportation barriers may contribute to a person with a disability not having program access.** This may result when, for example, public transportation is unavailable, or a participant does not have a drivers license. Barriers are removed by transporting between alternative program sites, and program relocation or schedule revisions.

3. **A third reasonable accommodation is providing auxiliary aids or services.** This type of assistance and support may come from an interpreter, reader, braille, sound amplification, text telephone (TTY), large print, augmentative and alternative communication systems like Boardmaker software, videotapes, a cassette recorder, interactive computer programs. Staffing options may include using leisure partners, providing behavioral support specialists, providing more staff training and/or increasing the number of staff resulting in a better staff-to-participant ratio.

4. **Removal of architectural barriers is considered a fourth reasonable accommodation.** This may include altering the path to enter a park or building as well as relocating a service to an accessible area, purchasing a pool lift, constructing a ramp, or installing automatic door openers. The Americans with Disabilities Act Accessible Guidelines (ADAAG) specifies the technical standards of accessibility. The U.S. Access Board is responsible for developing ADA accessibility guidelines. The Department of Justice (DOJ) enforces ADA compliance. The U.S. Access Board (www.access-board.gov) continues to develop and interpret standards. Outdoor Developed Areas and Play Areas (i.e., trails, beaches, picnic areas, and play areas and structures) and Recreation Facilities (i.e., pools, golf courses, amusement parks, and boating and fishing areas) are standards that have taken a number of years to prepare and evaluate (Hendy, 2001; McGovern, 2002; McGovern, 2001; Thompson, Hudson & Bowers, 2002). When guidelines like these are adopted by the DOJ, updating or constructing new areas must satisfy the intent of the criteria.

5. **A final reasonable accommodation is the removal of structured communication barriers.** A person may not understand communication media used due to a hearing, sight, or cognition impairment (Dattilo, 2002). If aural alarms warn of fire or natural disasters, visual alarms may need to be installed. Braille or large print may be used along with direction signage found at the entry way of a building or path. Audio cassettes also provide an alternative to reading the directions or rules in an activity area. A fitness partner may demonstrate proper use of exercise equipment, to a person who is deaf for example.

To make a blanket statement as to the type of accommodation that is reasonable with every person or situation is difficult. Each situation is individually assessed. ADA intends to support the rights of individuals with disabilities yet does not intend to impose an undue burden on the agency (Bullock & Mahon, 2000). Undue burdens may be economic, administrative or programmatic (Dattilo, 2002), and vary with the nature of the agency. The test of "undue burden to serve all community residents" for public leisure service agencies is more rigorous than for nonprofit agencies like the YMCA or private businesses like a health spa who serve "their members." Undue economic burdens consider cost of the accommodations in relation to the total agency operating budget and all of the agency resources. Number of staff available and their qualifications are assessed to determine administrative burden: For example, if a one-to-one staff-to-participant ratio and a registered nurse were requested on an adventure challenge activity, an administrator may determine the desired number of staff and nurse could not be provided without negatively impacting program access for the remaining participants. Consequently, staff would plan an alternative format for the outing. Lastly, if an accommodation would alter the fundamental nature of the program, undue programmatic burden results (Dattilo, 2002): One child with a mobility impairment on a hockey or soccer league team may cause an undue burden, because each of the other players must more closely assess their movements and safety in relation to the participant. Undue programmatic burden is determined by assessment. In this situation, staff may observe participants during practice sessions, document the nature of player contacts, and reassign playing teams. And if this fails, other reasonable accommodations might be offering skill development sessions or integrative non-competitive training.

Accessibility

Accessibility and usability are important to most people at some time in their lives; especially when a temporary limitation like a broken bone, environmental hazard like icy pathways, or a long-term adjustment like visual changes affect mobility and use or access to essential activities or resources (Getskow & Konczal, 1996). The phrase universal design refers to efforts to provide a meaningful range of options in all environments for all persons (Dattilo, 2002; Rogers, 2000; Smith, Austin, & Kennedy, 2001). Thus, universal design of a path of travel considers the needs of an individual who is using a wheelchair, laser cane, bicycle, motorized scooter, or baby stroller. The ADAAG serves as the primary accessibility guideline. This document is useful as an agency accessibility survey is planned and conducted. Yet, usability, like reasonable accommodations, is individually ascertained and situation-specific. Consequently, facility or area use policies are flexible and tolerant of individuals' diverse capabilities.

As previously noted, a policy statement (mission) institutionalized at the highest organizational level promotes acceptance of diverse capabilities. Incorporated in the policy is reference to the agency's intent to comply with ADA and to prepare a transition plan for barrier removal including structural modifications. Incorporating agency staff in the assessment of recreation facilities, outdoor areas, and playgrounds serves to train professionals about the actual physical accessibility guidelines, while also creating a sensitivity to usability and universal design features. A number of published survey forms outline design and accessibility elements (Bullock & Mahon, 2000; Dattilo, 2002; Hendy, 2001; Schleien, et al., 1997; Smith, et al., 2001; Thompson, et al., 2002). These resources with information from the U.S. Access Board assist agency staff as they develop surveys to assess facility and program support areas. Design features in several locations are important to assess and include: parking, entry routes, building entrances, interior travel routes, ramps and elevators, bathrooms, drinking fountains, phones, communication systems, seating, tables, workspaces or activity areas, and assembly areas. One survey format is to raise a series of questions that identify specific criteria in each service area (refer to Figure 1.1, Cincinnati Recreation Commission, Division of Therapeutic Recreation, 2002). After professionals have completed a survey responding to each question, they become aware of the standards and sensitive to the need for facility modifications prior to program delivery.

Accessibility guidelines for playgrounds, outdoor developed areas, and recreation facilities indicate what is to be accessible and explain how to achieve access. Play area guidelines were issued in 2000 and apply to newly built or altered areas (Thompson, et al., 2002). The guidelines require looking at play areas as a collection of individual components, then identifying the minimum number of components required to be accessible within the area. Standards address ground level and elevated components, ramp and transfer systems, and accessible surfaces. A summary of the guidelines is accessed through the Access Board website: www.access-board.gov/ play/summary.htm. Subsequent to the publishing of play area guidelines, guidelines for recreation facilities and outdoor developed areas were presented for review. Recreation facilities include amusement rides, boating facilities, fishing piers and platforms, golf courses and miniature golf, exercise equipment and machines, bowling lanes, and shooting facilities, and swimming pools, wading pools and spas. Accessibility guidelines were published September 3, 2002, and may be reviewed at www.access-board.gov/recreation/summary.htm. Outdoor developed areas are trails, beaches, picnic and camping areas. Attention is given to accessible routes and natural environmental conditions like terrain and surface characteristics. Information on the status of the guidelines is available at www.access-board.gov/outdoor/status.htm.

Universal design helps remove architectural, mobility and communication barriers. Assistive technology and computers also make environments more usable. Professionals plan capital improvements, e.g., pool lifts, electric door openers so areas are made more accessible to diverse users. Sensitive placement or reassignment of services, e.g., in the building nearer the parking lot, creates access, as do operating purchases like all-terrain or

Figure 1.1

Facility Accessibility Survey

Please Note: The areas of accessibility identified below include a sampling of the criteria for ADA compliance. For a complete listing of these standards please see the Americans with Disabilities Act Accessibility Guidelines (ADAAG)

Parking and Passenger Loading Zone

Are required number of accessible parking spaces provided?
Are accessible spaces the closest to facility entrance?
Are accessible spaces at least 96 inches wide with an adjacent access aisle 60 inches wide? (spaces designated as accessible van spaces require 96 inch wide access aisle)
Does each accessible space have a vertical sign unobscured by parked vehicles?
Are spaces and loading zone level, with no slope greater than 1:50?
Is there a pedestrian aisle (minimum 5 ft wide, 20 ft long) parallel to the vehicle pull-up space?

Total Parking in lot	Required Minimum Accessible Spaces
1 to 25	1
26 to 50	2
51 to 75	3
76 to 100	4
101 to 150	5
151 to 200	6
201 to 300	7
301 to 400	8
401 to 500	9
501 to 1000	2 % of total

Accessible (exterior) Route, Ground Surfaces, Pathways, Curb Ramps

Is there an accessible route linking public transportation stops and the facility entrance?
Is the accessible pathway free of steps and at least 36 inches wide?
Are accessible pathway surfaces stable, firm and slip-resistant?
Is the slope of the accessible pathway no greater than 1:20?
Is there a curb ramp wherever an accessible pathway meets a curb?

Figure 1.1 continued

Figure 1.1 – (continued)

Building Entrances, Stairs, Ramps, Doors

Is the accessible entrance connected by an accessible route to all accessible spaces within?
Is the accessible entrance to the building **not** a service entrance?
Is door handle mounted no higher than 48 inches above floor level?
Are handles, latches operable with one hand, without tight grasping or twisting?
Do doors have an opening force of 5 lbs or less?
Are doorways at least 32 inches in clear opening width?
Is the threshold no higher than ½ inch?
Do stairways have continuous handrails at both sides of all steps?
In any one flight do all steps have uniform riser height and tread width?
If there is a ramp, is the ramp slope 1:12 or less?
Is there a level landing at the top and bottom of each ramp, at least 60 inches long?

Interior Routes, Floor Surfaces, Corridors, Lobbies

Is there an accessible route connecting the accessible entrance with all accessible elements?
Are the floors in all accessible areas and routes stable, firm, and slip resistant?
Are changes of level greater than ½ inch treated with a ramp?
If carpet or carpet tile is used on the floor, is it securely attached?
If the accessible route is less than 60 inches wide, are there passing spaces at least 60 inches wide at reasonable intervals?

Elevators, Lifts

Are the elevator hallway call buttons centered at 42 inches above the floor?
Is there a visible and audible signal at each hoistway entrance to indicate which car is answering?
Do audible signals sound once for up and twice for down, or do they have verbal annunciators?
Is the time from when the elevator's arrival is signaled until doors begin to close at least 5 seconds?
Do elevator doors remain fully open for a minimum of 3 seconds?
Are elevator control panel buttons no higher than 48 inches above the floor?
Are controls designated by raised characters or symbols at least 1/32 of an inch high?
Is the button for the main entry floor designated by a raised star?
If a platform lift is installed, can it be used without assistance?
Is the lift platform at least 30 x 48 inches?
Is the highest operable part of a two-way communication system 48 inches (or less) above the floor?

Figure 1.1 continued

Figure 1.1 — (continued)

Rooms, Spaces, Assembly Areas

Do free standing objects mounted on posts project less than 12 inches into route of travel?
For tables/workspaces, is the top of the table or work surface between 28 and 34 inches from floor?
Is the table/workspace knee space at least 27 inches high, 30 inches wide, 19 inches deep?
Are the aisles between tables at least 36 inches wide?
Are light switches and other controls between 15 and 48 inches from the floor?
Is the required number of wheelchair locations in assembly spaces provided?
Are wheelchair spaces dispersed throughout the seating area?
Are the sightlines from these seating areas comparable to other viewing areas?
Is there a listening system for persons with severe hearing loss?
If listening system serves individual fixed seats, are seats within a 50 foot distance of viewing area?

Capacity of Seating/Assembly Area	Required Wheelchair Locations
50 to 75	3
76 to 100	4
101 to 150	5
151 to 200	6
201 to 300	7
301 to 400	8
401 to 500	9
501 to 1000	2 % of total

Bathrooms, Toilet Stalls, Sinks, Mirrors, Shower Stalls

Are the toilet rooms located on an accessible route?
Does no door swing into a required clear floor space at an accessible fixture?
Is the toilet stall at least 60 inches wide, 56 inches deep (59 inches if floor mounted model)?
Is the top of the toilet seat between 17 and 19 inches from the floor?
Are the grab bars mounted horizontally between 33 and 36 inches above the floor?
Are flush controls automatic or operable with one hand without tight grasping, twisting?
Is the lavatory rim or counter surface no higher than 34 inches above floor?
Are controls mounted no more than 44 inches above the floor?
Is there a clearance of at least 29 inches from the floor to the bottom of apron?
Are hot water pipes and drain pipes insulated or otherwise covered?
Can faucet be operated with one hand without tight grasping, twisting?
Does at least one mirror have a bottom edge no higher than 40 inches from the floor?
Is at least one of each dispenser type accessible and on an accessible route?
Can the dispenser be operated with one hand without tight grasping, twisting?
Where showers are provided, is at least one made accessible?
If transfer type shower, is the seat mounted between 17 and 19 inches from floor?
Is the seat on the wall opposite the controls with grab bars provided along control wall?

Figure 1.1 continued

Figure 1.1 – continued

Signage, Alarms, Detectable Warnings

Are signs mounted on the wall at the latch side of the door between 54 and 66 inches wide?
Do signs providing permanent identification of rooms have raised letters?
Are the raised characters or symbols between 5/8 inch and 2 inches tall?
Does the color of the characters and symbols contrast with the color of the background?
Do audible emergency alarms have an intensity and frequency that can attract attention of those with hearing loss?
Are detectable warnings (use of contrasting materials) on walking surfaces in places to indicate hazardous areas (stairs, vehicular traffic, etc.)?

Drinking Fountains, Telephones

Is there an accessible path of at least 36 inches clear alongside the drinking fountain?
Is the spout outlet no higher than 36 inches from the ground?
Is the water stream at least 4 inches high to allow the insertion of a cup under stream?
Are the controls located near the front edge and operable with one hand?
At each bank of telephones, is there at least one accessible phone?
Is there an accessible path of at least 36 inches wide alongside the telephone?
Is the highest operable part of the telephone 48 inches or less from ground (for forward approach) or 54 inches from ground if parallel approach is possible?
Is volume control provided on the telephone?
Does the telephone have pushbutton controls?
Is the cord from the telephone to the handset at least 29 inches long?

beach/float chairs. The International Symbol of Access (see Figure 1.2) is intended to identify universal design features. The symbol is used worldwide by organizations to denote physical accessibility, for example, parking stalls and program access, e.g., interpretive cassettes or availability of wheelchairs.

Policies and Procedures

Operating policies and procedures set the parameters for participant and staff decisions and behavior and govern management functions and program operations. They are written codes of conduct or guidelines that serve as standards to assure quality service delivery. Policies explain how goals will be achieved and establish limits within which a specified type of decision is made (O'Morrow & Carter, 1997). Some policies are broad in scope, while others leave little room for interpretation. Policies emerge over time from 1) management directives 2) decisions on behalf of consumer requests or appeals, and 3) interpretation of external standards emanating from laws, regulations, practice protocols, and professional guidelines (O'Morrow & Carter, 1997). While policies are broad guidelines for handling situations that arise, procedures are accepted ways to execute policies (Staffo, Boatright, & Hughes, 1999). Procedures usually outline the sequence of actions to perform work tasks in compliance with set policies. Consequently, procedures tend to be more numerous at the direct service level. Rules tend to regulate exactly how employees are to respond to specific situations as they interpret agency policies and departmental procedures. Along with policies and procedures, rules promote consistency in service delivery and assurance that standards guiding practice are being met.

Figure 1.2

International Symbol of Access

This symbol tells a person with a disability, particularly one using a wheelchair, that a building or facility is accessible and can be entered and used without fear of being blocked by architectural barriers. It should be displayed only on those buildings intended for public use. Used throughout the world, the symbol is recognized for its special meaning.

Policy statements are drawn from agency vision, mission and goal statements. An agency-wide inclusion policy taken from a therapeutic recreation mission statement (refer to page 14) describes how the goal of inclusion is to be accomplished by the agency (refer to Figure 1.3, Cincinnati Recreation Commission, n.d.). The statement sets guidelines as professionals assess, plan, and implement programs. Staff expectations as they interact with consumers are also delineated. A "tone" is set for creating positive attitudes as consumers request reasonable accommodations. Policy statements like this illustration are considered during hiring decisions and to select topics for agency-wide inclusion training. Reasonable accommodation policy statements that reflect welcoming language and awareness of diverse needs are found in agency operational manuals with inclusion statements and in program brochures distributed to participants. Examples from agency manuals and brochures are presented:

Individuals with disabilities are encouraged to register for general recreation programs. With your registration, please include information regarding your disability and accommodations needed...Reasonable accommodations will be made on an individual basis (Howard County Recreation & Parks, 2001, p. 65).

Figure 1.3

Policy Statement on the Inclusion of Individuals with Disabilities in Recreation Commission Programs

Meeting the recreational needs of a diverse community is fundamental to the purposes of the Cincinnati Recreation Commission. Including individuals with disabilities in all programs and services is required by law and is consistent with our intentions to serve all citizens. Our inclusion policy involves the following components:

- All programs must be developed and implemented in a manner which enables and encourages individuals with disabilities to participate

- All program promotions (flyers, program guides, etc.) must include a statement indicating our intention to include participants with disabilities and informing them of their right to request an accommodation

- Requests for information and/or to register must be addressed with a "yes first" response. Recreation Commission staff must respond affirmatively to questions regarding the acceptance of participants with disabilities (if otherwise eligible, age, placement openings, etc.)

- All staff, as indicated in the job descriptions, must be able and willing to assist individuals with disabilities in personal care tasks and/or other necessary accommodations

The Therapeutic Division's Inclusion Staff are available to assist with the inclusion process and should be contacted as soon as an inclusion situation arises.

The Department of Parks and Recreation offers a variety of accommodations to promote the participation of individuals with disabilities...Accommodations are provided based on the individual needs and abilities of each participant. Some examples of accommodations include:

- Sign Language Interpreters
- Large Print and Braille Brochures
- Adapted Equipment
- Assistive Listening Devices
- Accessible Facilities
- Trained Support Staff
- Accommodations for individuals with disabilities are available upon request. The Department of Parks and Recreation requests that the patron contact the facility two weeks in advance of the program start date. Additionally, the Department requests a 72-hour advance notice for the provision of sign language interpreters (Maryland-National Capital Park and Planning Commission, Prince George's County, Department of Parks and Recreation Inclusion Services Staff, 2000, p. 15).

NSSRA complies with the ADA and will make reasonable accommodations to enable people with disabilities to participate in and enjoy recreation programs. If you have a question about NSSRA's compliance, or feel that NSSRA has discriminated against you, please call Executive Director...(Northern Suburban Special Recreation Association, Spring, 2001, p. A).

The city of Boulder Parks and Recreation Department welcomes everyone to participate and enjoy programs and facilities regardless of race, color, disability, religion, national origin, pregnancy, age, military status, gender, gender identity, gender variance, or sexual orientation. If you have a disability and would like support for a program, please check the box on the registration form requesting an accommodation or contact an EXPAND staff member (City of Boulder Parks & Recreation, Spring, 2002, p. 2).

Examples of program policies appropriate to all participants including persons who register for inclusion services are also found in agency brochures:

The Department reserves the right:
- to deny registration or entry into a program when it deems necessary to assure public safety.

Parents please note: ...It is your responsibility to take your child to the leader and pick up your child from the leader immediately after the program. A fee will be assessed if your child is not picked up at the close of the program (Howard County Recreation & Parks, Fall 2001, p. 65).

Late Pick-Up Policy

If parents/guardians are not on time for picking up participants, a late fee will be assessed. After a ten-minute grace period, a $10 fee will be charged for every 15 minutes or portion thereof (Northern Suburban Special Recreation Association, Spring, 2001, p. A).

Unless otherwise noted, programs are for all ability levels. When registering, please use the following codes. Small Group: Participants who are independent or require minimal verbal prompting with personal care, hygiene, dressing, eating, balance and typical social behavior. **1 on 1:** Participants who need physical assistance with the previously mentioned skills should register for classes using the '1 on 1' class code (City of Boulder Parks & Recreation, Spring, 2002, p. 18).

Procedures identify protocols used to implement policies. Program procedures outline action plans to carry-out agency policies. One agency's procedures illustrate the inclusion process (Bullock & Mahon, 2000; Fairfax County Community and Recreation Services, Therapeutic Recreation Services, n.d.):

1. Upon registration, interview (phone or individual session) the individual and determine activity interests, skill level, and required accommodations.
2. Review the program brochure with the participant to select a program or class.

3. Once selected, review activity requirements, accommodations, transportation needs, scholarship needs, or other assistance or support needs.
4. Develop an accommodation plan with participant, caregiver, and staff outlining strategies and arrangements.
5. Send a copy of the plan to instructor, program coordinator, participant, and caregiver.
6. If appropriate, schedule participant, caregiver, and or staff training at least 48-72 hours prior to program start.
7. Document accommodations procured, cost, and administrative hours.
8. Complete a follow-up contact or visit within the first program week and at least once during program following the initial visit.
9. Evaluate the placement, accommodations, and participant outcomes.
10. Analyze program outcomes and accommodations, alter accommodation plan, review the support process and recommend future placement.

The APIE (assessment, planning, implementation, evaluation) process, referred to as the therapeutic recreation process, is a systematic procedure to deliver accountable services (Peterson & Stumbo, 2000). The APIE process is a universal procedure or protocol that is applicable across delivery settings. When it is used to design inclusion programs, the dynamics of the environment are analyzed and the results are individually unique inclusive plans (Sullivan & O'Brien, 2001). As shown in Figure 1.4, the APIE model outlines the inclusion process (Cincinnati Recreation Commission, Division of Therapeutic Recreation, 2002). The process outlines procedures to follow to assure reasonable accommodations and the maintenance of service quality. This particular model also supports collaboration between general recreation and therapeutic recreation professionals: A recommended professional best practice (Klitzing, 2002). Consequently, use of the APIE process is one benchmark to gauge quality or adherence to standards of best practice in inclusive programming (LeConey, Devine, Bunker, & Montgomery, 2000).

Quality Service Indicators

Service quality "has been defined as the degree of adherence to standards of good practice" (Peterson & Stumbo, 2000, p. 308). "Historically, quality referred to the achievement of some preestablished standard of service" (O'Morrow & Carter, 1997, p. 321). An emphasis on service quality and accountability has led to measurement of indicators like participant preferences, service consistency, effectiveness, efficiency and appropriateness (Hood, 2001; O'Morrow & Carter, 1997; Peterson & Stumbo, 2000). A variety of terms describe concepts of service quality and improvement: Quality assurance (QA), total quality management (TQM), and continuous quality improvement (CQI) are terms used to define agency initiatives to achieve and maintain standards of good practice. A commonly held perception is that quality of service is enhanced when standardized practices guide program delivery (Hood, 2001). Practice guidelines standardize services yet recognize individual preferences. Policies, procedures, and practice guidelines promote service consistency and ways to measure effectiveness, efficiency, and service appropriateness.

Quality service indicators are defined measures of service that denote quality or recommended professional practices. Use of the APIE process to design and evaluate individualized program plans is an indicator of quality in therapeutic recreation services. This procedure is integral to the standards of practice (SOP) of the American Therapeutic Recreation Association (2000) and the National Therapeutic Recreation Society (2003). These professional standards of practice also recommend additional quality indicators: Agency operational plans incorporate quality improvement programs, program evaluation and research, mission, goals and objectives that serve as evaluation blueprints, and recreation services that improve health, well-being and the quality of life. Properly trained and educated professionals are also indicators of quality service.

Quality service indicators are found in the NRPA Position Statement on Inclusion (NRPA, 1999). This paper suggests inclusion is most effective when support, assistance, and accommodations are present: Adjustments include but are not limited to qualified staff, adaptive equipment, alternative formats for printed or audio materials, trained volunteers, and/or flexibility in policies and program rules. Practices that remove physical and attitudinal barriers through environments that encourage choices and education and training of personnel are also recommended.

Figure 1.4

Inclusion Flow Chart

Participant (parent/guardian)
initiates contact

Through community center → TR section

Through community center

Center staff provides program info., assists with registration, contacts TR section

Through TR section

TR staff inquires/determines if inclusion is desired program option, contacts center staff

Center staff and TR/Inclusion staff work together (with participant, parent/guardian) to plan for successful inclusion experience

Assessment — Participant skills and areas for development relating to the inclusion program are assessed. Program/program environment assessed.

Planning — Inclusion Support Plan is developed, specific accommodations are prepared.

Implementation — Participant begins program, Inclusion Support Plan implemented with recommended accommodations.

Evaluation — Inclusion Support Plan is evaluated at pre-determined intervals, revisions made as needed.

Research on inclusive community programming tends to corroborate administrative and programmatic guidelines recommended in SOP and the inclusion position statement (Block & Conaster, 2002; Devine & Kotowski, 1999; Devine & McGovern, 2001; Klitzing, 2002; McDonald, 2002; Rizzo & Lavay, 2000; Schleien, et al., 1996). Collaborative planning among participants, caregivers, general recreation and therapeutic recreation professionals facilitates inclusion. An agency-wide inclusive mission and goals, marketing, and outreach strategies to individuals of all ability levels and from diverse backgrounds tend to encourage inclusion. Financial assistance and transportation during service provision reduce barriers encountered by participants. A proactive inclusionary practice is preparation and training of peers and professionals. Educational topics cover health issues, disability awareness, programming techniques and behavioral interventions, safety, transitions, accessibility, adaptive equipment, benefits of recreation, problem-solving scenarios to modify activities and documentation (Anderson & Heyne, 2000). Programmatic best practices incorporate skill level assessments; adaptations of materials, equipment, and experiences; use of behavioral techniques like reinforcement, partial participation, and peer coaches; environmental and task analyses; choices and alternatives that individualize experiences; and continuous monitoring and evaluation of the inclusion (APIE) process. Literature notes variation in the use of these procedures, yet supports service quality enhancement if these practices are in evidence. These administrative and programmatic procedures are therefore recognized as service quality indicators or inclusion best practices. The remaining chapters include examples and resources indicative of recommended best practices.

Risk Management

A partner of quality assurance and improvement is risk management. The intent of both quality and risk management is to develop procedures so feedback is proved to improve services (O'Morrow & Carter, 1997). Risk management procedures focus on reduction of accidents, severity of injuries, and financial losses. Risk management consists of written policies and daily practices that address professional and participant safety and proper use of programming resources. Risk management processes consist of (1) identifying the potential sources of risk; (2) evaluating the probability, severity and frequency of potential personal and financial losses; (3) determining how to avoid and or reduce loss exposure; and (4) implementing and evaluating policies, procedures, and standards of care that manage identified risks (Edginton, Hudson, & Lankford, 2001; O'Morrow & Carter, 1997).

A number of resources identify practices that promote risk and safety management. Professional documents like SOP (ATRA, 2000; NTRS, 2003) and the NRPA Position Statement on Inclusion (1999) provide program design and evaluation practices that maintain a standard of care and reduce harm and loss potential. Organizations like ACA (American Camping Association, www.ACAcamps.org), AEE (Association for Experiential Education, www.aee.org), and NPSI (National Playground Safety Institute) publish guidelines and conduct peer review of programs and facilities to assure standards are met. Likewise, standards legislated by law (ADA) and set forth by governing agents, CPSC (Consumer Products Safety Commission, www.cpsc.gov), OSHA (Occupational Safety and Health Administration), and EPA (Environmental Protection Agency) are designed to protect participants and create safe programming environments. Credentials from, for example, Wilderness Education Association (www.weainfo.org), American Red Cross (www.redcross.org), and American Heart Association (www.americanheart.org), are indicators of desired expertise. Professionals develop risk management plans pertinent to their services based on standards of a number of regulatory, governing, and professional guidelines.

Identifying and evaluating potential risk sources and losses, initial risk management steps, is an ongoing process, as the nature of participants, program experiences and supervision are dynamic. Assessment prior to participation identifies developmental abilities and capabilities in two critical areas: (1) ability to perform skills required to be successful in an activity, and (2) ability to complete supportive activity requirements like complying with supervisor directions and medication management. Pre-program interviews and or registration forms alert staff to potential for seizures, allergic reactions, and the need to monitor exposure to the sun or humid environments. Assessments identify skill level and social readiness like access to proper participation equipment (i.e., shoes) or adequacy of group interaction skills. Environmental stimuli trigger unanticipated behaviors like darting about or covering eyes/ears. A fundamental assessment question is, are consumers capable of comprehending risks inherent in activities?

A second area assessed as risks are identified and evaluated is the program itself. What are the skill requirements to successfully participate? What equipment is necessary, and how are the materials, equipment, and environmental resources used during the experience? What are the risks associated with program location? What rules are essential to safety? Is the activity developmentally appropriate (Jordan, 2001)? And, what skill progression and sequence is followed to complete the activity? Responses to these questions help professionals identify and evaluate inherent program risks and safety issues.

Staffing considerations are critical to assess when identifying and evaluating risk potential. What training, credentials, and past experiences with individuals with disabilities do staff possess? Are staff aware of the side effects or consequences of over- or under-medication? What have been their experiences with assistive devices or augmentative communication systems? Are staff certified and trained to conduct the activity (Jordan, 2001)? What is the staff-to-participant ratio? Are staff familiar with behavior or crisis management strategies? Are staff prepared to act in case of an emergency? Are regular safety checks conducted? Do staff document participant responses to activities? What types of supervisory skills do staff bring to the program? A professional's maturity, competence, skills and expertise greatly influence the maintenance of a safe experience and evaluation of the standard of care necessary to prevent consumer harm. Competent professionals maintain the type of supervision that enables good judgment and anticipatory responses.

Once potential risks are identified and evaluated, it is incumbent on the professional to identify procedures to avoid or reduce the potential for harm and loss: Then, procedures are put into place to evaluate practices so program improvements result. Decisions to avoid or reduce risk range from (1) not offering a program, to (2) purchasing insurance, and (3) alerting consumers to inherent risks with information (e.g., assumption of risk forms) as they register. Risk monitoring and control occur in a number of ways: Written supervisory plans outline staffing numbers and location (e. g., voice distance and visual contact), inspection and securing procedures, emergency plans, safety rules, participant management techniques, direct leadership tasks, and procedures to report resource conditions. Staff conduct safety inspections and complete risk management checklists to identify maintenance needs and appropriateness of environmental conditions. Staff training is recognized as a means to promote inclusion and assure program-specific competence. A common practice is to conduct safety drills in environments similar to programming situations. A number of forms are used to alert consumers to issues and the precautions to take to reduce harm. Registration forms may include activity specific permissions, medical history and medication information, emergency protocols, confidentiality releases, participant/parent/guardian releases, and or treatment/agreement to participate (Cincinnati Recreation Commission, 2003) (see Figure 1.5). Accident and incident forms report injury and potentially harmful situations with treatment procedures.

Quality and risk management plans are implemented with standards of care monitored by agency personnel and external regulators; for example, state health departments or agents conducting OSHA inspections. Job descriptions may incorporate risk management duties like facility opening and closing procedures or development of supervisory plans. Agencies may elect to use an insurance representative to conduct risk compliance visits. Common practice is to assemble manuals with policies, procedures, and rules that enhance service quality and attempt to minimize harm and loss. Another practice is to present guidelines to consumers during registration. This occurs via printed materials and required program orientations (Cincinnati Recreation Commission, 2002) (see Figure 1.6). Periodic review of accident and incident forms, workmens' compensations, financial statements, and contracts with vendors, identifies the nature and extent of harm and loss. Peer review by professional (American Camping Association) and governmental (fire department) agents facilitates staff awareness while assuring impartial evaluation of quality and risk practices.

Assessment considers each participant, the agency and community resources. This is the first step in an acknowledged approach (APIE) to design and deliver individually relevant services. Information gathered is used to develop a scope of service and programmatic boundaries. After a SWOT analysis, professionals write inclusion policies and procedures, prepare strategic plans, and organize quality and risk management documents. Options to secure necessary financial resources are known, as are alternative accommodations and accessibility strategies. Operation manuals, brochures, and registration forms provide professionals and participants with pertinent information and practices. The groundwork is laid to initiate design of inclusion plans with consumers having diverse backgrounds and programming needs.

Figure 1.5

Therapeutic Recreation
Participant Information Form

Please complete both the front and back pages and print all information on this form. Return this form with check payable to: Cincinnati Recreation Commission. Mail to: CRC, Therapeutic Recreation, 805 Central Avenue, Suite #800, Cincinnati, Ohio 45202 (or call (513) 352-4014 for more information).

I. Participant Information

First Name

Last Name

Date of Birth

Address **Street** **Apt #**

City **State** **Zip Code** **Gender**

Home Phone Number **Emergency Phone (other than home)**

Emergency Contact (other than parent) **Relationship**

Mother's Work Phone Number **Father's Work Phone Number**

Doctor's Name **Doctor's Work Phone Number**

School/Workshop **Teacher/Supervisor**

Group Home Agency **Agency Phone Number**

II. Disabling Condition

Please identify the participants' disabling condition. Circle all that apply to the participant and/or write in any disabling condition not listed:

Arthritis	Down Syndrome	Mental Retardation, Mild	Spina Bifida
Attention Deficit Disorder	Head Injury	Mental Retardation, Moderate	Spinal Cord Injury
Autism	Hearing Impairment	Mental Retardation, Severe	Injury Level: _____
Behavioral Disorder	Learning Disability	Muscular Dystrophy	Vision Impairment
Cerebral Palsy	Mental Illness	Multiple Sclerosis	Other: _____

Does participant walk independently? ☐ YES ☐ NO If not, what type of assistance is required? ☐ Wheelchair ☐ Walker
☐ Other (please specify): _____

Does participant dress independently? ☐ YES ☐ NO If not, what type of assistance is required? _____
_____

Does participant use bathroom/toilet independently? ☐ YES ☐ NO If not, what type of assistance is required? _____
_____

Does participant communicate through speech? ☐ YES ☐ NO If not, what type of communication is used? _____
_____

Additional information that would assist in programming for participant: _____
_____

Figure 1.5 continued

Figure 1.5 – (continued)

III. Medical Information

Please circle all that apply to participant:

Allergies (specify below)	Diabetes	Heart Condition	Shunt
Arthritis	Diet Restriction	Hepatitis Carrier	Tracheotomy
Asthma	Ear Tubes	High Blood Pressure	Other: _____
Atlantoaxial Subluxation	Glasses	Scoliosis	_____
Catheter	Hearing Aid	Seizures	

Please provide **specific** information for medical conditions we should be aware of (allergies, activity restriction, etc.): _____

_____

Does participant have seizures? ☐ YES ☐ NO   If yes, what type? ☐ Grand Mal ☐ Petit Mal ☐ Other _____

If yes, how often does participant have seizures? _____ Date of last seizure: _____

Please identify type, dosage and time of any medication participant is currently taking:

MEDICATION: Type _____   Dosage _____   Time _____

_____   _____   _____

_____   _____   _____

_____   _____   _____

IV. Swimming Information

Please answer the following questions if the participant is registering for a swim program.

Does the participant have swimming experience? ☐ YES ☐ NO   If yes, where? _____

Please explain participant's swimming skills (ie: face in water, float on front, etc.): _____

_____

Are there any precautions that need to be taken while the participant is in or around the pool? _____

_____

Does the participant need to wear ☐ Ear molds ☐ Ear plugs ☐ Bathing cap ☐ Other _____

Does participant have difficulty eating foods? ☐ YES ☐ NO   Does participant have difficulty drinking fluids? ☐ YES ☐ NO

If yes, for either, please explain. _____

_____

V. Participant / Parent / Guardian Release

As a participant or as a parent/guardian of the participant in this program, I recognize that there are certain risks of physical injury and I agree to assume the full risk of any injuries, damages or loss resulting from participation in any and all activities connected with or associated with such program. I agree to waive and relinquish all claims I may have, as a result of my or my son's/daughter's participation in the program, against the Cincinnati Recreation Commission, City of Cincinnati, and their agents, employees, staff and volunteers. I do hereby fully release and discharge the Cincinnati Recreation Commission, City of Cincinnati, and their agents, employees, staff and volunteers for any and all claims from injuries, damage or loss which I have or which may accrue to me on account of my son's/daughter's participation in the program. I further agree to protect, defend and hold harmless the Cincinnati Recreation Commission, City of Cincinnati, and their agents, employees, staff and volunteers from any and all claims resulting from injuries, damage or losses sustained by myself or my son/daughter or arising out of, connected with, or in any way associated with the activities of the program. I have read and fully understand this release form. **Before registration in this program is valid, this release form must be signed by the participant or the participant's parent or legal guardian.**

Signature of Participant / Parent / Guardian _____ Date _____

VI. Confidentiality Release

I, the undersigned, hereby authorize the Cincinnati Recreation Commission to utilize photographs, videotapes, voice recordings, etc,. of the participant to be used exclusively for promotion, advertising, and marketing of the Cincinnati Recreation Commission and its programs.

Signature of Participant / Parent / Guardian _____ Date _____

I, the undersigned, hereby authorize the Cincinnati Recreation Commission to contact school/work activity center concerning participant information that pertains to the recreation program.

Signature of Participant / Parent / Guardian _____ Date _____

Figure 1.6

Guidelines
for Parents & Guardians

We strive to achieve a safe environment and a positive program experience for all participants. Parents and guardians are asked to abide by the following guidelines:

Prior to participating in any T.R. program, each participant must have a current Participant Information Form, complete with parent/guardian signature, on file in the Therapeutic Recreation Office. Please include all information requested to help the T.R. staff take appropriate precautions when planning the program. It is essential that we have a phone number where the parent/guardian can be reached during the program hours.

The T.R. staff members are not responsible for the supervision of participants before or after the designated program times.

The T.R. staff members are not responsible for providing or arranging transportation from the center to the participant's home at the conclusion of the program.

If someone other than the parent/guardian will be picking up a participant at the conclusion of the program, advance written notification must be given to the program director.

A late pick-up fee of $5 for each quarter-hour will be assessed to any parent/guardian who is late picking up the participant at the conclusion of the program.

The T.R. staff members are not responsible for participants who travel independently to and from the program site once they have left the program site.

If a participant (who does not travel independently) leaves the program site during program hours, every effort will be made to return the participant to the program site. If this cannot be done without risk of injury to the participant or staff member, or if this results in lack of adequate supervision of the other participants, the parent/guardian will be contacted to take responsibility for the participant.

The following guidelines are used in managing behavior:
The T.R. staff members are instructed to use positive reinforcement and to provide a structured program in order to minimize negative behaviors.
If negative behavior should occur, a brief time-out is the approved method of behavior management.
If a behavior plan has been developed through school, or if you have specific techniques used at home, please inform the T.R. staff so we may support your efforts.

If, in the opinion of the T.R. staff, a participant becomes unmanageable and potentially dangerous to themselves, other participants or staff members, the parent/guardian will be contacted to take the participant home. If the parent//guardian is unable to be reached or does not respond shortly, the T.R. staff may be required to call for police assistance.

For participants with specific health/medical issues: Due to the physical requirements of some activities, participants with certain health/medical conditions may be asked to provide a physician's written consent prior to participation.

For participants requiring medication during program hours: All medication must be in proper prescription bottles with instructions for administration on the label. Please send only the exact dosage to be administered during the program hours, as staff are not permitted to accept larger doses. A medication waiver form must be completed and submitted in order for the T.R. staff to administer the medication.

Guidelines for Residential Agencies
If a group of four or more participants from a specific agency attend a T.R. program, we request a staff member from the agency attends the program and assists the T.R. staff in leading the activities. Larger groups of participants from a single agency may require additional agency staff.

In the event your agency will not be attending a program for which you have registered, please notify the T.R. office in advance. If the decision not to attend is made late, please notify the center where the program is to be held to inform the T.R. staff.

An agency may send an unregistered participant to a program in place of a registered participant if a Participant Information Form for the new participant has been submitted to the office and we are given advance notification of the substitution.

Agency staff attending events or outings must provide the necessary payment for meals and/or admission fees.

References

American Therapeutic Recreation Association. (2000). *Standards for the practice of therapeutic recreation and self-assessment guide* (2nd ed.). Hattiesburg, MS: Author.

Anderson, L., & Heyne, L. (2000). A statewide needs assessment using focus groups: Perceived challenges and goals in providing inclusive recreation services in rural communities. *Journal of Park and Recreation Administration, 18*(4), 17-37.

Block, M. E., & Conaster, P. (2002). Adapted aquatics and inclusion. *JOPERD, 73*(5), 31-34.

Bullock, C. C., & Mahon, M. J. (2000). *Introduction to recreation services for people with disabilities a person-centered approach* (2nd ed.). Champaign, IL: Sagamore Publishing.

Cincinnati Recreation Commission. (2002). *Facility accessibility survey.* (Available from Cincinnati Recreation Commission, Division of Therapeutic Recreation, 805 Central Avenue, Cincinnati, Ohio 45202).

Cincinnati Recreation Commission. (n.d.). *Policy statement on the inclusion of individuals with disabilities in Recreation Commission programs.* (Available from Cincinnati Recreation Commission, Division of Therapeutic Recreation, 805 Central Avenue, Cincinnati, Ohio 45202).

Cincinnati Recreation Commission. (2002). *Therapeutic Recreation, Fall & Winter 2002-2003 program guide.* [Brochure]. Cincinnati, OH: Author.

Cincinnati Recreation Commission. (2003). *Therapeutic Recreation, 2003 Spring & Summer programs.* [Brochure]. Cincinnati, OH: Author.

Cincinnati Recreation Commission, Division of Therapeutic Recreation. (2002). *Inclusion flow chart.* (Available from Cincinnati Recreation Commission, Division of Therapeutic Recreation, 805 Central Avenue, Cincinnati, Ohio 45202).

Cincinnati Recreation Commission, Division of Therapeutic Recreation. (2003.). *Mission statement.* (Available from Cincinnati Recreation Commission, Division of Therapeutic Recreation, 805 Central Avenue, Cincinnati, Ohio 45202).

City of Boulder Parks & Recreation. (2002). *City of Boulder parks & recreation spring 2002, April, May.* [Brochure]. Boulder, CO: Author.

City of Fort Collins Recreation Programs and Services for People with Disabilities. (n.d.). *ARO adaptive recreation opportunities aiming for independence.* [Brochure]. Ft. Collins, CO: Author.

City of St. Petersburg, Therapeutic Recreation. (2003). *Therapeutic recreation, January-May, 2003.* [Brochure]. St. Petersburg, FL: Author.

Dattilo, J. (2002). *Inclusive leisure services responding to the rights of people with disabilities* (2nd ed.). State College, PA: Venture Publishing, Inc.

Devine, M. A., & Kotowski, L. (1999). Inclusive leisure services: Results of a national survey of park and recreation departments. *Journal of Park and Recreation Administration, 17*(4), 56-72.

Devine, M. A., & McGovern, J. (2001). Inclusion of individuals with disabilities in public park and recreation programs: Are agencies ready? *Journal of Park and Recreation Administration, 19*(4), 60-82.

Edginton, C. R., Hudson, S. D., & Lankford, S. V. (2001). *Managing recreation, parks, and leisure services: An introduction.* Champaign, IL: Sagamore Publishing.

Fairfax County Community and Recreation Services, Therapeutic Recreation Services. (n.d.). *Staff training manual for community recreation integration.* Fairfax County, MD: Author.

Fitzgerald, C. (2003, April). *Inclusion and trends in therapeutic recreation.* Paper presented at the meeting of the NRPA Midwest/Southwest Regional Leadership and Professional Training Institute, Pueblo, CO.

Getskow, V., & Konczal, D. (1996). *Kids with special needs information and activities to promote awareness and understanding.* Santa Barbara, CA: The Learning Works, Inc.

Hendy, T. (2001). The Americans With Disabilities Act insures the right of every child to play. *Parks & Recreation, 36*(4), 108-117.

Hood, C. D. (2001). Clinical practice guidelines—A decision-making tool for best practice? In N. J. Stumbo (Ed.), *Professional issues in therapeutic recreation on competence and outcomes* (pp. 189-213). Champaign, IL: Sagamore Publishing.

Howard County Recreation & Parks. (2001). *Howard County Recreation and Parks, Fall 2001. Your guide to fun and adventure.* [Brochure]. Columbia, MD: Author.

Jordan, D. J. (2001). *Leadership in leisure services: Making a difference* (2nd ed.). State College, PA: Venture Publishing, Inc.

Klitzing, S. W. (2002). The best practices for successful inclusion. *Parks & Recreation, 37*(5), 60-65.

LeConey, S., Devine, M. A., Bunker, H., & Montgomery, S. (2000). Utilizing the therapeutic recreation process in community settings: The case of Sue. *Parks & Recreation, 35*(5), 70-77.

Maryland-National Capital Park and Planning Commission, Prince George's County, Department of Parks and Recreation Inclusion Services Staff. (2000). *Inclusion resource manual.* Prince George's County, MD: Author.

McDonald, J. (2002). Helping your counselors welcome all campers. *Camping Magazine, 75*(3), 24-27.

McGovern, J. (2002). U.S. Access Board adopts recreation facility accessibility guidelines. *Parks & Recreation, 37*(6), 44-49.

McGovern, J. N. (2001). A work in progress: Accessible trails, campsites, and other outdoor recreation areas. *Taproot, 13*(1), 22-27.

McGovern, J., & Wetherald, L. (2001). Inclusion comes into focus for parks and recreation get out active up! *Ability,* 62-69.

National Recreation and Park Association. (1999). *Position statement on inclusion.* Asburn, VA: The Association.

National Therapeutic Recreation Society. (2003). *Standards of practice for therapeutic recreation services and annotated bibliography.* Arlington, VA: Author.

Northern Suburban Special Recreation Association. (2001). *The benefits of special recreation with NSSRA, spring, 2001.* [Brochure]. Northbrook, IL: Author.

O'Morrow, G. S., & Carter, M. J. (1997). *Effective management in therapeutic recreation service.* State College, PA: Venture Publishing, Inc.

Peterson, C. A., & Stumbo, N. J. (2000). *Therapeutic recreation program design principles and procedures* (3rd ed.). Boston, MA: Allyn and Bacon.

Rizzo, T. L., & Lavay, B. (2000). Inclusion: Why the confusion? *JOPERD, 71*(4), 32-36.

Rogers, D. (2000). To the top: Challenge courses for persons with disabilities. *Parks & Recreation, 35*(3, 76-87).

Schleien, S. J., Germ, P. A., & McAvoy, L. H. (1996). Inclusive community leisure services: Recommended professional practices and barriers encountered. *Therapeutic Recreation Journal, 30*(4), 260-273.

Schleien, S. J., Ray, M. T., & Green, F. P. (1997). *Community recreation and people with disabilities* (2nd ed.). Baltimore, MD: Paul H. Brookes Publishing Co.

Smith, R. W., Austin, D. R., & Kennedy, D. W. (2001). *Inclusive and special recreation opportunities for persons with disabilities* (4th ed.). Boston, MA: McGraw Hill Higher Education.

Spencer, A. M. (2003). Accessibility and your playground a profile of facilities taking action. *Parks & Recreation, 38*(4), 40-49.

Staffo, D. F., Boatright, K., & Hughes, J. (1999). Organization structure and administrative operations. In B. van der Smissen, M. Moiseichik, V. J. Hartenburg, & L. F. Twardzik (Eds.), *Management of park and recreation agencies* (pp. 47-74). Ashburn, VA: National Recreation and Park Association.

Sullivan, A. K., & O'Brien, M. B. (2001). Inclusive programming at summer camp. *Parks & Recreation, 36*(5), 66-72.

Thompson, D., Hudson, S. D., & Bowers, L. (2002). Play areas and the ADA providing access and opportunities for all children. *JOPERD, 73*(2), 37-41.

Wegner, D., & Jarvi, C. K. (1999). Planning for strategic management. In B. van der Smissen, M. Moiseichik, V. J. Hartenburg, & L. F. Twardzik (Eds.), *Management of park and recreation agencies* (pp. 99-130). Ashburn, VA: National Recreation and Park Association.

CHAPTER 2

Personnel Resources

Leadership is an inherent characteristic of structured recreation experiences (Jordan, 2001). Professionals interact with participants in order to enhance well-being and accomplish a variety of physical, social, emotional, cognitive, spiritual, and leisure outcomes. The leadership provided has a tremendous influence on outcomes experienced by participants (Jordan, 2001). Success of inclusive programs is attributed "to specific roles fulfilled by strong and dedicated staff" (Sullivan & O'Brien, 2001, pg. 69). Additionally, there is general support and agreement that a CTRS (Certified Therapeutic Recreation Specialist) is the appropriately qualified person to oversee the inclusion process (McGovern & Wetherald, 2001).

The need for staff training to improve inclusion options and to prepare staff for inclusion experiences are acknowledged proactive accommodation practices (Dattilo, 2002; Devine & Kotowski, 1999; Devine & McGovern, 2001; Rizzo & Lavay, 2000; Schleien, Germ, & McAvoy, 1996). Further, there is a lack of awareness about individuals with disabilities as well as a fear of being unprepared and untrained to meet the needs of consumers in recreation programs (Anderson & Heyne, 2000). Training with all staff and volunteers on specific programming techniques, interventions, and inclusion strategies is critical to creating successful inclusion options.

This section addresses personnel issues and resources. Professionals assume a number of roles ranging from advocacy to assistance with consumer care. Agencies support inclusion with full-time and part-time professionals; seasonal staff, specialists, consultants, peer coaches, and volunteers. Staff composition impacts budget decisions and program consistency. Qualifications vary with the number of professionals available and types of positions held by staff. Staff training and supervision are recommended best practices. CTRSs and related professionals like special educators conduct training and provide staff support: Training varies from formal classroom experiences to individualized on-the-job support with single program participants. Training topics found helpful to the inclusion process are summarized with examples of training sessions provided. Supervision may commence with assessments and preparation of individual support plans or be available as needed to manage participant behaviors. Modifying the APIE process is individualized and ongoing; consequently, supervision is critical to the success of inclusion practices.

Staff Roles and Responsibilities

Roles and responsibilities of staff vary with the number and nature of positions on the organizational chart and the agency mission. In some instances, an agency may have only one CTRS agency wide for inclusion. When an agency's mission is to serve individuals with disabilities, each employee assumes responsibility for a particular inclusion function like training, marketing, and direct service delivery. If a therapeutic recreation unit exists, staff within the unit support general recreation staff agency-wide as inclusion services are delivered; and, they also may provide direct leadership during skill development programs so consumers develop skills necessary to experience some degree of inclusion.

Two general types of roles, administrative and direct service, are used to detail professional inclusion responsibilities. Administrative roles are similar to typical recreation manager duties that encompass organizing, planning, motivating, marketing, financing, staffing, and collaborating. Added responsibilities with inclusion relate to sensitivity awareness, advocacy, and facilitation. Managers oversee agency compliance with legal directives like ADA, professional mandates like the NRPA Position Statement on Inclusion, and external regulatory agents like NPSI (National Playground Safety Institute) and state health codes on day care. Managers guide review and revision of agency vision, mission, and goal statements, and develop agency transition plans to incorporate diversity awareness and facilitate support, assistance, accommodation, and barrier removal. Advocacy roles occur during advisory and support group meetings with caregivers and consumers. Managers oversee marketing initiatives that incorporate alternative media like large-print flyers, interpreters, or audio-cassettes. Hiring qualified professionals and conducting staff training are time-consuming tasks. Purchasing adaptive equipment, retrofitting buildings, and arranging accessible transportation alternatives are duties undertaken to comply with regulatory agents. A significant portion of time is devoted to overseeing implementation of the inclusion process by staff, consultants, and volunteers. This may involve safety and risk management planning and documentation. Ultimately, managers are responsible to maintain and improve service quality and participant satisfaction with available agency resources.

Direct service roles occur as inclusion is carried out through the TR process or APIE (assessment, planning, implementation, evaluation). These tasks are similar to those inherent in the delivery of structured recreation experiences. Variation results in order to make reasonable accommodations so participants meet eligibility criteria and have equal access to programs and services (Dattilo, 2002). Because these variations are often individualized, application of the APIE process to inclusion is both pre-planned and, at times, instantaneous. Assessment addresses the participant's potential for independent leisure functioning and takes into consideration environmental factors like facility accessibility, leader preparation and training, caregiver support, and the need for adaptations, consumer social skills training and/or peer coaches (LeConey, Devine, Bunker, & Montgomery, 2000; Schleien, et al., 1996). Planning may include the design of inclusion support plans and behavioral support plans that outline, for example, reinforcement strategies or partial participation steps. The unique aspect of planning in community settings is coordination among a number of professionals from various agencies like schools and vocational centers to maintain consistency in consumer plans (IEPs or IHPs) (LeConey, et al., 2000). Program implementation encompasses direct leadership as well as supportive tasks like monitoring behavioral interventions and compliance with medication or diet protocols; ensuring appropriateness of assistance, support and accommodations; and, assisting participants with personal care like eating or money management. Routine evaluation considers the impact of programs on client outcomes. Roles unique to evaluation with inclusion processes include determining future accommodation alternatives, evaluating leisure coaches, meeting with related professionals to incorporate outcome data in IEPs or IHPs, or on-site problem-solving and training with interpreters or recreation professionals to revise pre-program participant orientations (Anderson & Heyne, 2000). Application of the TR process to inclusion enables continuity in accommodations over extended time periods (LeConey, et al., 2000). Community residents may participate periodically over the course of several years. Evaluation documents participant response to service alternatives. Professionals facilitate participant transitions toward independent functioning among community services over extended time periods (Schleien, Ray, & Green, 1997).

Staffing Patterns

Application of the APIE process to inclusion standardizes the way professionals plan reasonable accommodations. Yet unique features of each community result in alternative approaches to support and assist inclusion of consumers (McGovern & Wetherald, 2001). Organizational charts present varying degrees of autonomy among staff responsible for inclusion and/or delivery of therapeutic recreation services. Four different approaches are found among service providers: One centralized approach occurs when therapeutic recreation including inclusion is the responsibility of an autonomous unit within an agency; a therapeutic recreation division in a public recreation agency represents this approach. A second centralized approach is found with special recreation districts that collaborate with several recreation districts to offer therapeutic recreation and inclusion services. One decentralized approach finds staff assigned to divisions throughout the agency to support inclusion; specialists in the respective divisions report to the division manager of sports, aquatics, and adult programs, for example. Lastly, a second decentralized approach is the hiring of one or more professionals as agency-wide inclusion specialists. This person reports to the agency manager like the recreation director or community services manager. Regardless of the organizational approach, commitment to inclusion becomes a shared responsibility among specialists and generalists who function as a team.

The agency structure affects the number of full- and part-time professionals, seasonals, resource persons, and volunteers used in an agency. In turn, the qualifications and responsibilities of professionals, support staff, and volunteers are influenced by agency structure. To illustrate, when an agency mission statement promotes inclusion in all service areas with a CTRS or a few therapeutic recreation specialists hired, job descriptions and responsibilities of all agency personnel include administrative and direct service tasks supportive of inclusion: If an autonomous unit is responsible for therapeutic recreation, responsibilities of other agency personnel may only include direct service tasks.

A centralized approach, exemplified by a therapeutic recreation unit in a public agency or a special recreation district, allows for greater consistency in service delivery to participants over extended time periods. This centralization of full-time qualified therapeutic recreation professionals also supports collaboration and rapport with other recreation staff (McGovern & Wetherald, 2001). When full-time professionals are employed, a number of seasonals, resource staff and consultants are hired as coaches, leisure companions, interpreters, and/or behavior specialists. In larger organizations, an inclusion manager or coordinator, may supervise one or more inclusion specialists, and have administrative responsibilities similar to other unit managers. The inclusion specialists report to the TR manager and perform direct service duties encompassed in assessment, planning, implementation, and evaluation of inclusion plans. Organizational charts from the Cincinnati Recreation Commission and the Fox Valley Special Recreation Association depict this centralized approach, refer to Figures 2.1 and 2.2. Job descriptions from two agencies, Cincinnati Recreation Commission and the Northern Suburban Special Recreation Association (NSSRA), detail the administrative duties of a division manager and the direct service duties of recreation specialists assigned to inclusion, refer to Figures 2.3-2.6.

With centralized approaches the separation of therapeutic recreation specialists from recreation generalists is created by the existence of separate units. There is a fine line between providing inclusion support and direct service assistance by therapeutic recreation specialists to general recreation staff. Generalists rely on specialists, yet with a TR division the perception might be that either the agency has met its inclusion responsibilities or that inclusion remains only the responsibility of the TR specialist. As a result of this perception, inclusion is not evident agency-wide. Another challenge arises during the budgeting process. Each unit manager develops his respective budget. Consequently, inclusion monies are budgeted to the TR division while persons are integrated into programs of units agency-wide. With special recreation districts the costs of reasonable accommodations may be billed to the park and recreation districts; this provides an incentive for cooperation as budgets are developed.

A decentralized approach is evident when qualified therapeutic recreation professionals are assigned to divisions throughout the organization or when a limited number of qualified therapeutic recreation professionals are hired to serve as agency-wide specialists. In either situation, a full-time qualified therapeutic recreation specialist (CTRS) may be hired to coordinate the agency's ADA program with part-time professionals assigned to divisions or as floaters throughout the agency: A second approach finds several qualified specialists hired agency-wide to supervise part-time, seasonals, and volunteers in particular areas like before and after school or summer day camp programs. In the first scenario, administrative duties are assumed by the full-time CTRS while in the second scenario, administrative and direct service duties are the responsibility of the full-time specialists. Job descriptions from Reno illustrate the varying nature of duties when one professional is hired as the agency ADA coordinator, refer to Figure 2.7, Therapeutic Recreation Specialist City of Reno, and part-time staff are hired as case managers, refer to Figure 2.8, Recreation Program Specialist IV, City of Reno.

In decentralized approaches the manager has the advantage of being able to hire staff as needed to meet consumer demands. Yet, management and service delivery is less consistent and more time consuming: To illustrate, the agency-wide coordinator may conduct peer coaches training with volunteers as needed resulting in numerous sessions rather than conducting quarterly agency-wide sessions as found in centralized agency management. A disadvantage of decentralized approaches is the supervisor-specialist relationship. A CTRS may

Figure 2.1

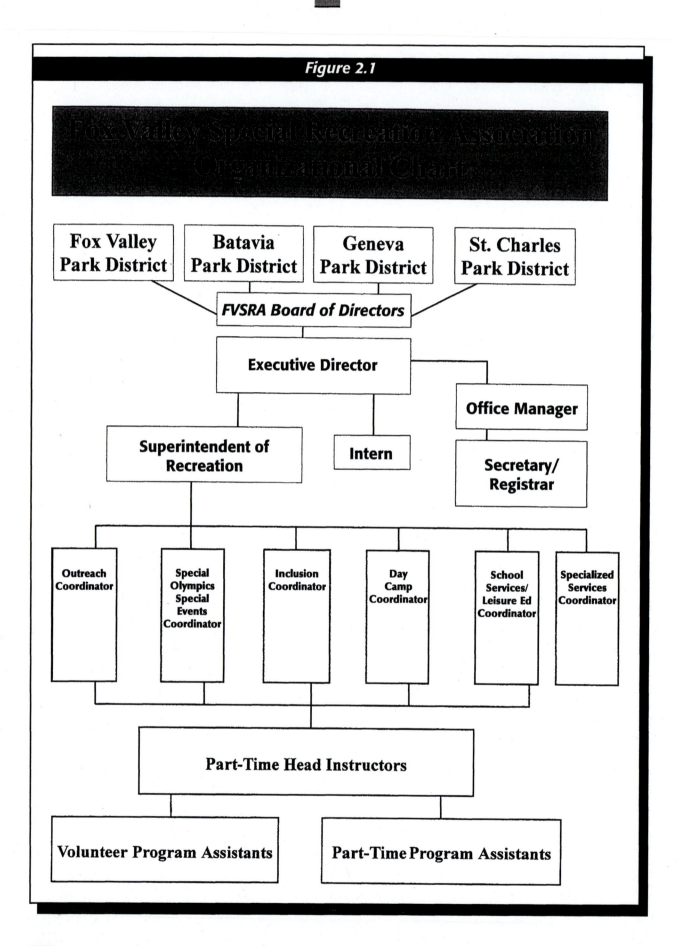

Fox Valley Special Recreation Association Organizational Chart

Fox Valley Park District | Batavia Park District | Geneva Park District | St. Charles Park District

FVSRA Board of Directors

Executive Director

Office Manager

Superintendent of Recreation

Intern

Secretary/ Registrar

Outreach Coordinator | Special Olympics Special Events Coordinator | Inclusion Coordinator | Day Camp Coordinator | School Services/ Leisure Ed Coordinator | Specialized Services Coordinator

Part-Time Head Instructors

Volunteer Program Assistants | Part-Time Program Assistants

Figure 2.2

I. Positions

The Division of Therapeutic Recreation (TR) operates with eight full-time positions and fifty part-time/ seasonal positions. These employees work together to provide a wide range of TR programs and inclusion services. Annual (full-time) positions include; Service Area Coordinator (SAC), Recreation Program Coordinator (RPC), and Community Center Director, (CCD). Part-time/seasonal positions include: Recreation Program Director and Recreation Leader. Position descriptions for the part time/seasonal positions are as follows:

Recreation Program Director: Under the immediate supervision of the Program Coordinator, the Recreation Program Director is the on-site supervisor and is responsible for the planning, implementation and evaluation of activities for a specific TR program. This position may involve the supervision of other part-time staff and volunteers assigned to the program. The program director must be 18 years of age or older.

Recreation Program Leader: Under the immediate supervision of the Recreation Program Director (or CCD), the Recreation Program Leader assists in the planning, implementation and evaluation of activities for a specific TR program. Assisting in the leadership of recreational activities may include group leadership as well as providing individual assistance. The Recreation Leader must be 16 years of age or older (Recreation Leaders working as Inclusion Support Staff must be 18 years of age or older).

**Therapeutic Recreation
Table of Organization**

```
                    ┌─────────────────────┐
                    │  Division Supervisor │
                    │        (SAC)         │
                    └─────────────────────┘

┌──────────────────────┐ ┌──────────────────────┐ ┌──────────────────────┐
│ Program/Inclusion     │ │ Program/Inclusion     │ │ Program/Inclusion     │
│ Coord. (RPC)          │ │ Coord. (RPC)          │ │ Coord. (RPC)          │
│ West Region           │ │ Central Region        │ │ East Region           │
└──────────────────────┘ └──────────────────────┘ └──────────────────────┘

┌────────────────┐ ┌────────────────┐ ┌────────────────┐ ┌────────────────┐
│ Program/        │ │ Program/        │ │ Program/        │ │ Program/        │
│ Inclusion       │ │ Inclusion       │ │ Inclusion       │ │ Inclusion       │
│ Specialist (CCD)│ │ Specialist (CCD)│ │ Specialist (CCD)│ │ Specialist (CCD)│
└────────────────┘ └────────────────┘ └────────────────┘ └────────────────┘

┌──────────────────────────────────────────────────────────────────────────┐
│ Recreation Program Directors, Recreation Program Leaders,                  │
│ Inclusion Support Staff                                                    │
│ (part-time / seasonal positions)                                           │
└──────────────────────────────────────────────────────────────────────────┘
```

Figure 2.3

JOB DESCRIPTION

COMMUNITY CENTER DIRECTOR (THERAPEUTICS)
(1-8-03)

Under the direct supervision of the T.R. RPC and the overall supervision of the T.R. Service Area Coordinator, this employee is responsible for providing a broad range of group and individual activities and services for participants with disabilities. Duties include:

Directing various T.R. programs as assigned on a seasonal basis by the T.R. Program Coordinator. Directing Therapeutic Recreation Programs includes the following components:

- Reviewing participant registrations, assessments and past program documentation to prepare for any medical/behavioral concerns and to develop appropriate program goals and individualized objectives.

- Planning the program activities and/or clearly delegating planning assignments to Recreation Leaders (part time staff). Assuring that planned activities are appropriate in terms of program goals and participant objectives. Assuring that activities are planned in detail with contingency plans for possible variables. Completing required planning documents specific to each program.

- Preparing for the program/activities by securing necessary equipment/supplies, confirming facility space and attending to all other planning details. This requires the CCD to communicate (well in advance) with the Program Coordinator as to the items needed and the procurement process.

- Supervising the Recreation Leaders (and volunteers) assigned to the program. Delegating activity leadership assignments and other duties relating to the program. Providing Recreation Leaders with on-going direction and support. Evaluating the performance of all staff assigned to the program. This includes the periodic performance reviews (written) required by the Division as well as regular feedback concerning progress and/or areas needing development.

- Monitoring program/activities for safety and success. Being alert to potential safety issues and assuring staff are acting in a safe manner. Making modifications to activities (as needed) to maximize participation and enjoyment.

- Maintaining clear and open communications with participants, parents/guardians, T.R. staff, volunteers and center staff. Informing of incidents, accidents, and issues pertaining to the program in an appropriate and timely manner. Providing opportunities for feedback, questions or suggestions concerning the program.

Figure 2.3 continued

Figure 2.3 – (continued)

- Evaluating program/activities in terms of quality standards and participant outcomes. Gaining input from staff, participants, and parents/guardians in determining recommendations and necessary revisions.

- Overseeing the care, cleanliness and upkeep of all facilities utilized. Reporting any maintenance concerns to Program Coordinator and center staff. Locking facilities, as may be required, at the conclusion of the program. Assuring the care and proper use of all TR Division equipment and supplies.

- May include assisting with transportation of participants for field trips, utilizing city vehicles.

- Accurately completing all departmental and divisional documentation requirements and submitting within designated time frames.

In addition to these duties related to program directing, the Community Center Director (Therapeutics) facilitates the inclusion of individuals with disabilities in general CRC programs. Responsibilities related to inclusion support include:

- Outreach; promoting inclusive program opportunities to individuals with disabilities through various promotional strategies (attending meetings, developing promotional materials, etc.).

- Assist in preparing CRC programs for inclusion through staff training/orientation, peer training, environmental analysis and barrier removal.

- Attend regional and service area meetings to develop contacts and keep current on region/service area programs.

- Assist individuals contacting the Division to identify and register for general CRC programs if this is the desired/available option.

- Respond to requests for inclusion support through:

    Assessing participant needs (observations, meeting with parent/guardian, contacting school, facilitating completion of the Assessment/Accommodation document).

    Developing and implementing the Plan For Accommodation based on the assessment information.

    Developing and overseeing the implementation of a Behavioral Support Plan (if needed).

Figure 2.3 continued

Figure 2.3 – (continued)

Working directly with participant within the inclusive program to determine effective techniques and to model appropriate interactions for center staff.

Orienting staff to the needs/abilities of the participant (specific communication techniques, behavioral interventions, activity adaptations, personal care tasks, etc.) and observe as they assist participant. Provide feedback and continuing support for staff.

Acting as liaison between parent/guardian and center staff in order to foster open communications and cooperation.

Continuing to monitor the inclusion placement, meeting with center staff to discuss progress, issues and strategies.

Providing summary documentation to record effectiveness of strategies and recommendations for future.

In addition to these program directing duties and inclusion support duties, the CCD is responsible for:

- Assisting with the planning and implementation of various Divisional events

- Contributing to the management and operation of the T.R. Division's central office (registration procedures, communications, etc.)

- Complying with all departmental/divisional policies and procedures. Asking supervisor for guidance and clarification of any unclear policy/procedure.

Note*   It is the Cincinnati Recreation Commission's policy to provide recreation programs in the most integrated setting, and to make reasonable accommodations on the basis of disability when necessary. This could include the provision of assistance with personal care tasks such as bathrooming, dressing, eating, etc.

Figure 2.4

Cincinnati Recreation Commission
Division of Therapeutic Recreation

Job Description
Therapeutic Recreation Leader for T.R. Programs and Inclusive Programs

T.R. Programs
Under the immediate supervision of the Program Director, the Recreation Leader is responsible for the following:

Duties

1. Plan and prepare for the program. This includes contributing ideas during planning sessions, securing materials and supplies, making trip arrangements, etc. It also includes developing activities for designated time periods or for groups of participants.

2. Activity Leadership, including the planning, preparation, and leadership of various recreation activities. This includes directing and controlling the activity through verbal directions and/or manual (hand over hand) assistance. It may involve individual assistance to a single participant or leadership of a group activity. The Recreation Leader helps the participant to develop activity skills and interests. This requires the ability to assess participants and adapt activities to match participant skills.

3. Monitoring participant safety throughout the program. The Recreation Leader provides continuous supervision of assigned participants from drop-off to pick-up time. Requirements include good judgement and the ability to recognize hazardous situation and prevent accidents. The Recreation Leader must be alert and able to physically control participants if necessary.

4. Assist participants with personal care tasks such as dressing, eating and bathroom usage. This includes both verbal directions and physical assistance as needed. It includes opening food/drink containers, spoon feeding, keeping face and clothing free of food, etc. Bathroom assistance may include lifting on/off toilet, wiping, diaper changing, hand washing, etc.

5. Provide verbal and physical (non-aversive) intervention as needed to manage disruptive or aggressive participant behavior. It may include the development of behavior management plans, or supporting behavior management strategies previously outlined. It requires the ability to use behavior management techniques such as positive reinforcement, redirection, setting limits, etc.

Figure 2.4 continued

Figure 2.4 – (continued)

6. Swim Instruction. The Recreation Leader must have good personal swim skills and be able to teach participants using the Division's sequential swim progression. This includes teaching the beginner swimmer (level I) as well as the more advanced swimmer (level III). The Recreation Leader must be aware of water safety concerns.

7. Complete assigned documentation requirements including Individual Recreation Plans, Swim Lesson Plans, and other Division documents. This also includes input into the daily and final program evaluations.

8. Attend staff meetings, in-service training and or other meetings designated by Division Supervisor, Program Coordinator or Program Director.

9. Assist with the care and proper use and storage of all Division equipment, supplies and facilities. Notify the Program Director of equipment or facility concerns. Help with the clean up and lock-up of facilities as needed.

10. May assist with transportation of program participants for field trips in city vehicles.

    In addition to these duties, the Recreation Leader is expected to interact positively with the program participants throughout the day. A high energy level and enthusiasm for the program activities is necessary. The Recreation Leader must model appropriate social behaviors and encourage the participants to interact positively with each other.

Inclusive Programs

The function of the T.R. Leader working in an Inclusive Program is to facilitate the participation of the individual(s) with a disability in the community recreation program. The T.R. Leader will work in cooperation/collaboration with the community center staff. The ultimate goal is to foster full participation of the individual(s) with a disability. In addition to those duties previously identified, the T.R. Leader working in an inclusive program will:

1. Provide assistance to the individual with a disability throughout the program. Participant's skill level will determine the degree of assistance needed within the activities. Areas of assistance may include physical assistance, verbal prompts, transferring, modeling, personal care needs and behavior management (assistance will vary depending on disability).

2. Facilitate social interaction between the individual with a disability and his/her peers. Encourage socialization throughout the program to promote friendship with other participants.

Figure 2.4 continued

Figure 2.4 – (continued)

3. Adapt activities so the participant with a disability can participate to their fullest potential. Efforts should be made to include the individual in every activity offered throughout the program.

4. Act as an advocate for the individual with a disability: to promote disability awareness and emphasize the similarities rather than the differences between participants.

5. Reinforce the Center Staff's instructions by repeating/rephrasing specific instructions.

6. Identifies when the individual with a disability needs an alternate activity.

7. Communicates with a variety of parties; parent/caregivers, community center staff, T.R. Program Coordinator and participant. You will act as the primary liaison between all those involved to maintain open communication/cooperation.

8. Provide the participant with supplemental skill training, which may be necessary for successful inclusion (activity skills, social skills, etc.)

9. Provide an evaluation of the participant's success within an inclusive setting.

The T.R. Leader working an in inclusive setting must possess the ability to problem solve and implement strategies. This employee must be capable of building working relationships with staff who are not employed through the T.R. Division.

Figure 2.5

Manager of Inclusion

Job Purpose   Assess, plan, implement, supervise, and evaluate placements of persons with disabilities in partner recreation programs, in cooperation with NSSRA partner agencies.

Accountability   Superintendent of Recreation

Qualifications

1. Graduate from accredited college or university with a BA/BS degree in Therapeutic Recreation or Parks and Recreation.

2. Minimum of two years full time experience planning and conducting recreation programs for people with disabilities. Must have experience in the training and supervision of seasonal employees and volunteers, recruitment, and the evaluation of employees and volunteers.

3. Must demonstrate knowledge of disabling conditions, and experience in planning a wide range of recreation activities.

4. Must demonstrate enthusiasm, and ability to work effectively with people with disabilities, NSSRA staff, NSSRA partner agency staff, teachers, parents of participants, and community contacts.

5. Must be able to work independently, solve problems, and convey a positive attitude to others. Must have strong written and verbal communication skills.

6. Knowledge of current standards of professional practice and ability to apply these standards to daily work.

7. Certification, or acquiring certification within one year of hire, by the Crisis Prevention Institute is required. CTRS with the National Council for Therapeutic Recreation Certification is required.

Duties

1. Receive and evaluate requests for recreation inclusion support, acting as the initial contact for all inclusion referrals, whether made by the participant, a partner agency employee, or another agency or individual.

2. Recruit and train part time staff and sign language interpreters for inclusive programs and special events.

3. Develop policies and procedures for use by NSSRA in coordinating inclusion support for the NSSRA partner agencies, consistent with NSSRA philosophy.

4. Prepare and verify timesheets for seasonal employees and submit for payroll processing.

5. Assist the Superintendent of Recreation in identifying training needs amongst the partner staff and coordinate training opportunities which will better enable the partners to support inclusive recreation placements.

6. Serve as the liaison between NSSRA and NSSED for inclusive recreation placements.

Figure 2.5 continued

Figure 2.5 — (continued)

7. Act as liaison on inclusion and referrals to member agencies.

8. Provide information and advice to families or individuals seeking inclusive recreation placements.

9. Supervise and evaluate the work of the Recreation Specialist assigned to Inclusion, the Recreation Specialist who coordinates cooperative programs, and other full time or part time staff as assigned.

10. Oversee expenditure of funds for sign language interpreters, companions, inclusion training, and other activities, and revenue derived from those activities.

11. Represent NSSRA through attendance at community meetings and functions, and address schools, parents, participants, park districts and other social service groups, to promote the availability of inclusion support through NSSRA.

12. Assist the Superintendent of Recreation in evaluating the effectiveness of inclusion placements and NSSRA policies, procedures, and support of inclusion.

13. Provide information to the NSSRA finance office, and assist when necessary in preparing invoices for inclusion support.

14. Attend in-service training, conferences, and professional development opportunities.

15. Prepare monthly reports on activity, or as often as requested.

16. Participate in the promotion of NSSRA in the partner agencies and within our community.

17. Participate in planning the annual budget, development of methods or materials for the evaluation of programs, and agency meetings which affect all employees and functions.

18. Perform other duties related to this job when necessary, or duties in the best interest of the Association.

Essential Functions

The Manager of Inclusion must, with or without reasonable accommodations, be able to perform the following functions:

1. Understand the need for assignments in partner programs, and explain such assignments to prospective employees.

2. Communicate effectively with large and small groups of people.

3. Prepare, receive, and understand written material, whether by mail, facsimile, or email.

4. Solve complex problems regarding demand for inclusion and availability of employees.

5. Lift and carry as much as 50 pounds for as long as 300 feet.

6. Work efficiently and effectively under pressure such as deadlines or emergencies.

Figure 2.5 continued

Figure 2.6

Recreation Specialist (assigned to Inclusion)

Job Purpose   Under the direction of the Manager of Inclusion, provide support to families and partner agency staff regarding recreation inclusion placements.

Accountability   Manager of Inclusion

Qualifications

1.   The ability to develop and implement recreation activities for individuals of all ages and abilities.

2.   Graduate from accredited college or university with a BA/BS degree in Recreation, Therapeutic Recreation, or a related field, with one year of experience with persons with a wide range of abilities.

3.   Certification in CPR and First Aid.

4.   Must demonstrate knowledge of disabling conditions, and experience in planning a wide range of recreation activities.

5.   Must demonstrate enthusiasm, and ability to work effectively with people with disabilities, NSSRA staff, NSSRA partner agency staff, teachers, and parents of participants.

6.   Must be able to work independently, and convey a positive attitude to others. Must have good written and verbal communication skills.

7.   Credentialling as a Certified Therapeutic Recreation Specialist (CTRS) with the National Council for Therapeutic Recreation Certification, or attaining certification within one year of the date of hire, is required. Alternative credentialling as a Certified Leisure Professional will be accepted.

Duties

1.   Respond to inquiries about inclusion, and evaluate the need for inclusion support.

2.   Under the guidance of the Manager of Inclusion, coordinate and evaluate the placement of staff, sign language interpreters, or other supports for recreation inclusion.

3.   Assist in the evaluation of cooperative programs with the partner agencies and other organizations.

Recreation Specialist (Assigned to Inclusion) Position Description

1.   Assist in training companions and interpreters, as well as partner agency staff when requested.

2.   Develop, implement, evaluate, and follow through on behavior or inclusion plans.

3.   Assist in the recruitment of part time staff and interpreters for placement in this area.

4.   Assist Manager of Inclusion in conducting observations of participants in the partner communities as requested, and complete all necessary observation forms and communication with;

Figure 2.6 continued

Figure 2.6 – (continued)

5. Attend program meetings, team meetings, inservices, and other meetings as scheduled.

6. Assist in solving problems at inclusion sites by changing program or behavior plans as necessary.

7. Assist in communication of opportunities available at NSSRA and the NSSRA philosophy to participants, parents, and other professionals, and present information about NSSRA to schools, families, participants, staff of partner agencies, and service clubs.

8. Assist in preparing and implementing behavior management strategies when necessary, to ensure safe involvement in recreation programs by people with disabilities.

9. Substitute for companions who are absent on short notice.

10. Assist in preparing payroll as requested.

11. Assist in preparing invoices for inclusion support as requested.

12. Develop skills and abilities necessary to carry out assigned duties, by attendance at meetings as required by supervisor.

13. Perform other duties as assigned which contribute to the availability of leisure services for people with disabilities or the efficiency and effectiveness of NSSRA.

RECSPECINC200101   12/99

report to a manager with limited inclusion experience. Or, general recreation staff who provide inclusion services and report to their division head may rely on the TR manager or specialist to assist with inclusion; consequently, the staff may feel as if they are reporting to two supervisors. As with the centralized approach, budgeting challenges arise. When consumers elect to register for several types of agency programs, each unit's financial needs to support inclusion may vary from season to season. Planning across units becomes crucial to support anticipated and immediate demand by consumers for particular services.

Roles and responsibilities vary with staffing patterns; yet, CTRSs hired in any agency may find their duties range from management to direct services during a specific program or while preparing for inclusion agency wide. Likewise managers find a number of factors discovered during assessment of community, and agency resources impact their ability to contribute to the success of inclusion agency wide. Each organization is unique in its service approach. The ultimate goal is to have all personnel equally prepared to deliver services to persons with and without disabilities, so the advantages and disadvantages of the centralized vs. decentralized approach become inconsequential; yet, in reality, each organization experiences a particular degree of inclusion readiness that necessitates an approach suited to the organization's culture.

In both organizational approaches, centralized and decentralized, a number of individuals may serve as volunteers, seasonals, and part-time employees. These persons have expertise in their respective professions like special education, yet may not be familiar with the nature and outcomes of accommodations in the leisure environment. Likewise, interns may have professional leisure experiences yet not be familiar with application of the TR process to inclusion or the specific behaviors of participants desiring support, assistance or accommoda-

Figure 2.7

CITY OF RENO

THERAPEUTIC RECREATION SPECIALIST

*Class specifications are intended to present a descriptive list of the range of duties performed by employees in the class. Specifications are **not** intended to reflect all duties performed within the job.*

DEFINITION

To plan, supervise, assign review and participate in the work of staff responsible for the provision of recreational services for persons with disabilities for the Parks & Recreation Department; to ensure work quality and adherence to established policies and procedures; and to perform the more technical and complex tasks of the work unit relative to assigned area of responsibility.

To provide a balance of inclusive and adaptive recreation programs and act as staff advisor on recreational components of the Americans with Disabilities Act.

SUPERVISION EXERCISED

Exercises direct supervision over technical and clerical staff.

ESSENTIAL FUNCTION STATEMENTS—*Essential responsibilities and duties may include, but are not limited to, the following:*

Essential Functions:

1. Plan, prioritize, assign, supervise, review and participate in the work of staff responsible for the operations of therapeutic recreation functions for the Parks & Recreation Department.

2. Establish schedules and methods for providing assigned recreation program or community services; identify resource needs; review needs with appropriate management staff; allocate resources accordingly.

3. Participate in the development of policies and procedures; monitor work activities to ensure compliance with established policies and procedures; make recommendations for changes and improvements to existing standards and procedures.

4. Recommend and assist in the implementation of goals and objectives; implement approved policies and procedures.

5. Oversee fund-raising efforts and grant preparation for recreation and community service programs; monitor grant funded programs to ensure compliance with established requirements.

6. Coordinate the Americans for Disability Act review of park and facility design, review requests for services and advise staff on the inclusion of persons with disabilities in all programs and services.

7. Maintain yearly calendar of programs and services available to persons with disabilities; provide information and resources to the public regarding upcoming programs and services.

8. Identify the needs of persons with disabilities living in the City and anticipate the needs of persons with disabilities (residents and non-residents) attending special events.

9. Conduct on-site inspections of parks, programs and facilities; ensure proper maintenance and safety requirements are adhered to; respond to inquiries from staff.

Figure 2.7 continued

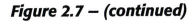

Figure 2.7 – (continued)

Essential Functions (continued):

10. Design and implement staff training programs which focus on disability awareness and of effective customer service.

11. Supervise the administration of various contracted recreational programs and classes; select instructors for classes, determine class locations and develop marketing and advertising materials.

12. Provide responsible staff assistance to the Director of Parks, Recreation & Community Service in the general administration of the Department; conduct operational studies and analyses involving budget, organization, procedures, policies or administrative problems.

13. Provide information and referral and consultation services to families needing assistance in determining appropriate recreation and leisure opportunities for participants with disabilities.

14. Monitor assigned departmental events to troubleshoot potential problems; investigate complaints regarding facilities, parks, programs or staff; identify issues and recommend corrective action.

15. Promote and coordinate specific activities within the therapeutic recreation program; prepare program event and facility marketing material including news releases, flyers, schedules of events, pamphlets and brochures.

16. Meet with public, private and community organizations to present and discuss issues and programs within the therapeutic recreation program; resolve complaints in a timely manner. Work in collaboration with community agencies and nonprofit organizations to ensure that programs are accessible to persons with disabilities.

17. Schedule usage of assigned recreational facilities for activities including special events; provide information and assistance to users of facilities.

18. Monitor and inspect recreational facilities for safety and proper maintenance; schedule maintenance and secure facilities.

19. Participate in the selection of assigned staff; provide or coordinate staff training; work with employees to correct deficiencies; implement discipline procedures.

20. Participate in the preparation and administration of the therapeutic recreation program budget; submit budget recommendations; monitor expenditures.

21. Prepare analytical and statistical reports on operations and activities.

22. Attend and participate in professional group meetings; stay abreast of new trends and innovations in the field of therapeutic recreation programs and services.

23. Perform related duties and responsibilities as required.

QUALIFICATIONS

Knowledge of:

Operations, services and activities of therapeutic recreation programs and services.
Principles and practices of planning, organizing and coordinating special and cultural events.
Principles and theories of inclusion for persons with disabilities.
Methods and techniques of developing therapeutic services and programs.

Figure 2.7 continued

Figure 2.7 – (continued)

Methods and techniques of grant preparation and administration.

Modern and complex principles, practices, tools and materials used in golf course maintenance.

Marketing theories, principles and practices and their application to therapeutic recreation program.

Principles and practices of public relations and customer service.

Principles of supervision, training and performance evaluation.

Principles and procedures of record keeping, business letter writing and basic report preparation.

Pertinent federal, state, and local laws, codes and regulations.

Ability to:

Supervise, organize, and review the work of lower level staff.

Select, supervise, train and evaluate staff.

Supervise and participate in the work of staff responsible for therapeutic recreation.

Coordinate the provision of downtown cultural and special events.

Oversee fund-raising and grant efforts for therapeutic recreation programs.

Oversee operations and use of assigned recreation facility.

Respond to requests and inquiries from the general public.

Coordinate the provision of contracted recreational classes to the public.

Recommend and implement goals and objectives for providing therapeutic recreational programs.

Elicit community and organizational support for therapeutic programs.

Research, analyze and evaluate new service delivery methods and techniques.

Interpret and explain city policies and procedures.

Prepare clear and concise reports.

Communicate clearly and concisely, both orally and in writing.

Establish and maintain effective working relationships with those contacted in the course of work including City officials and the general public.

Experience and Training Guidelines

Any combination of experience and training that would likely provide the required knowledge and abilities is qualifying. A typical way to obtain the knowledge and abilities would be:

> **Experience:**
>
> Four years of experience in the coordination of therapeutic recreation programs including one year of administrative or lead supervisory responsibility.

> **Training:**
>
> Equivalent to a Bachelor's degree from an accredited college or university with course work in therapeutic recreation and leisure services.

License or Certificate

Possession of a valid driver's license issued by the State of Nevada.

WORKING CONDITIONS

Environmental Conditions:

Office and field environment; travel from site to site; extensive public contact.

Physical Conditions:

Essential functions may require maintaining physical condition necessary for walking, standing or sitting for prolonged periods of time.

Figure 2.8

CITY OF RENO — Parks, Recreation, and Community Services
RECREATION PROGRAM SPECIALIST IV
(Temporary, Seasonal position)

Salary: Minimum:	$12.75 per hour	Maximum: $16.25

Definition
Under general supervision, performs work in the organization, direction, maintenance and/or supervision of facilities and/or programs; performs a variety of administrative functions in support of an assigned division: performs related duties as required.

Distinguishing Characteristics
This class is distinguished as having supervisory responsibility for the operations and programs of a recreation facility or program.

Examples of essential functions
Essential Functions may include, but are not limited to, the following:

1) Assists in supervising employees, instructs new employees on the various duties of their position.
2) Assists in the development of division and department policies, procedures, goals, and objectives.
3) Assists in organizing and supervising various special events.
4) Performs a variety of functions including answering phone calls, scheduling appointments, typing letters and memos, and maintaining files.
5) Prevents accidents through the enforcement of policies, rules, regulations, and ordinances governing the conduct of participants; observes for accidents within a program or facility.
6) Enforces policies, rules, and regulations regarding cleanliness of walks, floors, dressing rooms, of recreational facilities.
7) Assists in budget administration and evaluation.
8) Assists in making reports on attendance and activities of a recreational program or facility.
9) Conducts swimming, diving, and Water Safety classes, assists the Lifeguards in conducting aquatic training classes.
10) Enters the water to rescue persons in distress; resuscitates rescued swimmers; administers first aid to the injured and calls Emergency Medical Services (EMS) on serious accident cases.
11) Coordinates and supervises inclusion process.
12) Instructs staff on accommodation procedures regarding participants with special needs.
13) Perform related duties and responsibilities as assigned.

Working Conditions
*   Walks on various surfaces including uneven ground that may be slippery.
*   Tasks require physical condition necessary for walking, standing, or sitting for prolonged periods of time.
*   Conveys and exchanges verbal and written information.
*   Work may be performed outdoors in a variety of weather extremes.
*   Lifting, moving or carrying objects weighing up to fifty (50) pounds for short distances.

Minimum Qualifications
Age:	Must be at least 18 years of age
Education:	High school diploma or equivalent.
Experiences:	Five (5) years paid experience in program and/or facility coordination. Minimum of two (2) years supervisory experience.
Licenses:	Possession of a valid drivers license preferred.
Certifications:	Lifeguard Training, CPR, and First Aid required for aquatic positions. Certified Pool Operator and Water Safety Instructor certifications preferred for aquatic positions. Certified Therapeutic
Recreation	Specialist preferred for programs with special needs.

tions. Consequently, the use of job descriptions that delineate qualifications and responsibilities of volunteers, interns, and other part-time staff is a feature critical to the management of quality programs and services. Management may include the use of contracts that outline specific duties and training obligations. Adherence to safety protocols and professionally recognized practices is in the best interest of both the agency and individuals serving in a variety of supportive roles. Examples of intern and volunteer job descriptions, responsibilities and contracts illustrate the types of assistance provided by support personnel and the duties of full-time staff when agencies rely on interns and volunteers (refer to Figures 2.9-2.10).

Volunteerism offers the opportunity for inclusive programming. Individuals with and without disabilities may work together on community projects. Individuals with disabilities may provide support during general or inclusive programs. Regardless of the situation, benefits accrue to all involved (Miller, Schleien, Rider, Hall, Roche, & Worsley, 2002). When a volunteer program with persons having disabilities is operative, job descriptions and training practices similar to the agency's volunteer program with all community participants are developed to assure adherence to quality and risk management standards.

Training and Supervision

Preparation of peers and professionals through training and supervision is an acknowledged proactive inclusionary practice (Germ & Schleien, 1997; Rizzo & Lavay, 2000; Schleien, et al., 1996) and is positively correlated with employing a CTRS (Devine & Kotowski, 1999). Further, ongoing agency-wide training and supervision are recognized strategies to educate staff and volunteers about inclusion issues and strategies, updated ADA guidelines, funding alternatives, and accommodation practices (Dattilo, 2002; Devine & McGovern, 2001). A lack of staff training on programmatic issues like program modifications, implementation of behavior programs, and use of adaptive equipment is directly linked to limited provision of inclusive services (Devine & Kotowski, 1999). Training on how to include people with disabilities in programs and disability awareness (sensitivity to needs, general characteristics, and comprehension of participant capabilities to avoid the tendency to over-do or over-protect consumers) are identified as the most critical topics to the assurance of reasonable accommodations and equal access (Anderson & Heyne, 2000; Devine & Kotowski, 1999; McDonald, 2002). This section presents content recommended with staff and volunteers having inclusion assignments, training practices with adult learners, sample training outlines, and supervision scenarios that occur during inclusion experiences.

The initial step of training and supervision is to conduct a task or job analysis to identify skills necessary to implement inclusionary programs and services. This step also includes an assessment of current agency practices. An assessment of agency programming may reveal the need to infuse fundamental leadership and management best practices into agency-wide training and professional development plans with all personnel. Review of job descriptions, literature on inclusion, professional standards of practice, regulatory documents like ADA guidelines, and risk and quality improvement criteria reveal competencies essential to delivery of inclusion programs and services. Results of comparing job analysis information and professional practices with staff self-assessments of their knowledge, skills, and abilities reveal needed training content and supervisory areas. A primary training and supervision goal is to ensure staff growth and skill relevance to the application of the APIE process. A secondary goal is to foster supportive staff attitudes toward their inclusion roles. A recommended best practice is to incorporate training on inclusion into the general agency training areas; to illustrate, training on activity leadership during structured programs would include managing challenging behaviors of all children and persons with disabilities and adapting or modifying rules and equipment to accommodate the developmental needs of all participants.

Training is one of the most frequently identified strategies to prepare recreation staff to include individuals with disabilities in programs and services (Devine & McGovern, 2001). Successful inclusion occurs when a positive attitude and focus on participant abilities are expressed through a welcoming environment. Consequently, two topics, disability awareness and successful strategies to facilitate and promote positive community responses to inclusion, are fundamental to training with all agency personnel, volunteers, and patrons (Devine & McGovern, 2001; MacDonald, 2002). Another key topic is compliance with ADA mandates; in particular, how to make reasonable accommodations, satisfy accessibility regulations, and techniques to assist and support individuals as they meet eligibility criteria. Training on these topics facilitates compliance with specific regulations

Figure 2.9

CITY OF RENO - Parks, Recreation and Community Services

RECREATION PROGRAM SPECIALIST I - Supplemental
Therapeutic Recreation Intern
(Temporary, Seasonal position)

SALARY   Up to $8.00, based on experience

Definition
Under immediate supervision, assists in the on-going development and implementation of inclusion services and therapeutic recreation with in the PRCS department; performs related duties as required.

Distinguishing Characteristics
This class is distinguished as having responsibility for operations and programs within the Parks, Recreation, and Community Services Department.

Examples of Essential Functions
Essential functions include those identified in the Recreation Program Specialist I job description. Duties as assigned may also include but are not limited to, the following:

1)   Collects payments, registration, and reservations for recreational facilities.
2)   Greets customers, answers phone calls, and provides customer service as directed.
3)   Record keeping activities for various programs.
4)   Assists in instructing staff on inclusion and therapeutic recreation techniques.
5)   Responsible for organizing, supervising, and set up/dismantle of a special event/program.
6)   Responsible for the development, implementation, and evaluation of a special project.
7)   Responsible for completing a case study as assigned by supervisor.
8)   Prevents accidents through the enforcement of policies, rules, regulations, and ordinances governing the conduct of facility patrons.
9)   Enforces policies, rules and regulations regarding facilities and programs.
10)   May, under direction, assist with the teaching of water safety, swimming and diving, and assists in recreation based special events.
11)   Clean up and light maintenance around the facility.
12)   Assists in making reports on attendance and activities of the facility or program.
13)   Leads or instructs participants in programs.
14)   Prepares supplies for programs.
15)   Reports to supervisor in area of responsibility.
16)   Provides information on Department activities to public.
17)   Open and close facility including securing, doors, windows, and all other surrounding areas.
18)   Facilitates inclusion of people of all abilities into activities and or classes.
19)   Assists with providing inclusive recreation environment and accommodating participants with special needs.
20)   Supervise and schedules structured activities for participants in various programs.
21)   Prepares, attends and participates in necessary staff training, in-services, and meetings.
22)   Completes all assignments and projects as assigned.
23)   Communicates openly and effectively with supervisor, other city staff, participants, parents/care-givers, and volunteers to provide excellent customer service.
24)   Completes all assessment, documentation and evaluations as assigned.

Figure 2.9 continued

Figure 2.9 – (continued)

Working Conditions
- Walks on various surfaces including uneven ground that may be slippery.
- Tasks require physical condition necessary for walking, standing, or sitting for prolonged periods of time.
- Conveys and exchanges verbal and written information.
- Work may be performed outdoors in a variety of weather extremes.
- Lifting, moving or carrying objects weighing up to fifty (50) pounds for short distances.

Minimum Qualifications

Age:	Must be at least 18 years of age
Education:	Two (2) years of college or university coursework. Major in Recreation or Therapeutic Recreation preferred.
Experience:	Previous experience working with people with disabilities preferred.
Licenses:	Possession of a valid drivers license. Provision of evidence of an acceptable driving record.
Certifications:	CPR, and First Aid required. Lifeguard Training or Water Safety Instructor certifications preferred.
Independence:	Ability to work independently and as part of a team.

Supervision: Interns are supervised by a full-time CTRS.

Hours: Interns are required to work 40 hours a week for a minimum of 12 consecutive weeks, equal to 480 hours. They may not work less than 20 hours during any given week. Additional hours per university requirements may apply.

Compensation: Interns are eligible for a wage of up to $8.00 an hour for the duration of their internship pending the availability of funds. This position expires upon the completion of the internship. The City does not provide additional benefits or room and board.

Application Procedure: Internship candidates must send a Letter of Interest and resume to initiate the application process. The Dept. will then send a formal letter and application. Employees may not start until the application process is completed including the submission of the formal City of Reno Employment Application, interview, background check, reference check and employment orientation. All university contracts must be signed and submitted before the internship commences.

Deadline for Applications:

Season	Deadline for Letter of Application
Fall	May 1
Winter/Spring	October 1
Summer	February 1

Send all inquiries and letters of application to the following:

Inclusive Recreation - Internship
c/o Andy Fernandez
City of Reno
Parks, Recreation and Community Services
1301 Valley Road
Reno, Nevada 89512

Figure 2.10

VOLUNTEER RESPONSIBILITIES

Under the supervision of the program director and/or assistant directors, volunteers in a therapeutic recreation program are responsible for assisting with or leading a variety of activities and supervision of participants.

The volunteer is responsible for:

1. Assisting in monitoring the safety of program participants, visitors, supplies, and equipment.

2. Assisting in planning diversified leisure activities based on the needs and interests of the participants according to the continuum method.

3. Notifying program director (at home or work) in case of absence. (Call one day or evening ahead, if possible.)

4. Attending at least one day of program each week for the entire program session.

5. Leading and/or assisting in conducting assigned activities.

6. Reporting progress and problems with participants and program to director and assistant directors.

7. Assisting with the evaluation of program and participants.

8. Dressing appropriately by wearing clothes that will allow you to be actively involved in activities (e.g., wear gym shoes and loose fitting, comfortable clothes).

9. Being enthusiastic!

10. Being dependable and adaptable to various situations.

Figure 2.10 continued

Figure 2.10 — (continued)

VOLUNTEER CONTRACT

The Cincinnati Recreation Commission, Division of Therapeutic Recreation agrees:

    a. To train volunteers to a level that will enable them to begin their work confidently.

    b. To continue their training to whatever extent is necessary to maintain continuing competence.

    c. To provide volunteers with working conditions equal to those of paid employees.

    d. To make written evaluations of each volunteer's job performance at regular and suitable intervals and to provide references on request.

    e. To offer volunteers promotion to more responsible jobs within the volunteer program.

    f. To include volunteers in staff planning and evaluating when possible and generally promote their understanding of division workings and decisions.

The volunteer agrees:

    a. To work a certain number of hours a week according to a schedule acceptable to the program director.

    b. To become thoroughly familiar with the policies and procedures (written and verbal) set forth by the division for volunteers.

    c. To be prompt and reliable in reporting for work and to provide the division with an accurate record of hours worked by signing in and out.

    d. To attend orientation and training sessions and undertake continuing education as necessary to maintain competence.

    e. To respect the function of the program director and staff and to contribute fully to a smooth working relationship between staff and volunteers.

    f. To accept the division's right to dismiss any professional volunteer for poor performance, including poor attendance.

    g. To notify the division at least one week in advance of resignation or requested leave of absence.

    h. To exercise caution when acting on the division's behalf and to protect the confidentiality of all information relating to the division and its participants.

| _____ | _____ | _____ | _____ |
| Program Director | Date | Volunteer | Date |

while preparing recreation environments for inclusion (Devine & Kotowski, 1999; Devine & McGovern, 2001). General training topics relevant to all personnel include: benefits of recreation, meaning of inclusion, managing challenging behaviors, safety, documentation, appropriate modifications, accessible transportation, and general program and leadership management skills presented in the chapters on direct service (4) and participant motivation and management. (6)

Managers of inclusion support benefit from training on: assessment, behavior management, volunteer recruitment and training, team building, caregiver interactions, activity adaptations, assistive devices, activity and task analyses, and individualizing instruction (McGovern & Wetherald, 2001). Direct service staff and volunteers benefit from training topics on the APIE process like: transfers, personal assistance, crisis intervention, alternative communication like sign language or symbol picture systems, medication side effects, seizure management, orthopedic and prosthetic devices, documentation on support and behavior plans and incident reports, structuring program time, and managing program transitions and "down time." Managers and direct service staff benefit from practicing time management and stress reduction or burnout avoidance techniques. The practice of strategies to accommodate participants with challenging disruptive behaviors using resource personnel like behavior specialists as trainers is a topic important to program safety. Also, training opportunities that help caregivers sustain their own recreation behaviors helps to foster consumer participation and encourage collaboration with professionals.

A CTRS hired agency-wide or from the therapeutic recreation division may assume primary training responsibilities on inclusion for the agency. A second scenario finds professionals in the human resource division responsible for agency-wide training. They may rely on assistance from the CTRS/TR division as they develop and implement agency-wide training and staff development programs. Persons who manage and provide direct inclusion services come from a variety of educational and experiential backgrounds. They may vary in age from 16 to 60, or be teen companions, RSVP or consumer volunteers. Also, staff and volunteers may assist with one special event for a limited time or serve as leisure buddies over extended time periods during seasonal programs. Thus, training preparation takes into consideration factors like these as well as the completed job analyses, staff self-assessments, and agency wide program assessments. A number of guidelines are recommended with adults to foster retention and application of information and inclusionary practices.

1. Site-specific administrative and program practices with specific cases or problems is received favorably and promotes positive attitudes and practices.
2. Explanation of why it is important to correctly implement the APIE process creates an understanding of inclusion roles and tasks.
3. Staff review of their job descriptions that have been revised to include statements on inclusion support helps staff plan how to accommodate and assist consumers.
4. Awareness training with children and youth who patronize programs serves as a staff training technique by requiring staff to assist the children as therapeutic recreation professionals present inclusion scenarios. Children may raise questions adults would hesitate to ask.
5. Demonstration of correct as well as incorrect procedures, like documenting behavior plans, helps trainees distinguish right from wrong.
6. Content coverage from general leadership techniques like reinforcement to specific types of reinforcers, for example, facilitates application.
7. Training priorities are determined by considering the critical nature and frequency of behaviors and skills. Therefore, important topics to cover include seizure management, activity adaptation, social skill reinforcement, and behavior management skills like redirection and setting limits.
8. Reliance on the primary senses and hands-on techniques with case studies authenticates experiences.
9. Including rewards for attending training sessions and acknowledging the humor and emotional challenges of therapeutic relationships encourages participation.
10. Comparing and contrasting activity formats like structured vs unstructured programs and line vs circle formations helps staff experience the outcomes of various leadership strategies and articulate the pros and cons of each.

Training on inclusion occurs during new staff orientations, over lunch breaks, during in-service days, or by attending workshops and professional meetings. Some topics like phone registration are presented with printed material then followed by role-playing. Others like universal precautions or lifts and transfers are presented by peer experts from other health and human service agencies. Regardless of training format, managers prepare and retain outlines to document the nature of training, trainee attendance, and recommended practices. Training outlines illustrate the range of topics from the APIE process to specific behavior management strategies (refer to Figures 2.11-2.13). The materials found in the direct services, individuals with disabilities, and motivating and managing participants, Chapters 4-6, are useful training resources. A recommended best practice is to include inclusion training in the agency's comprehensive human resource development program with qualified professionals dedicated to training in this area.

Supervision permeates managerial responsibilities and is critical to ensure that appropriate levels of support and assistance facilitate accomplishment of reasonable accommodations. And, due to the dynamic nature of participant behaviors and program interactions, ongoing feedback enables adaptation and modification of individual support and behavior plans. Participant response to planned events is influenced by medication levels, variance among group member abilities, program location, transitions and changes, and staff expertise, to name a few. Consequently, the nature of supervision varies and is influenced by the manner in which the APIE process is delivered. To illustrate, staff may be involved daily with a consumer and his/her leisure buddy until a support plan is fully implemented over a definitive time period; or, another scenario might have the CTRS training general recreation staff prior to assessment and program delivery with intermittent visits during implementation and program evaluations (refer to Figure 2.7, the Therapeutic Recreation Specialist position description for the City of Reno). Yet another situation may find, as a result of initial assessments, that additional assistance or a one-on-one companion is the recommended accommodation in the support plan. If this occurs, an inclusion specialist might indefinitely provide behavior supervision (refer to Figure 2.4, the Cincinnati Recreation Commission Therapeutic Recreation Leader for TR Programs and Inclusive Programs job description). The one-on-one companion then balances the companion role so the participant interacts as independently as possible in social experiences while the companion assumes roles supportive of other staff present in the program. Thus, supervision occurs in a number of ways that intend to promote independence and success during the immediate experience while preparing for alternative future placements.

Supervision with staff and volunteers supports their continued growth and receptivity to inclusionary experiences. Modifying the APIE process to individualize experiences is a continual process of assessment and re-assessment. Through case reviews, observations, role playing, and critical incidents, diverse participant needs are identified and alternatives are created to access experiences. Documentation of the types of inclusion assistance provided helps staff prepare training programs and identify budget staffing needs (refer to Figure 2.14, the Inclusion Assistance Tracking Form used by the Cincinnati Recreation Commission (n.d.)). Effective training and supervision efforts contribute to program consistency and a welcoming attitude among service providers.

Training and supervision are major managerial responsibilities (refer to Figures 2.3 and 2.5, the Community Center Director (Therapeutics), Cincinnati Recreation Commission, and the Manager of Inclusion, Northern Suburban Special Recreation Association, job descriptions). Yet as noted in the literature and professional studies, training is essential to successful inclusion experiences.

Figure 2.11

**Therapeutic Recreation
Inclusion Training "Retreat"
April 17, 2003**

Session Agenda/Outline

I. Inclusion and the CRC; Where We've Been, Where We're Going

II. Overview of the Americans with Disabilities Act (Title II, implications for recreation)

III. The Inclusion Process, The Program/Inclusion Specialist's Role in Providing
Inclusion Support

   A. Program Promotion, requirements for notification

   B. "Intake" Procedures, the Registration Process

   C. **Assessment** (determining need for accommodation)

        1. Participant Assessment (Assessment/Accommodation document,
school observations, program observations,
IEP, parent meeting, etc.)

        2. Program/Environment Assessment (environmental analysis)

   D. **Planning** (determining strategies for providing accommodation, identifying
resources, individual behavior plans, etc.)

   E. **Implementation** (providing accommodation through training, orientation and
support for center staff, building relationships with center staff,
etc.)

   F. **Evaluation** (monitoring the effectiveness of accommodation through follow-up)

IV. Documentation Requirements for Inclusion

Figure 2.12

Planning for Accessibility

Inclusion Training for SRC's, SAC's & RPC's

**Creating a Supportive Recreational Environment and Using
Effective Strategies that Work for Participants with Disabilities**

Date: May 28, 2003

Time: 9:00am – 12:00pm

Location: Drake Hospital, Room E

Target Audience: **Administrators &
                               Program Directors**

Agenda:

☆   **Americans with Disabilities Act and Section 504
      A Snapshot of our Participants with Disabilities
      and Their Needs**
      Presenter: J. Bruce Kramer, Regional Autism Coordinator

☆   **Setting Up a Successful Environment, Strategies that Work**
      *Presenter: Donna Murray, Ph.D. Treatment Director of the Kelly
                     O'Leary Center for Autism spectrum Disorders*

☆   **Supporting the Staff**
      *Presenter: Charlene Younger, Community-Based Team Leader,
                     Community Integrated Training and Education (CITE)*

☆   **Agency Support-Who Can Help and How to Access Them**
      *Presenters: Agency Representatives from the Community
                     Organizations which support students with disabilities*

This workshop is designed for those who provide support to participants with disabilities in
summer camps and recreation activities. They are provided through the collaborative efforts of the
Hamilton County Autism Spectrum Disorder Task Force, The Kelly O'Leary Center for Autism
Spectrum Disorders, Children's Hospital, Division of Developmental Disabilities, Hamilton County
Board Of Mental Retardation and Developmental Disabilities, The Resident Home, Cincinnati
Recreation Commission, Camp Country Club and select YMCA sites in Hamilton County

Questions? Please call Stephanie Knarr @ 352-4055

Figure 2.13

Pre-Summer Behavior Management Training
for Region Day Camp Staff

I. Introduction
   ☆ Overview of session
   ☆ Inclusion Philosophy/Departmental responsibilities under ADA
   ☆ Benefits of recreation, developmental aspects of recreation

II. Environmental Strategies
   ☆ Structuring the program
       ("Evaluating Program Structure" hand-out, group work)

   ☆ Group Supervision
       *   Prevention, the best intervention!
       *   Pro-active management techniques
       *   Positive reinforcement (rules for reinforcement)

III. The "A,B,C's" of Managing Behavior

   Behavior rarely occurs as a separate, isolated incident

   A (Antecedent)   Most behavior occurs as a response to some prior stimulus
                         Recognizing the prior stimulus, or "antecedent", is critical in
                         determining how to respond to an individual's behavior

   B (Behavior)   Behavior, for this session, refers to any action (or non-action)
                         by a program participant determined to be detrimental to the
                         program or individual(s)

   C (Consequence)   The immediate response of the staff member (and
                         others) to the participant's behavior is either a
                         positive or negative reinforcement for the behavior.
                         Negative reinforcement, also known as a
                         "consequence", is meant to extinguish the behavior

   ☆ Recognizing and understanding antecedents

   ☆ Rules for consequences (appropriateness, least restrictive to more restrictive, etc.)

   ☆ Enforcing consequences (setting limits)

   ☆ Group Work: List observed behaviors, identify possible antecedents, identify
               appropriate consequences

IV. Addressing Chronic Behaviors/Individual Behavior Plans

   ☆ Behaviors as "symptoms" of a disability, behaviors associated with (ADD,
       autism, etc.)

   ☆ Importance of documentation, evidence of accommodation efforts,
       Individual Behavior Plans

   ☆ Policy on physical restraint, CPI training program

Figure 2.14

Inclusion Assistance Tracking Form

TR Staff: _____   Date(mmyy): _____

N e w	Date	Region/ Center	Time	Reason for visit
☐	___ ___/_____	_____	☐Observation ☐Meeting ☐Training ☐A&A ☐Office_____ ☐Other _____
☐	___ ___/_____	_____	☐Observation ☐Meeting ☐Training ☐A&A ☐Office_____ ☐Other _____
☐	___ ___/_____	_____	☐Observation ☐Meeting ☐Training ☐A&A ☐Office_____ ☐Other _____
☐	___ ___/_____	_____	☐Observation ☐Meeting ☐Training ☐A&A ☐Office_____ ☐Other _____
☐	___ ___/_____	_____	☐Observation ☐Meeting ☐Training ☐A&A ☐Office_____ ☐Other _____
☐	___ ___/_____	_____	☐Observation ☐Meeting ☐Training ☐A&A ☐Office_____ ☐Other _____
☐	___ ___/_____	_____	☐Observation ☐Meeting ☐Training ☐A&A ☐Office_____ ☐Other _____
☐	___ ___/_____	_____	☐Observation ☐Meeting ☐Training ☐A&A ☐Office_____ ☐Other _____
☐	___ ___/_____	_____	☐Observation ☐Meeting ☐Training ☐A&A ☐Office_____ ☐Other _____
☐	___ ___/_____	_____	☐Observation ☐Meeting ☐Training ☐A&A ☐Office_____ ☐Other _____
☐	___ ___/_____	_____	☐Observation ☐Meeting ☐Training ☐A&A ☐Office_____ ☐Other _____
☐	___ ___/_____	_____	☐Observation ☐Meeting ☐Training ☐A&A ☐Office_____ ☐Other _____
☐	___ ___/_____	_____	☐Observation ☐Meeting ☐Training ☐A&A ☐Office_____ ☐Other _____
☐	___ ___/_____	_____	☐Observation ☐Meeting ☐Training ☐A&A ☐Office_____ ☐Other _____
☐	___ ___/_____	_____	☐Observation ☐Meeting ☐Training ☐A&A ☐Office_____ ☐Other _____
☐	___ ___/_____	_____	☐Observation ☐Meeting ☐Training ☐A&A ☐Office_____ ☐Other _____
☐	___ ___/_____	_____	☐Observation ☐Meeting ☐Training ☐A&A ☐Office_____ ☐Other _____
☐	___ ___/_____	_____	☐Observation ☐Meeting ☐Training ☐A&A ☐Office_____ ☐Other _____
☐	___ ___/_____	_____	☐Observation ☐Meeting ☐Training ☐A&A ☐Office_____ ☐Other _____
☐	___ ___/_____	_____	☐Observation ☐Meeting ☐Training ☐A&A ☐Office_____ ☐Other _____

References

Anderson, L., & Heyne, L. (2000). A statewide needs assessment using focus groups: Perceived challenges and goals in providing inclusive recreation services in rural communities. *Journal of Park and Recreation Administration, 18*(4), 17-37.

Cincinnati Recreation Commission, Division of Therapeutic Recreation. (n.d.).
> *Inclusion Assistance Tracking Form*
> *Inclusion Training Retreat*
> *Job description Community Center Director Therapeutics (2003)*
> *Job description Therapeutic Recreation Leader for TR Programs and Inclusive Programs*
> *Planning for Accessibility*
> *Pre-Summer Behavior Management Training for Region Day Camp Staff*
> *Therapeutic Recreation Table of Organization*
> *Volunteer Contract*
> *Volunteer Responsibilities*

(Available from Cincinnati Recreation Commission, Division of Therapeutic Recreation, 805 Central Avenue, Cincinnati, Ohio 45202).

City of Reno—Parks, Recreation, and Community Services. (n.d.).
> *Recreation Program Specialist I—Supplemental Therapeutic Recreation Intern*
> *Recreation Program Specialist IV*
> *Therapeutic Recreation Specialist*

(Available from City of Reno—Parks, Recreation, and Community Services, PO Box 1900, Reno, Nevada 89505).

Dattilo, J. (2002). *Inclusive leisure services responding to the rights of people with disabilities* (2nd ed.). State College, PA: Venture Publishing, Inc.

Devine, M. A., & Kotowski, L. (1999). Inclusive leisure services: Results of a national survey of park and recreation departments. *Journal of Park and Recreation Administration, 17*(4), 56-72.

Devine, M. A., & McGovern, J. (2001). Inclusion of individuals with disabilities in public park and recreation programs: Are agencies ready? *Journal of Park and Recreation Administration, 19*(4), 60-82.

Fox Valley Special Recreation Association. (n.d.). *Organizational chart.* (Available from Fox Valley Special Recreation Association, 1 North Lincolnway, North Aurora, IL 60542).

Germ, P. A., & Schleien, S. J. (1997). Inclusive community leisure services: Responsibilities of key players. *Therapeutic Recreation Journal, 36*(1), 22-37.

Jordan, D. J. (2001). *Leadership in leisure services: Making a difference* (2nd ed.). State College, PA: Venture Publishing, Inc.

LeConey, S., Devine, M. A., Bunker, H., & Montgomery, S. (2000). Utilizing the therapeutic recreation process in community settings: The case of Sue. *Parks & Recreation, 35*(5), 70-77.

McDonald, J. (2002). Helping your counselors welcome all campers. *Camping Magazine, 75*(3), 24-27.

McGovern, J., & Wetherald, L. (2001). Inclusion comes into focus for parks and recreation get out active up! *Ability,* 62-69.

Miller, K.D., Schleien, S.J., Rider, C., Hall, C., Roche, M., & Worsley, J. (2002). Inclusive volunteering: Benefits to participants and community. *Therapeutic Recreation Journal, 36*(3), 247-259.

Northern Suburban Special Recreation Association. (n.d.).
> *Manager of Inclusion*
> *Recreation Specialist assigned to Inclusion* (Available from Northern Suburban Special Recreation Association, 3105 MacArthur Blvd., Northbrook, Illinois 60062).

Rizzo, T. L., & Lavay, B. (2000). Inclusion: Why the confusion? *JOPERD, 71*(4), 32-36.

Schleien, S. J., Germ, P. A., & McAvoy, L. H. (1996). Inclusive community leisure services: Recommended professional practices and barriers encountered. *Therapeutic Recreation Journal, 30*(4), 260-273.

Schleien, S. J., Ray, M. T., & Green, F. P. (1997). *Community recreation and people with disabilities* (2nd ed.). Baltimore, MD: Paul H. Brookes Publishing Co.

Sullivan, A. K., & O'Brien, M. B. (2001). Inclusive programming at summer camp. *Parks & Recreation, 36*(5), 66-72.

CHAPTER 3

Marketing and Advocacy

Leisure and health care professionals are in a competitive market to attract and retain customers (burlingame, 1998; Siegenthaler, 2000). Marketing tools are used to survey consumer needs, identify gaps, and develop products and services appropriate to consumers, caregivers, and the community. Adding value to services, or delivering more than customers expect is generally regarded as essential to the success of establishing and maintaining long-term relationships or exchange relationships with consumers. Inclusive services through community agencies often are provided to consumers over extended time periods. Thus, the importance of establishing and maintaining communication is key.

Marketing and various communication tools are used by managers and direct service staff in the management and delivery of programs and services. To create program access entails: 1) developing formal compliance statements, 2) creating alternative information formats, 3) removing communication barriers, and 4) ensuring information is accessible and usable by individuals with disabilities (Dattilo, 2002). Creating a welcoming and positive attitude and becoming aware of individual needs, rather than making assumptions based on labels, are necessary to remove participation barriers and establish helping relationships (Fink, 2001). Advocacy roles are assumed by managers and direct service staff when they assist and support consumers as they gain reasonable accommodations and manage naturally occurring challenges associated with physical and attitudinal accessibility (Dattilo, 2002).

A marketing plan is developed from information gathered during the SWOT analysis (refer to Chapter 1, Defining the Service: Assessing the Community and Agency). Format for the plan follows the APIE outline. The first portion of this section considers the importance and steps in designing marketing or action plans. Marketing tools are used to inform consumers of the agency's intent to comply with ADA and to enable participants to enter into programs: Training is a marketing tool that supports inclusive programming. These topics are presented in the second section. The closing portion considers the role of advocacy in creating and maintaining community relations.

Marketing Plans

Marketing is a dynamic process that uses a number of strategies to achieve specific outcomes. These outcomes promote professional values, gain resources to meet programming needs, accomplish agency and department goals, and assure that quality customer services result in long-term relationships. Strategic market planning aligns agency resources with consumer needs and expectations. A marketing plan results from the SWOT analysis and is guided by the agency vision and mission (refer to Chapter 1, Defining the Service: Assessing the Community and Agency). Results of the SWOT analysis guide programming decisions and identify communication tools effective with various audiences. A marketing plan uses the APIE process to identify communication tools and strategies effective with internal and external audiences to support therapeutic recreation and inclusionary services.

The initial step in the development of a marketing plan is to conduct a needs assessment. A needs assessment identifies consumers' recreation and personal needs and agency readiness. This includes 1) expectations of external audiences (persons outside the agency or inclusion program) and internal audiences (persons within the agency or associated with the inclusion program), 2) their awareness and sensitivity to individuals with disabilities, 3) status of services and resources devoted to therapeutic recreation and inclusion; and, 4) types of reasonable accommodations that may be necessary to create program access. Marketing surveys are used to gather data from internal and external audiences. The Internet, focus groups, program brochures, personal interviews, observations, and drop-off/pick-up forms collect data from consumers, caregivers, and community members. Specific market segments are assessed as shown in a survey targeting persons with physical disabilities, Figure 3.1, Therapeutic Recreation Adapted Sports Survey, (Cincinnati Recreation Commission, 2002).

In the second step, planning, action plans are written to identify how the agency intends to deliver programs and services and accomplish specific marketing goals with each internal and external audience or market segment. To illustrate, one goal of the inclusion process is to ensure that individuals with disabilities are aware of agency programs and services. An action plan, therefore, identifies alternative promotional and informational approaches that include an ADA compliance statement or program mission so persons with sight, hearing or cognitive impairments have the opportunity to register or enroll in desired programs and services. Action plans describe services available to consumers and accessibility of the location or the "place" (in marketing terms) of the service. Funding options or pricing alternatives to support and assist in programming are explained: While financial adjustments of program fees to specifically accommodate inclusion are not recognized as one of the reasonable accommodations, scholarships, sliding fee structures, and third-party reimbursement are allowable strategies. The manager provides information on these alternatives through policies and procedures developed to promote access.

In step three, implementation, programs and services are delivered. Marketing plans include strategies to support and educate consumers and constituents as services are delivered. For example, therapeutic recreation staff facilitate participant advisory groups, community awareness days, sibling inclusion training, and staff in-services with general recreation personnel. In actual program delivery, staff use augmentative and alternative communication (AAC) systems and computer assistive devices to remove communication barriers during program registration and delivery. Action plans outline how these accommodations are used with each audience to promote access and support inclusion.

Evaluation is the final step in the marketing process. Goals prepared for each marketing audience as a result of the needs assessment are evaluated to determine if the marketing plan resulted in pre-planned outcomes. Each step of the marketing action plan is critiqued. To illustrate, evaluation questions appropriate to each step are presented: Assessment—Were all potential consumers made aware of the agency's inclusion opportunities through alternative promotional strategies? Is each agency employee aware of the agency statement on inclusion? Planning—Was the agency ADA compliance statement and/or agency mission statement supported through policy and procedural adjustments that created reasonable physical accommodations and program access? Do agency employees have the opportunity to participate in sensitivity training? Implementation—Were communication methods used during program delivery to adapt or modify experiences commensurate with participant functioning abilities? Are general recreation managers aware of the support responsibilities of peer coaches or buddies who participate in their programs? Evaluation—Are the communication strategies and tools being used by the agency helping to achieve the agency mission of consumer satisfaction and the establishment of long-term relationships with all participants? Are agency employees supporting reasonable accommodations through their interactions with participants, caregivers, and the community-at-large?

ADA Compliance and Marketing Tools

Professionals providing inclusive services communicate their intent to comply with ADA to internal and external audiences. Internal audiences are persons within the agency and the consumers and caregivers who

Figure 3.1

Cincinnati Recreation Commission

Therapeutic Recreation Adapted Sports Survey

Are you interested in sports?

The T.R. Division is in the process of determining which sports and activities to offer for individuals with physical disabilities. Over the past few years we have provided a variety of sports programs and events and we are asking for your help in planning for the future.

The following survey is intended to help us determine the level of interest in specific activities and to understand some of the factors which contribute to participation. Please take a few minutes to complete and return and help us develop programs which meet your interests!

I. Please rank the following activities using this rating scale:

1 = very interested   2 = somewhat interested   3 = not interested

archery	____	golf	____
target shooting	____	tennis	____
(air guns, etc.)		basketball	____
fishing	____	softball	____
rowing	____	track and field	____
kayaking	____	hand cycling	____
sailing	____	volleyball	____
scuba	____	football	____
swimming	____	rugby	____
water skiing	____	bowling	____
snow skiing	____	bocce	____
horseback riding	____	pool/billiards	____
cart driving	____	ping pong	____
martial arts	____	other (please write in):	
(karate, tai chi, etc.)		_____	
climbing/rappelling	____	_____	
road racing	____	_____	
(5 k, 10 k, marathons, etc.)		_____	

Figure 3.1 continued

Figure 3.1 – (continued)

II. Additional Participation Factors

For the sports/activities you indicated you were very interested in, how often would you like (be available) to participate in each?

Please circle number indicating your preferred frequency of participation;
1 = every week   2 = every other week   3 = once per month   4 = once or twice per year

activity				
_____	1	2	3	4
_____	1	2	3	4
_____	1	2	3	4
_____	1	2	3	4

What day(s) and time(s) are best for your participation? Please place a check mark next to all days and times you would be able to participate in your activities of interest.

Weeknights: Mon ____ Tues ____ Wed ____Thurs ____ Fri ____
Saturday: morning ____ afternoon ____ evening ____
Sunday: morning ____ afternoon ____ evening ____

Is transportation to/from program locations an issue? Yes____ No____
If yes, please indicate any limitations or complications due to transportation.

_____

What method of announcing program information works best for you? (check all that apply)

Monthly Newsletter _____   Direct Mail (flier) _____   E-Mail _____   TR Division web site _____
Other (please specify) _____

Are you interested in coaching or assisting in the development of any program/activity?
Yes ____ No ____   If yes, please indicate program/activity: _____

Optional Information: Name_____
                        Address _____
                        City _____ State _____ Zip_____
                        Phone _____
                        E-mail _____

Thank you for your time in completing this survey. Please mail to the following address:
Cincinnati Recreation Commission
Attn: Therapeutic Recreation
805 Central Ave. Suite 800
Cincinnati, OH. 45202

benefit from programs and services. External audiences include those persons who interface with the agency and whose support and assistance are necessary to ensure reasonable accommodations. The general public, politicians, volunteers, community partnering agencies, resource providers such as vendors of adapted equipment, accessible transportation providers, the media, and external funding sources are key external audiences. Marketing tools identified in the action plan to communicate with these audiences include: 1) personal contact; 2) agency-controlled tools such as brochures, listservs, videos; and 3) public media such as the Internet, TV, radio, newspapers, and accessible signage. Assistive technology is a multi-purpose tool that enables two-way communication between service providers and consumers equalizing and facilitating inclusive leisure experiences.

Marketing inclusive options commences with the intent to achieve access identified in an agency ADA compliance statement communicated to all potential internal and external audiences through marketing avenues appropriate to each particular audience. The message sent to potential audiences describes the range of choices and transition steps to accommodate requests like relocation, renovation, purchase of alternative communication devices, or use of leisure buddies (Dattilo, 2002). Internal audiences like general recreation staff find ADA compliance statements in policy documents, personnel manuals, and training materials. External audiences are made aware of program options and procedures for requesting accommodations through program brochures, the Internet, volunteer recruitment, and focus group meetings. Incorporation of ADA statements in agency-wide brochures or on the agency website reminds all staff and community residents that the possibility of participation by an individual with a disability may occur with any service at any time. Compliance statements are presented in a variety of alternative formats. Audio cassettes, TTY's, large-print media, braille, and accessible signage are used so persons with cognitive, visual, or hearing limitations may access information. An example statement in a program guide sent to consumers and disseminated throughout the community illustrates the intent to comply with ADA, informs consumers of leisure options, and encourages constituents to seek assistance (see Figure 3.2, Inclusion Programs, Cincinnati Recreation Commission, 2002). Further, therapeutic recreation staff distribute a flyer with similar information throughout the agency and in correspondence to consumers and agency resource providers (see Figure 3.3, Inclusion and Recreation). Communication that encourages consumers to request assistance benefits the agency by allowing adequate time for staff to prepare the accommodations. The use of the Internet to communicate to both internal and external audiences allows staff access to a wide range of potential benefactors while permitting frequent program updates. The NSSRA website presents types of support and assistance available to partner agencies and consumers requesting services (http://www.nssra.org/programs/inclusion/index.htm, 2002), refer to Figure 3.4.

After the intent to comply with ADA is communicated to various audiences, the next step is to facilitate entry into programs or access to services. A registration process is the usual conduit. A number of challenges may occur as consumers attempt to enroll. Staff apprehension, limited funding or transportation access, reliance on first-come-first-serve or in-person registration, ownership of personal or safety equipment (tennis racket or helmet), participant or caregiver fear of non-acceptance causing incomplete registration information, and timely access to medical records are potential barriers. Social access may also be a challenge. Consumers may wish to participate with others who share the same communication methods (Oliva & Simonsen, 2000) like ASL or AAC systems with visual display formats or digitized speech output.

A number of communication tools and strategies facilitate registration processes. Personal contact in the form of an advocate to assist a consumer to register or training staff as they use the agency TTY to respond to a consumer with articulation difficulties fosters a welcoming environment. Helpful agency media include the use of large print with on-line registrations or the availability of fax or e-mail registration. Public avenues like human interest stories during the evening news or community awareness fairs promote participation benefits while making registration more accessible.

Marketing is important to assure audience support consumer participation as programs and services are delivered. Customer service commences with front-line staff and direct service personnel as consumers enter a facility or attend a program. Performance of these individuals reflects upon the entire organization (Siegenthaler, 2000). The nature of personal contact and staff modeling during one-on-one interventions or as leisure buddies influences consumer perceptions. The manner in which staff interact with consumer-operated assistive devices like wheelchairs or amplification systems projects either an accommodating attitude or a reluctance to welcome consumers. Personalizing delivery using activity analysis becomes second nature as staff respond to consumer abilities and preferences using age-appropriate and person-first language. Comfort with alternative activities

Figure 3.2

Inclusive Programs

In addition to the TR programs in this guide, **all** programs offered by the Cincinnati Recreation Commission are available for participants with disabilities. Furthermore, if an individual requires additional assistance in order to successfully participate, an accommodation may be requested.

The Cincinnati Recreation Commission operates more than forty community/senior centers located in neighborhoods throughout the city. These centers offer a variety of programs for participants of all ages.

The TR Division's "Inclusion Team" was created to assist individuals with disabilities in paricipating in these communiy / senior center programs.

The Inclusion Staff will:
a) assist you in identifying a Cincinnati Recreation Commision program that fits your needs and interests.
b) assist you in the process of registering and (if necessary) requesting an accommodation.
c) assist Community Center staff in providing necessary accommodation and other supports for successful participation.

To find out more about the many recreational opportunities available to you through inclusive participation, please call Stephanie at (513) 352-4055 or complete and submit the form on page 12.

Here are a few programs offered by the Cincinnati Recreation Commission:
- before and after school day camp programs
- extended day summer camps (see page 6)
- aerobic classes (jazzercise, aquacize, tai bo,)
- karate, (tae kwon do, tai-chi)
- Weight training (fitness center orientations available)*
- dance (square, line, hip-hop, ballet)
- arts and crafts (ceramics, painting, jewelry, crochet)
- tumbling, gymnastics and creative movement

* Three fitness centers offer wheelchair accessible weight training machines, (individuals using wheelchairs do not need to transfer out of chairs to operate machines.)

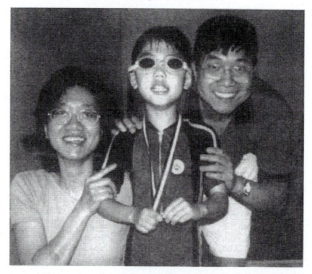

Figure 3.3

INCLUSION and RECREATION

All programs offered by the Cincinnati Recreation Commission are available for participants with disabilities. Participants are not limited to programs offered through Therapeutic Recreation. Furthermore, if an individual requires additional assistance in order to successfully participate, an accommodation may be requested.

The Cincinnati Recreation Commission operates more than forty community/senior centers located in neighborhoods throughout the city. These centers offer a variety of programs for participants of all ages.

Some of the many programs offered by the Cincinnati Recreation Commission:
- Before and after school day camp programs
- Summer day camps
- Aerobic classes (jazzercise, aquacize, tae bo, chair)
- Karate, (tae kwon do, tai-chi)
- Weight training (fitness center orientations available)*
- Dance (square, line, hip-hop, ballet)
- Arts and crafts (ceramics, painting, jewelry, crochet)
- Tumbling, gymnastics and creative movement
- Team Sports
- Youth Sports (Basketball, Flag Football, Soccer)

  * Three of our fitness centers are equipped with accessible weight training machines (does not require wheelchair users to transfer)

The "Inclusion Team" was created to assist individuals with disabilities in participating in these community/senior center programs.

The Inclusion Staff will:

- Help you to identify Cincinnati Recreation Commission programs fitting your needs and interests.

- Help you in the process of registering and (if necessary) requesting an accommodation.

- Assist Community Center staff in providing necessary accommodations and other supports for successful participation.

To find out more about the many recreational opportunities available to you through inclusive participation, please call Stephanie at (513) 352 – 4055.

Figure 3.4

INCLUSION –
THE BENEFITS
ARE ENDLESS

Inclusion | Get Included | Inclusion Companions

Northern Suburban Special Recreation Association provides a recreational choice for people with disabilities.

programs

funding

news

staff

partners

Some people with disabilities prefer to have recreation opportunities in **traditional recreation programs** with people who do not have disabilities. To meet this need, NSSRA provides **training, support staff and assistance** to partner park districts and local recreation departments so inclusive recreation can be enjoyed by all. This **joint effort** provides inclusion support in the form of extra staff, sign language interpreters, adapted rules and policies, behavior management training, disability awareness training, and any other services necessary to include your child.

Who Do We Want?

YOU!

High School Students

Caring People

College Students

People 14 years & up

Special Education Majors

Moms with Kids in School

Volunteers

People with Skills to Share

Senior Citizens

Drivers for NSSRA Vans

People Who Love Kids

Interns

Sign Language Interpreters

Figure 3.4 continued

History & Mission | Individuals Served | Recreation Programs
Inclusion & Accessibility | Location | Governance & Staff | Funding
Intergovernmental Cooperation | Safety | Information

programs

funding

news

staff

partners

INCLUSION & ACCESSIBILITY

NSSRA works closely with the partner park districts and cities to enable inclusive participation in recreation programs conducted by the partner agencies. Recognizing that some people with disabilities prefer to have recreation opportunities in recreation programs with people who do not have disabilities, NSSRA provides training, extra staff, or other assistance to partner park district or recreation department staff that will enable participation by people with disabilities in inclusive leisure settings.

Participation in inclusive programs has grown tremendously, and is expected to continue to grow faster than any other NSSRA operation. NSSRA also provides the partner agencies with information about making new and existing recreation facilities and areas accessible to people with disabilities.

http:Hwww.nssra.org/about/inclusion-and-accesibility.htm

and equipment modifications supports a trial-and-error approach until strategies result in successful participation outcomes. Reward and recognition highlight successes. Videos, photos and e-mail capture successes and document experience benefits.

Managers use a variety of marketing techniques to support inclusive programming. An initial responsibility is to assure consumer confidentiality and autonomy. One approach is to require release statements with program registration. As shown in the illustration (Cincinnati Recreation Commission, 2002), these releases identify the forms of marketing and contacts that are permitted during programming (see Figure 3.5, Confidentiality Release). Managers craft policies that allow for privacy as medications are dispensed or "out of control" behaviors are handled away from the public eye. Like direct service personnel, the personal conduct of a manager is assessed by constituent groups and reflects upon the reputation of an agency. Responding to a reporter in a matter-of-fact manner when answering questions about consumer behaviors, careful proofreading of media documents, keeping in mind person-first language, or allowing an extra hour off for staff who have been managing challenging behaviors are managerial actions that contribute to consumer integrity, program credibility, and community relations.

Figure 3.5

Therapeutic Recreation
Participant Information Form

Please complete both the front and back pages and print all information on this form. Return this form with check payable to: Cincinnati Recreation Commission. Mail to: CRC, Therapeutic Recreation, 805 Central Avenue, Suite #800, Cincinnati, Ohio 45202 (or call (513) 352-4014 for more information).

I. Participant Information

First Name

Last Name

Date of Birth

Address   **Street**   **Apt #**

City   **State**   **Zip Code**   **Gender**

Home Phone Number   **Emergency Phone (other than home)**

Emergency Contact (other than parent)   **Relationship**

Mother's Work Phone Number   **Father's Work Phone Number**

Doctor's Name   **Doctor's Work Phone Number**

School/Workshop   **Teacher/Supervisor**

Group Home Agency   **Agency Phone Number**

II. Disabling Condition

Please identify the participants' disabling condition. Circle all that apply to the participant and/or write in any disabling condition not listed:

Arthritis	Down Syndrome	Mental Retardation, Mild	Spina Bifida
Attention Deficit Disorder	Head Injury	Mental Retardation, Moderate	Spinal Cord Injury
Autism	Hearing Impairment	Mental Retardation, Severe	Injury Level: _____
Behavioral Disorder	Learning Disability	Muscular Dystrophy	Vision Impairment
Cerebral Palsy	Mental Illness	Multiple Sclerosis	Other: _____

Does participant walk independently? ☐ YES ☐ NO If not, what type of assistance is required? ☐ Wheelchair ☐ Walker
☐ Other (please specify): _____

Does participant dress independently? ☐ YES ☐ NO If not, what type of assistance is required? _____

_____

Does participant use bathroom/toilet independently? ☐ YES ☐ NO If not, what type of assistance is required? _____

_____

Does participant communicate through speech? ☐ YES ☐ NO If not, what type of communication is used? _____

_____

Additional information that would assist in programming for participant: _____

_____

Figure 3.5 continued

Figure 3.5 – (continud)

III. Medical Information

Please circle all that apply to participant:

Allergies (specify below)	Diabetes	Heart Condition	Shunt
Arthritis	Diet Restriction	Hepatitis Carrier	Tracheotomy
Asthma	Ear Tubes	High Blood Pressure	Other: _____
Atlantoaxial Subluxation	Glasses	Scoliosis	_____
Catheter	Hearing Aid	Seizures	

Please provide **specific** information for medical conditions we should be aware of (allergies, activity restriction, etc.): _____

_____

Does participant have seizures? ☐ YES ☐ NO   If yes, what type? ☐ Grand Mal ☐ Petit Mal ☐ Other _____

If yes, how often does participant have seizures? _____ Date of last seizure: _____

Please identify type, dosage and time of any medication participant is currently taking:

MEDICATION: Type _____   Dosage _____   Time _____

IV. Swimming Information

Please answer the following questions if the participant is registering for a swim program.

Does the participant have swimming experience? ☐ YES ☐ NO   If yes, where? _____

Please explain participant's swimming skills (ie: face in water, float on front, etc.): _____

Are there any precautions that need to be taken while the participant is in or around the pool? _____

Does the participant need to wear ☐ Ear molds ☐ Ear plugs ☐ Bathing cap ☐ Other _____

Does participant have difficulty eating foods? ☐ YES ☐ NO   Does participant have difficulty drinking fluids? ☐ YES ☐ NO

If yes, for either, please explain. _____

V. Participant / Parent / Guardian Release

As a participant or as a parent/guardian of the participant in this program, I recognize that there are certain risks of physical injury and I agree to assume the full risk of any injuries, damages or loss resulting from participation in any and all activities connected with or associated with such program. I agree to waive and relinquish all claims I may have, as a result of my or my son's/daughter's participation in the program, against the Cincinnati Recreation Commission, City of Cincinnati, and their agents, employees, staff and volunteers. I do hereby fully release and discharge the Cincinnati Recreation Commission, City of Cincinnati, and their agents, employees, staff and volunteers for any and all claims from injuries, damage or loss which I have or which may accrue to me on account of my son's/daughter's participation in the program. I further agree to protect, defend and hold harmless the Cincinnati Recreation Commission, City of Cincinnati, and their agents, employees, staff and volunteers from any and all claims resulting from injuries, damage or losses sustained by myself or my son/daughter or arising out of, connected with, or in any way associated with the activities of the program. I have read and fully understand this release form. **Before registration in this program is valid, this release form must be signed by the participant or the participant's parent or legal guardian.**

Signature of Participant / Parent / Guardian _____ Date _____

VI. Confidentiality Release

I, the undersigned, hereby authorize the Cincinnati Recreation Commission to utilize photographs, videotapes, voice recordings, etc,. of the participant to be used exclusively for promotion, advertising, and marketing of the Cincinnati Recreation Commission and its programs.

Signature of Participant / Parent / Guardian _____ Date _____

I, the undersigned, hereby authorize the Cincinnati Recreation Commission to contact school/work activity center concerning participant information that pertains to the recreation program.

Signature of Participant / Parent / Guardian _____ Date _____

Managers devote time and resources to training efforts as programs and services are delivered. Training is a marketing tool to help front line and direct service personnel develop attitudes and skills necessary to provide quality programs and project a welcoming and accommodating atmosphere. Sensitivity and awareness training help professionals project a "positive attitude towards a participant with special needs even when he or she presents inappropriate behaviors" (Fink, 2001, p. 61). Likewise, training on APIE and needs of particular individuals encourage professionals to promote recreation participation among individuals who share the same communication methods and assistive devices. Support of caregiver training fosters awareness of agency compliance processes and programming guidelines that intend to create safe and positive programming environments. Managers are challenged to balance the responsibilities of various general and therapeutic recreation staff as inclusive services are offered. To illustrate, the provision of teen or adult social experiences may not be a typical general recreation offering, yet is a requested inclusion program: As a result, managers assign and reassign staff to support requests agency-wide, such actions require diplomacy, negotiation skills and financial savvy. Thus, a major managerial responsibility during program delivery is creating supportive work and participation environments through personal, agency, and public media and human resources within and external to the agency.

Advocacy and Community Relations

Developing and cultivating relations and resources are primary tasks of managers (O'Morrow & Carter, 1997; Smith, Austin, & Kennedy, 2001). Establishing and maintaining long-term relationships with key community sources is as important as nurturing long-term relations with consumers and caregivers. Networking and partnering build positive impressions, generate access to needed resources, and interpret the inherent values of therapeutic recreation. Managers who collaborate are building networks that promote access and cost containment (O'Morrow & Carter, 1997).

Managers use a number of marketing strategies to build community relations. Needs assessments identify constituents' preferences. Professional presentations to college classes, during conferences, and before support groups or service organizations create awareness and avenues to access funding and volunteers. Managers become members of civic and professional groups to gain information, disseminate results of efficacy studies, and to identify equipment, facility, and transportation resources. Managers volunteer their services to conduct inclusion trainings, for example, to build relations and awareness of the significance of recreation as a therapeutic tool. When managers support participation of their agencies in community health fairs, the role of recreation as a prevention and education tool is being promoted. Focus groups and program advisory committees are conduits to gaining awareness of expectations and resource availability. Lastly, responsibility for preparation of an agency or department marketing plan lies with the manager. Managers garner resources and information so staff maintain and enhance the quality of consumer programs and services.

Managers advocate on behalf of 1) consumers, 2) their agency, and 3) the therapeutic recreation profession. First, managers ultimately are held accountable for satisfying consumer needs. Second, agency compliance statements are designed and interpreted to an array of internal and external audiences. And, thirdly, managers participate in professional networks influential in setting local, state, and national legislative agendas, and professional standards. Consequently, a positional responsibility of managers is advocacy.

Managers are responsible for delivery of programs and services that satisfy consumer expectations. As managers articulate transportation, financial, and volunteer needs, they are responding to consumer requests. When managers meet with consumers and caregivers, they are attempting to, for example, remove barriers, improve service quality, and increase awareness of therapeutic recreation benefits (Broida & Wenzel, 1995). Managers promote self-advocacy when they encourage consumers to participate on agency-wide advisory committees or complete needs assessments.

A second area of advocacy for managers is within the agency. Prior to ADA, a therapeutic division focused on needs of the community and designing special programs to meet these needs; since the enactment of ADA, a division or agency examines the general service offerings within the agency in order to create access and inclusion. To this end, advocacy may include: conducting in-services on inclusion and volunteer management; circulating articles among staff or placing them in the reading file; coordinating inter- and intra-agency accessibility workshops; preparing collaborative funding proposals; serving as internship supervisors; developing efficacy studies to document outcomes; writing ADA compliance statements and transition plans, and developing and promoting new programs and services. Advocacy occurs informally during conversations with CEOs and formally through system-wide dissemination of brochures, fact sheets, home page updates, and CDs depicting scope and intent of therapeutic recreation. The need for advocacy within the agency is ongoing as managers and direct service staff encourage and assist other agency staff to "think inclusively."

A third advocacy area is the profession. As a therapeutic recreation professional, the manager articulates the nature and outcomes of therapeutic experiences to colleagues with backgrounds in management and business, the public at-large, legislators, third-party payers, regulatory and accrediting bodies, and researchers. These efforts attempt to garner or justify resources, influence the content of laws or policies, and promote the inclusion of therapeutic recreation as a viable, reimbursable, essential health and human service. E-mail campaigns, lobbying, encouraging a consumer to testify, attending ATRA and NTRS legislative forums, coordinating events during National Therapeutic Recreation Week, presenting efficacy study outcomes, and recognizing outstanding agencies or professionals are forms of professional advocacy (Broida & Wenzel, 1995). "Advocacy is a force for change" (Broida & Wenzel, 1995, p. 22). Through professional organizations, professionals gain mutual support and the power of numbers to be heard. Professional organizations are conduits to access those who influence standard setting, funding, and ultimately, the direction taken by professionals implementing inclusion services.

Marketing and advocacy are ongoing responsibilities directed toward enhancing customer services while garnering resources and interpreting the benefits of therapeutic recreation. The nature of these responsibilities is influenced by the maturity, size, and organizational structure of an agency. When one CTRS guides agency inclusion, a major portion of the professional's time may be devoted to marketing. On the other hand, in larger, mature organizations, functions like marketing are centralized with professionals hired to market all agency programs. With this scenario, one or more CTRSs may supply timely information to the marketing department to support agency-wide inclusion practices. Whether centralized or decentralized or one or several CTRSs manage therapeutic recreation, successful agencies are ones in which all personnel use marketing and advocacy tools to articulate the role of inclusion as an integral component of quality recreation services.

References

Broida, J. K., & Wenzel, K. (1995). Shaping our future through advocacy. In NTRS/NRPA, *Impacting public advocacy an advocacy manual for therapeutic recreation* (pp. 22-31). Arlington, VA: NTRS/NRPA.

burlingame, J. (1998). Customer service. In Brasile, F., Skalko, T. K., & burlingame, J. (Eds.), *Perspectives in recreation therapy issues of a dynamic profession* (pp. 249-264). Ravensdale, WA: Idyll Arbor, Inc.

Cincinnati Recreation Commission. (2002). *Therapeutic recreation, Fall & Winter 2002-2003 program guide.* [Brochure]. Cincinnati, OH: Author.

Cincinnati Recreation Commission. (n.d.). *Therapeutic recreation adapted sports survey.* (Available from Cincinnati Recreation Commission, Division of Therapeutic Recreation, 805 Central Avenue, Cincinnati, Ohio 45202).

Dattilo, J. (2002). *Inclusive leisure services responding to the rights of people with disabilities* (2nd ed.). State College, PA: Venture Publishing, Inc.

Fink, D. B. (2001). Carlton plays tee-ball: A case study in inclusive recreation. *Parks & Recreation, 36*(8), 54-61.

Northern Suburban Special Recreation Association. (n.d.). *Inclusion & accessibility. Inclusion—the benefits are endless.* Retrieved July 2, 2002, from http://www.nssra.org/programs/inclusion/index.htm

Oliva, G. A., & Simonsen, A. (2000). Re-thinking leisure services for deaf and hard of hearing persons: A new paradigm. *Parks & Recreation, 35*(5), 78-85.

O, Morrow, G. S., & Carter, M. J. (1997). *Effective management in therapeutic recreation service.* State College, PA: Venture Publishing, Inc.

Siegenthaler, K. L. (2000). Hello operator front-line staff performance reflects the entire organization. *Parks & Recreation, 35*(4), 100-104.

Smith, R. W., Austin, D. R., & Kennedy, D. W. (2001). *Inclusive and special recreation opportunities for persons with disabilities* (4th ed.). Boston, MA: McGraw Hill Higher Education.

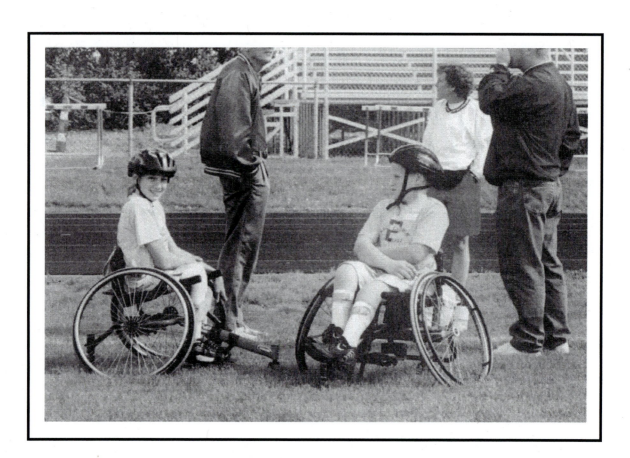

CHAPTER 4

Direct Services

An agency's scope of service is greatly influenced by its organizational structure (Bullock & Mahon, 2000). Organizational structure influences leisure options available to individuals with disabilities. These options range along a service continuum from participation in all available offerings through specialized programs to in-home services (Fox Valley Special Recreation Association, Summer 2002). A number of approaches are used to incorporate persons with disabilities into agency services. The SWOT analysis reveals organizational structures, leisure options, and prevailing practices employed to deliver therapeutic recreation services (refer to Chapter 1 Defining the Service: Assessing the Community and Agency).

The APIE process is fundamental to delivery of quality, accountable, relevant therapeutic recreation programs (Carter, VanAndel, & Robb, 2003; Peterson & Stumbo, 2000). Agency vision and mission statements and organizational structures guide development of both individual and group programs. Assessment, similar to the needs assessments completed during the agency and community SWOT analysis, identifies consumer needs and resources available to plan individual and group programs. During the planning step of the APIE process, goals and objectives of individual and group programs are developed, inclusion support plans, formative evaluations, and specific accommodations including behavior support plans are prepared. Implementation involves program delivery. Inclusion support plans are delivered with recommended accommodations. Leadership influences the success or failure of program results, and during program implementation direct leadership is most apparent (Jordan, 2001). Evaluation, the final step of the APIE process, determines if individual and group outcomes are achieved. Inclusion support plans and accommodations are evaluated at pre-determined intervals with revisions made to improve program effectiveness. Feedback on consumer performance and outcomes of specific interventions validates recommended inclusion practices (Lee, McCormick, & Perkins, 2000).

This section reviews organizational structures, program and service options and approaches used to extend recreation services to all individuals. An agency's scope of service is defined in philosophical statements (vision, mission, goals, and objectives). Individual and group programs are designed, delivered, and evaluated within the parameters of the agency structure and philosophy. A focus of this section is the step-by-step application of the APIE process as it is carried out to evaluate and deliver inclusion options along the service continuum.

Organizational Structure

Organizational structure affects the way in which an agency carries out its mission; and, consequently, determines program options. As presented in Chapter 2, Personnel Resources, organizational charts reveal four operating patterns. One scenario finds special recreation districts created for the sole purpose of supporting and assisting recreation districts as they deliver services, including inclusion, to their member districts. This pattern is evident throughout the state of Illinois. With this operating pattern, the APIE process is used to plan services along the continuum from specialized or segregated to inclusive and in-home programs (Wachter & McGowen, 2002).

A second pattern finds a special division or department, like the Division of Therapeutic Recreation of the Cincinnati Recreation Commission, dedicated to services with individuals with disabilities (Bullock & Mahon, 2000). This centralized approach is administered by a manager with CTRS credentials who reports to a general recreation supervisor. The advantage of this structure is the opportunity to garner financial support equitable to other agency divisions yet challenges result from attention given to "consumer differences" and the potential service duplication (Bullock & Mahon, 2000). Services range along the continuum from specialized or segregated programs and events to inclusion and in-home leisure education.

A third approach has specialized staff assigned to divisions throughout the agency. In this decentralized approach, general recreation staff benefit from specialists' expertise, yet the challenge becomes general staff abdicating their responsibility to provide programs that include all participants (Bullock & Mahon, 2000). With this approach, inclusion is assured to some extent in all agency offerings; especially if a CTRS is hired at the senior management level to supervise specialists agency-wide, (refer to the City of Reno Therapeutic Recreation Specialist job description, Figure 2.7, Personnel Resources Chapter 2). The use of resource personnel and available time of specialists' influence the range of services.

A fourth structure, also a decentralized organizational pattern, is evident when inclusion specialists are hired agency-wide to support general recreation staff (Bullock & Mahon, 2000). Although specialized programs are offered, the intent is to accommodate individuals in routine agency offerings. A disadvantage is the potential absence of a managerial voice at decision-making levels who advocates for, for example, transportation and scholarship funds and supports the specialized staff. Agency-wide specialists develop and lead programs using the APIE process; provide training and consults to general recreation staff; support volunteers and resource personnel; and, advocate for reasonable accommodates agency-wide.

Organizational structures are dynamic. Staff roles and assignments are reassessed as administrators address issues of accessibility and social inclusion while attempting to abide by ADA directives. Consequently, managers are experimenting with combinations of the four identified patterns: Therapeutic recreation divisions are hiring inclusion specialists and assigning them to work either in specific divisions or agency-wide with general recreation staff (structures two, three and four) (refer to Cincinnati Recreation Commission job descriptions, Figure 2.3 and Figure 2.4 in Personnel Resources Chapter 2); another operational pattern finds a senior-level CTRS-qualified therapeutic recreation manager hired and reporting directly to the agency manager while supervising CTRS-qualified staff assigned to specific agency divisions (modifications of structures two and three), (refer to City of Reno job descriptions, Figure 2.7 and 2.8 in the Personnel Resources Chapter 2). Alternative structures evolve as managers evaluate consumers' responses to inclusive practices.

Leisure Options and Inclusion Approaches

Legislation, ADA in particular, combined with health care reform have resulted in therapeutic recreation re-evaluating its role in healthcare settings (Sylvester, Voelkl, & Ellis, 2001). Greater consideration is being given to services along the care continuum from inpatient into the community and private homes (in-home services) where persons released from shorter hospital stays are continuing their recuperation and living out their lives. TRSs apply the APIE process during brief treatment sessions in acute care settings and in private homes as a result of patient referrals and in preparation for inclusion. Managers and direct service personnel rely on a number of approaches to extend program options to consumers as they transition along the care continuum, whether it be from inpatient through in-home or specialized to socially inclusive options.

Approaches and levels of acceptance have been labeled as segregated, integrated, and inclusive programming (Schleien, Ray, & Green, 1997) or physical integration, functional and social inclusion (Schleien, Green, & Stone, 2003). Segregated programs serve only people with disabilities. Specialized programs are developed by TRSs using the APIE process with the intent of improving functional skills necessary for leisure involvement (Peterson & Stumbo, 2000). Participants tend to be homogeneous with respect to their needs or nature of desired programs: For example, aquatics with youth with autism or adults in cardiac rehab or a New Year's Eve dance with adults with developmental disabilities represent programs designed to improve functioning and address specific interests. Physical integration recognizes and assures the participant's right to access (Schleien, et al., 2003).

During integrated programs individuals with and without disabilities participate side by side. Functional inclusion occurs as reasonable accommodations are made so participants function successfully in a program or service (Schleien, et al., 2003). Integrated programs may be planned from the onset or result because one or more persons has an interest in the activity or desire to develop a skill. Individuals with disabilities may elect to register for programs available to any consumer; or, through reverse mainstreaming, persons without disabilities are involved in programs with persons having disabilities, unified sports programs of Special Olympics exemplifies this approach (Wachter & McGowen, 2002). Integrated programs use leisure buddies or coaches, siblings, staff, and volunteers to assist and support participants; in some instances, persons participate without support once registration is completed. Community reintegration includes outpatients with family members and care providers in leisure awareness outings, special events such as performances, and in-home assessments. The intent of integrated programs is to practice skills, promote adjustment, and facilitate the highest possible level of independent leisure functioning.

The third approach involves inclusion in experiences available to all consumers. In the zero-exclusion approach, programs are planned from the onset to incorporate anyone who selects the experience (Sylvester, et al., 2001). This approach relies on high levels of assessment and collaborative application of the APIE process to plan, implement, and evaluate programs and services. Social inclusion, the highest acceptance level, is evident when participants have positive interactions with peers during recreation (Schleien, et al., 2003). Welcoming attitudes supportive of friendship building exemplify socially inclusive experiences.

The initial focus of inclusion was on community-based leisure options. With the concept of a care continuum extending from inpatient to in-home services as a result of legislation and health care reform, CTRSs are called upon to apply a preventative and wellness approach to deliver recreation and therapeutic recreation options across all human service sectors. The APIE process and clinical decisions are made so reasonable accommodations result in meaningful outcomes. To illustrate, general recreators (CPRP) and specialists (CTRS) work side by side in recreation centers, confer with one another as discharged patients request services, visit private homes to complete pre-program assessment and accommodation forms, and plan wraparound programs and summer day camps with teachers. This approach focuses on consumer ability, preference, and social inclusion while de-emphasizing the clinical or community nature of the setting. The terms, segregated, integrated, and inclusion describe programs. Person-centered or individualized approach refers to the application of the APIE process across the care continuum to achieve socially inclusive experiences. An agency's scope of service and ADA statements may use a variety of terms to describe the nature of offerings presented to all consumers.

Essential Components of Successful Programming

The APIE process is recommended as a professional best practice and standard protocol to prepare and deliver accountable services resulting in individualized inclusive plans (Klitzing, 2002; Peterson & Stumbo, 2000; Sullivan & O'Brien, 2001). As shown in the inclusion flow chart used by one agency to deliver inclusion services, APIE is both a programming process resulting in measurable outcomes and a standard to gauge the effectiveness of delivery and adherence to best professional practices (Cincinnati Recreation Commission, n.d.; LeConey, Devine, Bunker & Montgomery, 2000; Lee, et al., 2000) (refer to Figure 1.4, Inclusion Flow Chart in Defining the Service: Assessing the Community and Agency in Chapter 1). In this section, APIE is applied to design individual inclusion plans. This occurs after the SWOT analysis of community and agency resources has determined the scope of service and intent of offerings (refer to Chapter 1 Defining the Service: Assessing the Community and Agency). Armed with information from the SWOT analysis, the planner is attuned to the consumers' needs and available resources to support and assist with program accessibility and preparing accommodations.

Preparation of individualized programs and group programs that meet individual objectives commences with assessment of participant skills and the program environment. During planning, inclusion support plans with accommodations including behavior support plans if appropriate are written. Individual support plans are then implemented; and, lastly, plans are evaluated and revised at predetermined intervals. Practical application of the APIE process varies. Tasks are unique to each agency, because the mission, organizational structure and inclusion options vary among providers along the care continuum.

Assessment

Needs assessment, the SWOT analysis, reveals community and organizational information on current and potential participants, status of physical and programmatic accessibility, and preparedness of staff to carry out reasonable accommodations. As a result of the analysis, staff are cognizant of the types of support, assistance, and training necessary to facilitate outcomes implied in the agency mission and goal statements. Assessment with individual consumers results in an understanding of their needs, preferences, and resources. Participant skills and developmental areas and the program and its environment are assessed. The process includes a number of tasks presented in Figure 4.1 (assessment includes) (Cincinnati Recreation Commission, n.d.). Outcomes of individual assessments enable development of individual and program goals and objectives and program accommodations.

Common practice is to request assessment information as participants register. Agency-developed forms require self-reporting or caregiver response or on-line, in person, phone or mailed return (refer to Figure 4.2, Registration Questions, Cincinnati Recreation Commission, n.d.). On occasion, staff complete forms during participant interviews (refer to Figure 4.3, Therapeutic Recreation Inclusion Services Intake Form). Submittal of medical or recent physical information from consumers' physicians may also be required. Home visits are conducted to administer standardized or agency-specific inventories. Staff may also assess participants by observing them as they participate in initial program sessions. Staff obtain academic and social work reports through interagency planning sessions. In some instances, staff request information from colleagues as consumers participate, refer to Figure 4.4 (Dear Teacher) (Cincinnati Recreation Commission, n.d.). Information provided by teachers and care providers supplements information gathered by staff and is helpful in targeting goals and objectives common to settings across the care continuum.

A number of standardized instruments are available for purchase or, in some instances, may be used with permission if data are forwarded to the developer to aid in further refinement of the tool (burlingame & Blaschko, 2002; Stumbo, 2002). The programmer's intent and the focus of each instrument influence use of specific tools. Several general categories of tools include: 1) Inventories, interest or preference questionnaires like satisfaction scales or activity checklists; the Leisurescope Plus and STILAP are examples of participation assessments. 2) Diagnostic tools such as the Leisure Diagnostic Battery and the General Recreation Screening Tool assess factors influencing participation and abilities necessary to be successful during experiences. 3) Disability-specific tools such as the CERT (Comprehensive Evaluation in Recreation Therapy) and the LCM (Leisure Competence Measure) have been developed to assess performance in physical rehabilitation; information is helpful to plan transitions and referrals. And, 4) Psychometric tests that assess functioning in developmental and behavioral areas like those used to assess mental capacity or measure developmental levels provide programmers insight into consumers' capacities and potential. Scores reported by teachers may help CTRSs make decisions on age-appropriate activities or the participant's ability to comply with safety rules or the leader's directions. Triangulated evaluation, using one or more tools or sources of assessment information, enables professionals to develop plans having outcomes relevant to a number of delivery settings over extended time periods.

Individual participant assessment information is gathered on agency-developed forms as consumers request services or as they enroll in seasonal programs. Once assessments are completed, the data are used over a period of time and to plan accommodations in multiple programs (i.e., forms are periodically updated and maintained in agency files). An example of a skill assessment form completed by participants/caregivers illustrates types of information helpful to planning a number of agency programs (refer to Figure 4.5, Cincinnati Recreation Commission Therapeutic Recreation Participant Skill Assessment, n.d.). Comprehensive agency assessments include two major sections, one gathers information on the consumer the other on the program: This is illustrated in the form used by the Cincinnati Recreation Commission, Assessment and Accommodation Request (n.d.) (refer to Figure 4.6). Agency generated tools gather information that allows professionals to contact caregivers, education and social service colleagues, seek medical assistance in emergency situations, assess readiness for social inclusion, determine foundational skill levels, identify existing supports and resources, gauge family expectations, express interests, and permit release of information (refer to Figure 4.6, Part A, Participant Information on Assessment and Accommodation Request).

Figure 4.1

Assessment – Participant skills and areas for development relating to the inclusion program are assessed. Program/program environment assessed.

Includes:

Meeting with participant (parent/guardian) to discuss program and possible accommodations (registration process should provide participant/parent/guardian with a process to formally request an accommodation).

Completing a formal, written assessment to determine participant skills, areas needing development, activity interests, motivating factors, etc. (assessment must relate to the inclusion setting).

Checking documentation from previous program participation (TR programs, other centers, etc.)

Contacting school teacher, job coach, etc. to gain additional information (school IEP, etc.)

Contacting other professionals who may be involved with the participant (case manager, physical therapist, speech therapist, etc.)

Observing participant at school, work, or recreation programs

Identifying medical/safety concerns, activity restrictions, etc.

Determining method of communication, assessing communication skills

Observing the inclusion program to determine:
        Program factors (structure, activities, etc.)
        Staff factors (number, abilities, attitudes, training needs, etc.)
        Facility factors (space, noise level, accessibility, etc.),
        Peer factors (age range, skills/interests, acceptance, etc.)

Establishing starting date, days/times attending

Information that is gathered is necessary to plan relevant consumer outcomes. Types of demographic and health information include: gender, cultural heritage, disability information, medications and administration routines, allergies, heart conditions, dietary habits, seizure status, physician, emergency contacts, hospital, transportation provider, family or caregiver (who may or may not come into contact with the participant), use of assistive and adaptive devices like personal prostheses or ramps, and behavioral traits like startle responses to sudden noises or self-abusive reactions and management strategies to accompany responses. Functional abilities in self-care, ADL, expressive and receptive communication, reality orientation, ambulation and mobility, fitness levels, protective responses, and social interactions like awareness of social amenities, responses to

Figure 4.2

Registration Questions

What do I do when someone with a disability (or their parent/guardian) asks about registering for a community center program?

The Cincinnati Recreation Commission welcomes people with disabilities to participate in all programs. In addition to a welcoming attitude, staff should be aware the CRC is required to offer and provide accommodations, if accommodations are needed for successful participation.

First and most importantly, when asked if participants with disabilities are eligible to participate in center programs, the answer must always be "yes"! The issue of disability should never be used to restrict the individual's participation. In addition, it is not appropriate to <u>refer</u> the individual to the programs offered by the Therapeutic Division (or to another center). While it may be appropriate to <u>inform</u> the individual of the Therapeutic programs, staff must be very careful not to suggest this (TR) would be a better placement due to their disability. The individual's eligibility for the program may only be determined based on the same criteria as those without disabilities. Examples of allowable criteria would be; age restrictions, payment procedures, and participant limits (meaning <u>no</u> additional participants will be accepted).

Once it has been determined which community center program is wanted, the registration process begins. The registration process for individuals with disabilities is the same as for other participants with the exception of the **Assessment/Accommodation Request**. If the participant (parent/guardian) has indicated they have a disability, the staff member should ask if they think they might need any additional assistance (accommodation) in order to participate in the program. Very often, the participant (parent/guardian) will not know what assistance is needed. They may not know much about the program or the expectations for participation. The Assessment/Accommodation Request document was designed to provide us with a better understanding of the participant's abilities and what assistance (if any) might be necessary. At this point it is recommended you contact the Therapeutic Division for assistance in completing the Assessment/Accommodation document and determining what steps are needed in providing the accommodation.

Question: What if the participant (parent/guardian) does not mention disability and it is apparent the participant has a disability?

This can be a very touchy issue, as some parent/guardians do not want additional attention brought to their child. Or perhaps they feel by making this known their child won't be welcome in the program. Either way, staff must be very tactful in asking questions regarding a participant's abilities and make it clear we are asking these questions in an effort to provide the best possible care. If, despite our efforts, the parent/guardian refuses to acknowledge there is a disability, then we are not required to provide accommodations. Keep in mind that it is very likely the parent/guardian will acknowledge a disability if/when behavioral issues warrant the removal of the child.

Figure 4.2 continued

Figure 4.2 – (continued)

Question: What if the participant (parent/guardian) acknowledges the disability but refuses an accommodation?

The Americans with Disabilities Act makes it very clear a participant with a disability is not required to accept an accommodation. Even when it is apparent that some form of accommodation is necessary, the parent may, for whatever reason, decline the accommodation. If this is the case, it is very important to document the accommodation was offered and declined. Again, if/when the child's behavior leads to dismissal, the parent/guardian may feel differently about an accommodation. In some cases an accommodation can be provided in a discreet way. It may be possible to increase the staff ratio for the participant's group without making this an <u>individualized</u> accommodation.

strangers or members in a group are foundational to successful and safe participation. A report of past and current program participation patterns and adaptations is helpful as is identification of consumer interests and preferences and caregiver resources and expectations. Release of school information (IEP) and documentation of medication regimens or behavioral interventions as well as permission to release or use consumer information during program delivery supports and protects participants and managers during therapeutic and inclusive experiences.

The second area considered during the assessment step in the APIE process is the program and the environment in which the consumer anticipates or has requested to participate. Assessing the nature of the experience identifies the competencies participants need to enter into and achieve success during inclusionary experiences (Bullock & Mahon, 2000). Recommended accommodations result from this assessment. Reference to Part B on the Cincinnati Recreation Commission Assessment and Accommodation Request (n.d.) (refer to Figure 4.6) illustrates the nature of the information to be collected. Information on each type of reasonable accommodation defined by ADA, policies, procedures and practices; transportation; auxiliary aids or services; architectural barriers; and, structured communication barriers pertinent to specific activities, program areas, and facilities is critical to delivery of equitable services. Managers and direct service personnel of general recreation programs and inclusive services are interviewed, observed, and voluntarily provide information to complete program information forms. Consumers and caregivers may attend and participate in these assessments so they become oriented to the experiences and aware of the recommended accommodations.

General program assessment information includes: 1) Activity or experience profile, intent of the activity, skill and behavioral requirements, equipment and resources used, and place and time of the experience (Bullock & Mahon, 2000); 2) Nature of leadership and supervision and preparation or training of the staff; 3) Program format, schedule, timing of multiple activities, peer interactions, and transitions during the program; and, 4) Access to program transportation, and areas and facilities. Outcomes of program assessment reveal the level of readiness for inclusion and, when compared to individual assessments, the types of accommodations that might be realistically made to enable consumer inclusion.

As a result of completing individual and program assessments, programmers collect and organize information used to document supports, assistance, and barrier removal enabling consumer participation. As shown in Part C, Plan for Accommodation, Assessment and Accommodation Request (n.d.), (refer to Figure 4.6) summarized information identifies resource adjustments, and roles and responsibilities of inclusion specialists and general recreation staff. Forms used to summarize assessment data are also designed to allow ongoing documentation so evaluation and revision in accommodation recommendations occur routinely as consumers transition among services over extended time periods.

Figure 4.3

Therapeutic Recreation / Inclusion Services
Intake Form

Contact Date ____/____/____ Staff Taking Call/Contact_____

Caller s Name_____Phone (____)_____

Agency/Organization Name (if applicable)_____

Address_____Zip_____

Participant Name_____Birthdate____/____/____

Primary Disability (check) ____autism ____down syndrome ____mental retardation (other)

    ____cerebral palsy ____spina bifida ____spinal cord injury ____head injury

    ____arthritis ____emotional/behavioral (ADHD, etc.) ____hearing impaired

    ____vision impaired ____other (please explain)_____

Action Requested ____general information ____send TR program guide
(check all that apply)
    ____add to mail list ____specific program request_____

    ____inclusion info requests* (region/center/program)_____

    * Forward inclusion information requests to appropriate coordinator

Inclusion request details_____

_____

_____

Additional Comments_____

_____

_____

Confirmation of Action
(initials of staff completing action)

Participant/Prof. Added to Mail List _____   Program Guide Mailed _____

Other Program Material Mailed _____   Inclusion Action Initiated _____

Additional Action Requested/Taken _____   _____

Figure 4.4

Cincinnati Recreation Commission™

Dear Teacher:

Your student, _____, is currently participating in a recreational program through the Cincinnati Recreation Commission. We would appreciate any information you can give us concerning the child's behavior and skills at school to more effectively meet his/her needs during the recreational program. Please check below all areas that apply to this child.

I.   Language Skills

    1. Does the child communicate verbally?   o Yes   o No

    2. Can the child speak and be understood?   o Yes   o No

    3. Can the child follow simple verbal directions?   o Yes   o No
        If yes, which ones?_____

    4. Does the child have a speech or hearing difficulty?   o Yes   o No
        If yes, please exlpain._____

    5. Does the child have receptive language?   o Yes   o No

II   Social Skills

    1. Does the child seem to enjoy interacting with peers?   o Yes   o No

    2. How does the child socially interact with people? (i.e. smile, initiate contact, etc.)
        _____

    3. Does the child relate well with groups? oYes o No   To one or two children? oYes o No

        _____

    3. What are a few of the child's favorite indoor activities? _____

        _____

        Outdoor Activities?_____

        _____

III.   Cognitive

    1. Can the child sort? o Yes   o No

Figure 4.4 continued

Figure 4.4 Continued

2. Can the child match? o Yes o No

3. Does the child know colors? o Yes o No

4. Can the child sequence? o Yes o No

5. Can the child identify body parts? o Yes o No

6. Does the child understand dangerous situations (i.e. crossing the street)? o Yes o No

IV. **Behavior**

1. Does the child exhibit any behavior problem? o Yes o No
   If yes, please explain. _____

3. What type of behavior management does the child respond to best?

   o Positive Reinforcement   o Time Out

   o Withdrawal of reinforcers   o   Token system

   Please specify other special methods used _____

V. **Motor Skills**

1. Does the child require any Therapy?

   Physical o Yes o No Occupational o Yes o No   Speech   o Yes o No

2. What specific skills are being developed? (i.e. walking, head control, etc.) _____

   _____

3. What therapeutic equipment does the child use? _____

   _____

4. Is the child tactilely defensive?   o Yes   o No

5. Can the child work puzzles?   o Yes   o No
   What other fine motor skills does the child have? _____

   _____

6. Can the child walk independently?   o Yes   o No

Figure 4.4 continued

Figure 4.4 Continued

RELEASE OF INFORMATION

We (I), hereby agree and consent for The Cincinnati Recreation Commission to request information from our (my) child's schoolteacher concerning behavior and skills in the school environment. We (I), understand that this information will be utilized to help meet our (my) child's needs most effectively during the recreation program. We (I), also understand that without this information it will be difficult to appropriately place our (my) child within the recreation program.

_____

Child's Name

_____

School

_____

School Phone

_____

Parent or Guardian's Signature

_____

School Address

_____

Child's Teacher (Full Name)

Cincinnati Recreation Commission, Division of Therapeutic Recreation, 805 Central Avenue, Suite 800, Cincinnati, OH 45202

Figure 4.5

Cincinnati Recreation Commission
Therapeutic Recreation
Participant Skill Assessment

Participant's Name _____ Birthdate ___/___/___
                   first   last

Program/Location _____ Date _____

This Skill Assessment was designed to provide us with the information needed to plan appropriate activities and develop individual recreation plans. Please be as thorough as possible in completing the following sections:

I.   Disability Information

Place a check next to each that apply to the participant and/or write in any disabling condition not listed:

___Autism	___Attention Deficit Disorder	___Vision Impaired
___Down Syndrome	___Behavior Disorder	___Other (please
___Severe Mental Retardation	___Cerebral Palsy	describe)
___Moderate Mental Retardation	___Spina Bifida	_____
___Mild Mental Retardation	___Head Injury	
___Learning Disability	___Hearing Impaired	_____

II.   Skill Assessment

Place a check next to each statement that applies to the participant. Please use the comment section to identify additional skills and/or areas of difficulty.

A.   Dressing (putting on, taking off clothing)

___1. Needs total physical assistance with dressing, undressing
___2. Needs some physical assistance with dressing, undressing
___3. Dresses, undresses with verbal directions
___4. Dresses, undresses independently
___5. Ties own shoelaces

Comments/Areas of difficulty: _____

_____

Staff Comments: _____

Figure 4.5 continued

Figure 4.5 – (continued)

B.   Eating/Drinking

__1. Takes pureed/soft foods from a spoon
__2. Drinks from a cup with assistance
__3. Drinks from a cup independently
__4. Able to chew semi-solid food
__5. Finger feeds if food is pre-cut
__6. Able to use straw to drink
__7. Able to grasp; use spoon
__8. Able to unwrap, open containers
__9. Able to open drink containers

Comments/Areas of difficulty: _____
_____

Staff Comments: _____
_____

C.   Personal Care (toileting, washing)

__1. Wears diaper (Attends/Depends)
__2. Shows discomfort in being wet
__3. Indicates need to use toilet (gives advance notice)
__4. uses toilet with physical assistance (needs help wiping, etc.)
__5. Uses toilet with verbal direction
__6. Uses toilet independently
__7. Washes hands with physical assistance
__8. Washes hands with verbal direction
__9. Washes hands independently

*Please include any information on catheterization or menstruation care in the comments section

Comments/Areas of difficulty: _____
_____

Staff Comments:_____
_____
_____

Figure 4.5 continued

Figure 4.5 — (continued)

D.   Communication

__1. Unable to communicate needs/wants
__2. Communicates needs/wants with gestures or other non-verbal behavior
__3. Communicates needs/wants with basic sign language
__4. Communicates needs/wants with word symbol board or similar device
__5. Communicates needs/wants with one or two word statements
__6. Communicates through partial or complete spoken sentences
__7. Speaks clearly, can usually be understood
__8. Able to recall and relate information accurately

Comments/Areas of difficulty: _____

_____

Staff Comments:_____

_____

E.   Receptive Language

__1. Reacts or responds to various sounds
__2. Able to distinguish between different sounds
__3. Recognizes own name when called, spoken to
__4. Responds appropriately to simple one-step directions (within capabilities)
__5. Responds appropriately to two or three step directions (within capabilities)
__6. Responds appropriately to directions given collectively to a small group of participants
__7. Responds appropriately to directions given collectively to a larger group (6 or more)
__8. Asks questions if unsure or needing more information

Comments/Areas of difficulty: _____

_____

Staff Comments:_____

_____

Figure 4.5 continued

Figure 4.5 – (continued)

F.   Mobility

__1. Walks with full physical assistance
__2. Walks with some physical assistance
__3. Walks independently.
__4. Able to maintain balance over uneven surfaces
__5. Walks up/down steps with physical assistance
__6. Walks up/down steps independently
__7. Able to walk continuously for 15 or more minutes
__8. Able to maintain balance while running

Comments/Areas of difficulty: _____

_____

Staff Comments:_____

_____

G.   Mobility (for wheelchair/walker/crutch user)

__1. While lying on a mat, is able to roll-over
__2. Able to crawl or scoot short distance
__3. Able to sit on floor/mat unsupported
__4. Uses a manual wheel chair
__5. Uses a motorized wheelchair
__6. Uses a walker or crutches
__7. Wheels self in wheelchair short distance
__8. Wheels self in wheelchair longer distance
__9. Able to transfer in/out of wheelchair with assistance
__10. Able to transfer in/out of wheelchair independently
__11. Able to negotiate minor barriers (doors, sloped surfaces, etc.)

Comments/Areas of difficulty: _____

_____

Staff Comments:_____

_____

Figure 4.5 continued

Figure 4.5 — (continued)

H.   Motor Coordination

__1. Follows movement of objects with eyes
__2. Able to reach toward objects
__3. Able to touch, grasp objects
__4. Able to release a grasped object when directed
__5. Able to transfer object from one hand to another
__6. Able to catch a ball rolled
__7. Able to catch a ball bounced
__8. Able to catch a ball tossed form a short distance
__9. Able to kick a stationary ball
__10. Able to kick a rolling ball

Comments/Areas of difficulty:_____

_____

Staff Comments:_____

_____

I.   Social/Behavioral

__1. Demonstrates awareness of others
__2. Responds to interaction of others
__3. Aware of personal space, maintains appropriate distance
__4. Will initiate interaction with others
__5. Will play/interact cooperatively with another participant
__6. Will play/interact cooperatively with a small group of participants
__7. Able to identify and take responsibility for personal belongings
__8. Is aware of safety concerns when out in the community (traffic, staying with group, etc.)
__9. Manages frustration, controls anger
__10. Able to adjust to changes in routine

What (if any) situations are likely to cause the participant to act out or misbehave?

_____

Please identify any behavior management techniques used at home or school which reduce or discourage negative behavior.

_____

_____

Staff Comments:_____

Figure 4.5 continued

Figure 4.5 — (continued)

J.   Activity Skills, Leisure Interests

__1. Participation in activities requires much prompting/assistance
__2. Participation in activities requires some prompting/assistance
__3. Participation in activities requires little prompting/assistance
__4. Will participate in an activity of interest;
          __five minutes   __ten minutes   __15 minutes or more
__5. Understands directions (left, right, over, under)
__6. Understands basic number concepts
__7. Understands concepts of time
__8. Identifies colors
__9. Able to work a simple puzzle
__10. Will indicate an activity preference
__11. Will sit and watch a video/program for 30 minutes or longer

What are the participant's three favorite indoor activities?_____

_____

What are the participant's three favorite outdoor activities?_____

_____

Staff Comments:_____

_____

K.   Swimming

__1. Non-swimmer, requires individual attention in water
__2. Puts face in water
__3. Will submerge entire head under water
__4. Can float on front
__5. Can float on back
__6. Swims short distance in shallow water
__7. Able to swim in deep water

Comments/Areas of difficulty: _____

_____

(staff comments will appear in swim progression documents)

Figure 4.5 continued

Figure 4.5 – (continued)

School Information

In an effort to provide a goal-directed program, it is helpful for us to have information from the participant's school. We encourage you to provide us with a copy of the participantís Individual Education Plan (IEP) and to complete the following questionnaire. If you grant permission for us to contact the participantís school/teacher, please sign the waiver below.

School Name_____Teacher_____

School Address_____Zip Code_____

School / Teacher Phone Number_____

Participant's Special Education Classification (if known)_____

Is the participant in an inclusive classroom? Yes____ No____ If yes, how much of the participant's day (approximately) is spent in the inclusive classroom?

_____

Does the participant have a personal assistant / aide during the school day? Yes____ No____ If yes, how much time (approximately) does the assistant / aide spend with the participant?

_____

Please identify any recreational skills or areas of development (school I.E.P., etc.) that you would like to see emphasized in the day camp program: _____

_____

_____

School Contact Release (optional)

I, the undersigned, hereby authorize the Cincinnati Recreation Commission to contact the participantís school concerning information which may pertain to the recreation program.

Participant Name_____

Parent/Guardian Signature_____date_____

Thank you for your time and assistance!

Figure 4.6

Cincinnati Recreation Commission
ASSESSMENT and ACCOMMODATION REQUEST

This form is intended to assist in identifying accommodations which may be necessary for successful participation. Please complete as thoroughly as possible. Thank you.

Part A PARTICIPANT INFORMATION (to be completed by participant/parent/guardian)

Participant _____ Date of Birth _____

Address _____City _____Zip _____ Phone _____

Parent/Guardian _____Home Phone _____ Work Phone _____

Participants School/Workshop/Employer   Teacher/Supervisor's Name (Phone Number)

_____   _____

I.   Disability Information

Place a check next to each that applies to the participant and/or write in any disabling condition not listed:

___Autism   ___Attention Deficit Disorder   ___Hearing Impaired
___Down Syndrome   ___Psychiatric Disability   ___Vision Impaired
___Severe Mental Retardation   ___Cerebral Palsy   ___Speech Impaired
___Moderate Mental Retardation   ___Spina Bifida   ___Other
___Mild Mental Retardation   ___Head Injury   _____
___Learning Disability   ___Behavior Disorder   _____

Does participant walk independently? Yes_____ No _____ If no, please identify any mobility devices used or assistance needed (wheelchair, walker, etc.)

_____

Does participant have seizures? Yes_____ No _____If yes, please indicate type_____
Date of most recent seizure _____

Medications taken: (type, time, dosage, purpose)_____

_____

Allergies (include food/medications/other), activity restrictions, special diets or other medical concerns:

_____

Figure 4.6 continued

Figure 4.6 – (continued)

Cincinnati Recreation Commission
ASSESSMENT and ACCOMMODATION REQUEST

II.   Skill Assessment
Please check each statement that applies to the participant. Please use the comment section to identify additional skills needed and/or areas of difficulty.

Eating/Drink
__ Drinks from a cup
__ Able to use straw to drink
__ Able to grasp; use spoon
__ Able to unwrap, open containers
__ Able to open drink containers

Bathrooming (toileting, washing)
__ Wears diaper (Attends/Depends)
__ Indicates need to use toilet
__ Uses toilet with physical assistance
__ Uses toilet independently
__ Washes hands independently

Comments/Areas of difficulty:

_____

Communication (please check all that apply)

__ Unable to communicate needs/wants
__ Communicates with gestures, signs or non-verbal behavior

__ Communicates using basic sign language

__ Uses one or two word statements
__ Uses a communication device to
        communicate
__ Uses partial or complete spoken sentences

Comments/Areas of difficulty:

_____

Receptive Language (please check all that apply)

__ Recognizes own name when called
__ Reacts or responds when spoken to

__ Responds appropriately to one-step directions

__ Responds appropriately to two or three step directions
__ Responds appropriately to directions when in a small
        group
__ Responds appropriately to directions when in a larger
        group

Comments/Areas of difficulty:

_____

Motor Coordination (please check all that apply)

__ Able to catch a ball rolled
__ Able to catch a ball bounced
__ Able to catch a ball tossed from a short distance

__ Able to kick a stationary ball

__ Able to kick a roling ball
__ Able to grasp small objects (beads, pencil, etc.)
__ Able to grip/grasp larger objects (tennis ball, racquet,
        etc.)

Comments/Areas of difficulty:

_____

Figure 4.6 continued

Figure 4.6 – (continued)

Cincinnati Recreation Commission
ASSESSMENT and ACCOMMODATION REQUEST

Social/Behavioral   (please check all that apply)

__ Shows interest in others
__ Will play/interact cooperatively with others

__ Will sit quietly to watch a program, show, movie, etc.
__ Can identify and take responsibility for
    personal belongings

__ Is tolerant of others, not easily agitated or annoyed
__ Is aware of safety concerns when out in the community (traffic, staying with group, etc.)

__ Will play/interact cooperatively within a group

Comments/Areas of difficulty:
_____

Does your child swim independently _____yes _____no

If no, please explain?_____
_____

Please identify any activities, games, hobbies, etc. the participant enjoys or has expressed interest in:
_____
_____

Please explain any behavior management techniques used at home or school which eliminate or reduce negative behaviors:
_____
_____

(This portion of the Assessment & Accommodation needs to be completed if the participant is under 18 years of age.)

Does your child have an aide/ personal assistant at school?   ❑ Yes   ❑ No

If so, how much time is the aide/ personal assistant with your child?_____
_____
_____

Please describe your child's classroom?   ❑ Special Ed   ❑ Inclusive   ❑ Both

Please be specific regarding the structure of the classroom environment_____
_____

How many students are in your child's classroom? _____
_____

Additional comments, suggestions: _____
_____

Figure 4.6 continued

Figure 4.6 – (continued)

RELEASE OF INFORMATION

I, _____ (Parent/Guardian Care Provider) hereby give my permission for you to release the information requested below for my child. I understand this information will be used to plan appropriate activities for my child. Please initial all methods you give permission for release of information.

_____   IEP Information

_____   Completion of Teacher Questionnaire

_____   Inclusion Specialist Observation

_____   Teacher / Inclusion Specialist Phone Conversation

Signature of Parent/Guardian _____ Date
_____

MULTI – MEDIA RELEASE FORM

I, undersigned, hereby authorize the Cincinnati Recreation Commission to utilize (including but not limited to) photographs, videotapes, and/or voice recordings, etc. of the participant listed to be used exclusively for promotion, advertising, and/or marketing of the Cincinnati Recreation Commission and its programs, facilities, and/or services. The images may be repeatedly used at any time and I will not seek recourse or payment for the use of the aforementioned materials from the Cincinnati Recreation Commission.

Signature of Participant/Parent/ Guardian _____ Date
_____

Figure 4.6 continued

Figure 4.6 – (continued)

Cincinnati Recreation Commissionn
ASSESSMENT and ACCOMMODATION REQUEST

Name_____   Program/ Yr. _____

Part B   RECOMMENDATIONS for ACCOMMODATION (to be completed by Inclusion Specialist)

Identify potential areas of concern relating to program activities, program environment, staffing, and/or participant abilities:

_____

_____

_____

Supports/accommodations recommended for successful participation. Including: activities, interventions, skill training, adaptations, management strategies and communication techniques (include aspects of the program that could benefit the inclusion process).

_____

_____

_____

_____

_____

I have reviewed the recommended support(s) / accommodation(s) and agree with the stated plan for inclusion.

_____   _____   _____
     Participant/Parent/Guardian   Date   Inclusion Specialist

I have reviewed the recommended support(s) / accommodation(s) and would like to request the following revision(s) / addition(s) to the plan for inclusion:

_____

_____

_____

_____

_____   _____   _____
     Participant/Parent/Guardian   Date   Inclusion Specialist

Figure 4.6 continued

Figure 4.6 – (continued)

Cincinnati Recreation Commission
C. PLAN FOR ACCOMMODATION

Participant Name:_____Plan Date_____

Program/Center

_____

Day(s)/Time(s) of Program_____

Center Staff Name(s) and Phone Numbers _____

I. Summarize accommodations needed for successful participation:

_____

_____

_____

II.   Resources needed? How provided?

_____

_____

_____

Inclusion Specialist's role, frequency and schedule of on-site support

_____

_____

_____

IV.   Center Staff's role/responsibilities relating to Inclusion Plan:

_____

_____

_____

V.   Evaluation/Recommendations (Summary of Inclusion Support Plan at the conclusion of the on-site support stage)

_____

_____

_____

_____
             Inclusion Specialist

The organizational structure, staff roles and assignments, and the agency's approach to inclusion influence who completes assessments, where completed forms are stored and how information is shared among program managers and direct service personnel. The integrity and confidentiality of consumers is considered as the data are used to prepare the location and staff and to design support and behavioral plans—the next APIE step.

Planning

The second major step in the APIE process is planning. This involves two tasks: 1) developing individual support plans, and 2) preparing the accommodations necessary to deliver programs (refer to Figure 1.4, Inclusion Flow Chart in Defining the Service: Assessing the Community and Agency in Chapter 1). After a number of sub-tasks are completed participant support and behavior plans are written and accommodations are in place to deliver inclusive services (refer to Figure 4.7, planning includes, Cincinnati Recreation Commission, n.d.). The nature of this step is unique to each agency. To illustrate, in some settings inclusion plans are developed and monitored by inclusion specialists while in others therapeutic recreation specialists partner with general recreators

---

Figure 4.7

Planning – Inclusion Support Plan is developed, specific accommodations are prepared. (Assessment and Accommodation Request)

Includes:

Summarizing assessment data (primary need for inclusion support and recommended accommodations)

Identifying the "inclusion team", convening and gaining input from all those needing to be involved in the inclusion support plan

Identifying participant objectives, achievement measures

Identifying specific inclusion strategies, adaptations, interventions to be used

Identifying resources needed, how provided

Clarifying roles/responsibilities

Establishing clear channels of communication

Developing behavioral support plan (if needed)

Staff preparation, training and orientation

Participant/peer preparation strategies (disability awareness program)

Identifying Inclusion Specialist/support staff schedules, observations, meetings, dates to review support plan, etc.

and other team members to design inclusion options. This planning process is applicable across settings; forms and procedures are modified to enable design of consumer-oriented programs.

Individual Support Plan. An individual support plan contains 1) assessment information, 2) participant goals and objectives, 3) experiences/interventions, 4) staff roles and responsibilities, 5) accommodations, and 6) evaluation information (refer to Figure 4.6, Cincinnati Recreation Commission Assessment and Accommodation Request, Part C Plan for Accommodation, n.d.). The *assessment summary* establishes the need for accommodations and the baseline to judge improvements in behavioral areas noted in participant goals and objectives. Participant goals and objectives are prepared in concert with members of the inclusion team and identify outcomes desired from participation. These statements are the foundation for preparing interventions, adaptations, staff, program resources; and if necessary, developing behavior support plans.

Goals and Objectives. Participant goals and objectives are similar in format to agency goals and objectives, refer to Goals and Objectives in Chapter 1 Defining the Service: Assessing the Community and Agency. The focus is on participant outcomes rather than overall direction of the agency. Through participation, consumers benefit in five behavioral areas: cognitive, affective, physical, social, and spiritual. In each area, goals are written to describe improvements, changes, or acquisition of new behaviors (refer to Figure 4.8, Cincinnati Recreation Commission Therapeutic Recreation Individual Goal Sheet, n.d.). Following each goal statement, objective statements are written to measure outcomes derived from specific programs/interventions. To illustrate, each behavioral area is defined with goal and objective statements describing the nature of anticipated outcomes.

Cognitive behaviors are concerned with thinking or mental activity and can be as simple as recalling the score or as complex as creating a music script. Cognitive skills are evident as consumers learn directions from one location to another or in the decisions made as one leisure experience is selected over another.

Goal: To improve decision-making skills

Objective: During a leisure awareness program, participant will select one leisure experience from three choices and state one reason for the choice at least once.

Affective behaviors occur during expression of emotions through verbal and nonverbal communication and gestures. Emotional responses range from responding to or showing an interest in a leisure project to selecting a preferred recreation experience and valuing outcomes of an experience or relationship.

Goal: To improve ability to express feelings

Objective: During a group activity, participant will identify or label at least once correctly feelings of joy, guilt, fear, frustration or anger.

Physical behaviors are concerned with movement and the sensation of motion. Balance, coordination, manipulation, strength, endurance, and perceptual, fine and gross motor movements are among the behaviors improved during therapeutic experiences. Most experiences require the use of physical skills; however, these skills are more evident in activities like swimming and walking than in drama or reading.

Goal: To improve gross motor coordination

Objective: During frisbee golf, participant will increase throwing and catching accuracy by 25% from initial to last session of program by hitting course targets.

Social behaviors are evident during interaction with others. Cooperation, sharing, taking turns, listening and the display of social etiquette are exemplary behaviors.

Goal: To improve cooperation with others

Objective: During partner and group activities, participant will assist or support and share or take turns with at least one other person at least 50% of the session to complete a project or a game.

Spiritual behaviors are linked to feelings of well-being and peace of mind. Subjective evaluations of relaxation, friendship, wilderness experiences and values garnered from music reflect spirituality.

Goal: To express acceptance of a state of health or well-being

Objective: During a skill development class, participant will identify three adaptations or accommodations used in a particular recreation experience that help achieve successful participation levels.

Each properly worded objective is comprised of 1) condition or circumstance under which the behavior is developed, 2) action verb that describes an observable and measurable performance or skill to be developed or changed by a specific program or intervention, and 3) criterion or performance level, such as degree of accuracy

Figure 4.8

CINCINNATI RECREATION COMMISSION
THERAPEUTIC RECREATION

INDIVIDUAL GOAL SHEET

Participant's Name_____Date_____

Staff Completing_____ Program Location _____

Identify two goals per participant

Physical
❏Improve fine motor skills (grasp, etc.)
❏Improve gross motor skills (run, jump, etc.)
❏Improve coordination (eye-hand, eye-foot)
❏Increase range of motion
❏Improve posture
❏Increase spatial awareness
❏Improve chair handling/usage
❏Other (specify below)

_____
_____

Cognitive
❏Increase attention span (staying on task)
❏Improve ability to follow directions
❏Improve directionality (left, right, etc.)
❏Improve ability to solve problems
❏Improve cause-effect understanding
❏Increase understanding of time concepts
❏Improve fact retention skills (names, etc)
❏Other (specify below)

_____
_____

Social
❏Increase awareness of others
❏Increase ability to make/maintain eye contact
❏Increase ability to initiate positive interaction
❏Increase ability to listen (without interrupting)
❏Decrease inappropriate interactions with others
❏Improve cooperation (share, take turns)
❏Improve social etiquette (please, thank you, etc.)
❏Improve ability to express thoughts/opinions
❏Improve ability to engage in conversation
❏Other (specify below)

_____
_____

Emotional / Behavioral
❏Improve ability to identify feelings
❏Improve ability to express feelings
❏Increase confidence, assertiveness
❏Increase trust in others
❏Improve impulse control
❏Increase ability to manage frustration
❏Improve ability to ignore negatives
❏Improve ability to tolerate others
❏Other (specify below)

_____

Recreation / Leisure Activity
❏Increase awareness of activity interests
❏Improve ability to make activity choices
❏Increase awareness of leisure resources
❏Increase level of participation
❏Increase independence in participation
❏Improve leisure skill (specify below)

_____
_____

Self Help / Safety
❏Increase independence in using bathroom
❏Increase independence in eating, drinking
❏Increase independence in dressing
❏Improve personal hygiene skills
❏Increase awareness of safety concerns
❏Other (specify below)

_____
_____

(over)

Figure 4.8 continued

Figure 4.8 – (continued)

PROGRESS NOTES
(Identify activities and interactions used to promote goal)

Goal 1:_____

Date:_____   _____
                        _____
                        _____

Date:_____   _____
                        _____

Date:_____   _____
                        _____
                        _____
                        _____

Goal 2:_____

Date:_____   _____
                        _____
                        _____

Date:_____   _____
                        _____
                        _____

Date:_____   _____
                        _____
                        _____

FINAL EVALUATION
(summary statement / recommendations for future programs)

Goal 1: _____
_____
_____
_____

Goal 2: _____
_____
_____
_____

or percent of time or number of participants expected to minimally display the performance or behavior. In each behavioral area, covert outcomes like thinking or having fun are desired, yet they are not seen or heard: So, overt indicators are used to describe invisible outcomes. For instance, to measure thinking, a staff might ask a participant, "How many blocks is the park from your house?" or observe laughing and gestures that express happiness as indicators for having fun.

Experiences/Interventions. Goal and objective statements lead to the identification of experiences or interventions likely to support consumer achievement of desired outcomes; as noted in the illustrations, some objectives actually state desired experiences or nature of the intervention. Through activity and task analyses, skill requirements, degree of difficulty, and sequence to master or perform skills are determined. After conducting these analyses, professionals identify alternative experiences or intervention processes and desired steps to achieve outcomes specified by goals and objectives.

Activity analysis. Activity analysis occurs as each potential experience is reviewed to determine the number, level, and types of behaviors inherent with the experience. Each experience is broken down into skills displayed from each of the behavioral areas; then within each area, skill complexity is explored. Initially completed on paper, this process once familiar is less time consuming and automatic as staff and consumers select alternative experiences to achieve desired outcomes.

In the cognitive, affective, and social domains, a natural hierarchy exists from the least to the most complicated skill along a continuum. To illustrate, knowledge is the lowest, while synthesis is the highest level of thinking: Receiving is the least complex, with characterization the most complex emotion: And, intra-individual experiences require fewer social skills than any other form of social interaction. Within the physical area, frequency, speed, and duration when added to an activity increase its complexity. When a number of skills are concurrently used, like riding a bike, the activity is more difficult than when fewer skills and sensations are used. Spiritual behaviors are found within each of the other domains and are the participant's interpretations of experiences according to a particular worldview; consequently, hierarchical interpretation of spirituality is nonexistent (refer to Figure 4.9 for an outline of skills in each behavioral area).

Task analysis. The number, degree of difficulty, and types of behaviors inherent in experiences are known after activity analysis. From this information, staff develop skill progressions or sequences identifying prerequisites, skill sequences, and follow-up experiences. A task analysis results in listing by complexity every step to master a skill and perform an activity successfully. Each step listed in a sequence may be a behavior defined in a participant objective. Consequently, by examining activity and task analyses completed on a number of experiences, professionals decide which experience best enables the accomplishment of participant goals and objectives. With these processes, staff become familiar with alternative experiences/interventions to achieve desired participant outcomes. An example is presented in Figure 4.9, Therapeutic Use of Activities.

Staff Roles and Responsibilities. Assessment, and activity and task analyses consider both the consumer and the experience (Bullock & Mahon, 2000). Staff roles and responsibilities are guided by consumer needs and the nature of the activity and environment in which the experience occurs. Staff roles are identified after comparing assessment information to results of activity and task analyses that examine program features including 1) rules, procedures, and regulations governing experiences 2) equipment and resources used in experiences, and 3) place, time, location, and peer interaction during the program. Staff determine the types of support, assistance and program adaptations that result in *reasonable accommodations*. Also staff identify and participate in additional preparation and training needed before programs are implemented. One accommodation for staff and consumers may be information, orientation, and practice prior to inclusion experiences. A final outcome of comparing consumer assessments to activity and task analyses is the need for staff to write behavioral support plans. These plans are written during the planning phase if staff determine that program features require adjustment so the consumer and peer participants will be safe and successful in the experience.

Generally there are four types of adaptations staff identify during the planning phase that do not create undue burden and lead to reasonable accommodations: Staff may 1) modify their relationship and interactions with participants, 2) alter the behavioral expectations, 3) adjust rules and procedures; and 4) change the resources used during the experience (refer to Figure 4.10, Adapting Recreational Experiences for examples of each adaptation). A training document on adapting recreation activities presents questions and principles that guide staff as they plan for maximum participation and enjoyment (refer to Figure 4.11, Cincinnati Recreation Commission, n.d.). Staff record recommended adaptations and accommodations on the individual inclusion support plan, and if appropriate, write individual behavior support plans.

Figure 4.9

THERAPEUTIC USE OF ACTIVITIES

Activity Analysis

The study of an activity to establish the number, level, and types of behaviors inherent in the activity with the purpose of selecting an activity to achieve specific outcomes.

Behaviors are present in four areas in every activity yet at any given time one is probably more evident or necessary to the completion of the activity than are behaviors from the other areas.

Cognitive

Intellectual behaviors are presented in a hierarchy from those requiring less to those requiring more skill.
- Knowledge or recall of facts such as name and activity title.
- Comprehension such as interpretation of scores or summarization of the leader's directions.
- Application such as manipulation of figures to determine scores of others.
- Analysis such as the breakdown of steps to complete a task.
- Synthesis or design such as creating a picture or motor pattern from the leader's directions.
- Evaluation such as the decisionmaking or judgement to select one activity over another considering the influencing variables.

Questions the leader might ask to determine the cognitive requirements of an activity include:
- Does the activity involve luck or chance?
- How many steps and rules are involved in the activity?
- What levels of math, reading, spelling, comprehension, memory, and recall are involved?
- How much creativity is involved in the activity?
- How much concentration is involved in the activity?

Affective

Emotional behaviors are also presented from the least to the most complicated.
- Receive such as that demonstrated when listening or attending to music or someone talk.
- Respond such as showing interest in or reacting to an activity that one likes.
- Value such as showing appreciation or commitment to a particular leisure experience.
- Organize such as that shown when one accepts the responsibility for behavior during an activity.
- Characterize such as that demonstrated when one displays consistent behavior during an activity.

Questions the leader might ask to determine the affective requirements of an activity include:
- Which emotions are openly expressed during the activity: joy, guilt, pain, anger, frustration, fear, and/or frustration?
- Which of the above emotions must be hidden during an activity?
- Does the activity provide for accomplishment and recognition leading to improved selfc-oncept?
- Is emotional stress created or relieved during the activity?
- When and how frequently is emotional control needed during the activity?

Physical

The physical requirements of an activity include several behaviors that become more complicated as the participant is required to increase the speed, duration, and frequency with which the skill is displayed. Motor behaviors include balance, manipulation, coordination, sensation, gross, fine, and perceptual movements, body position, endurance, cardiovascular fitness, and fundamental skills such as standing, walking, grasping, throwing, rolling, bending, etc.

Figure 4.9 continued

Figure 4.9 – (continued)

Questions the leader might ask to determine the physical requirements of an activity include:

- What body parts are required during the activity?
- What body positions are required during the activity? Which of the senses are used during the activity?
- What degree of range of motion, endurance, and fitness is required by the activity? Are rest breaks built into the activity?
- How much handeye or eyefoot coordination is used in the activity?

Social

The social behaviors in an activity become more complicated as more people participate in the experience. These behaviors are also influenced by communication, selfconcept ' the nature and tinting of rewards, and the degree of structure given to the activity by the leader.

The interaction patterns that may occur during an activity include:

- Intraindividual occurs when one daydreams.
- Extraindividual occurs when one plays cards.
- Aggregate occurs when several people are each doing the same thing yet no one is interacting as in parallel play of children.
- Interindividual occurs as one person competes against another such as in playing cards.
- Unilateral occurs when three or more people play against the person who is it as in King of the Mountain.
- Multilateral occurs when three or more people are competitive yet no one is it as in poker.
- Intragroup occurs when two or more people cooperate to accomplish a task like rowing a boat.
- Intergroup occurs when two or more groups compete as in a sports contest.

Questions the leader might ask to determine the social requirements of an activity include:

- How many people are required and in what interaction pattern will they participate?
- What is the proximity of participants to one another and is physical contact required?
- What degree of modeling is involved in the activity? Are sharing, taking turns, and waiting required?
- Which verbal and nonverbal communication skills are used? Are etiquette and manners important to the activity?

Task Analysis

The study of an activity to identify the sequence from first to last of skills the participant must demonstrate to complete the whole activity with the purpose of presenting a stepbystep breakdown listing the skills from their initial or least difficult to the last or most difficult skill of the total experience.

Examples of task analysis are presented:

Objective: To throw and retrieve a horseshoe to a stake
Sequence: 1. Grasp horseshoe
                2. Hold horseshoe and swing arm
                3. Release horseshoe toward target area
                4. Walk toward target area
                5. Pick up horseshoe
                6. Walk back to starting mark

Objective: To stop and start a cassette recorder
Sequence: 1. Extend finger to play button
                2. Push play button down
                3. Extend finger to stop button
                4. Push stop button down

Figure 4.10

ADAPTING RECREATIONAL EXPERIENCES

1. Adjust the leader-participant relationship
   a. Modify the leader's communication and interaction methods
   b. Modify the degree of control by the leader
   c. Use various intervention processes, such as reality orientation
   d. Regroup participants

2. Alter the behavioral expectations of the experience
   a. Physical modifications
      Coordinate fewer body parts
      Reduce the number of items to be dealt with
      Reduce the speed of the task
   b. Cognitive modifications
      Simplify the organizational pattern
      Reduce the number of facts to be recalled
      Alter the number of steps involved to complete the project
      Select from fewer alternatives
   c. Affective-social behaviors
      Reduce the number of participants
      Increase the structure
      Modify the reward, intrinsic to extrinsic
      Allow more or less freedom of choice

3. Modify the procedures or rules
   Adjust the size or the space in which the activity occurs
   Alter the number of players or positions
   Allow more time or a greater number of actions
   Substitute actions
   Adjust the number of body parts used
   Alter distances
   Adjust the time allowed to score or win
   Permit assistants
   Develop new ways to do the activity

4. Modify the resources
   a. Supplies and equipment
      Modify the size and weight of materials
      Adjust the color of materials
      Alter the grip of rackets
   b. Areas and facilities
      Modify texture of surface
      Adjust size of geographic area used
      Decrease noise within the area
      Assure accessibility
      Control heat, light, electricity
   c. Supportive aspects
      Adjust the number of staff and their assignments
      Alter tirring (daily, weekly) of experiences
      Add rest intervals

Figure 4.11

Adapting Recreation Activities
For
Maximum Participation and Enjoyment!

Providing age appropriate activities for individuals with disabilities is often difficult due to their lack of skill in various activities. A primary purpose of Therapeutic Recreation programs is to develop skills which allow individuals to participate with their peers (with or without disabilities).

A starting point for every TR program is to consider the activities engaged in by individuals of the same age range <u>without</u> disabilities. What skills are needed for participation in these activities? How are these skills developed?

The most common approach to skill development and participation in age appropriate activities is known as "activity adaptation". Beginning with the original activity, areas of difficulty are identified and simplified to allow for successful participation.

Age Appropriate Activity
What skills are needed for participation?
↓

(Your) Participant's Skills and Areas Needing Development
↓

What Aspects of the Activity Might Cause Difficulty?
(compare skills emphasized in activity to participant skills)
↓

How can the Activity be Modified to Reduce the Need
for Skill in Areas of Difficulty?

Principles of Activity Adaptation

- Adapt to increase participation and/or independent participation

- Adapt only when necessary, don't assume an adaptation is needed

- Adaptations should be made on an individual basis

- Begin with the slightest adaptation needed

- De-emphasize the adaptation, focus on those aspects of the activity that remain the same

Figure 4.11 continued

Figure 4.11 – (continued)

Techniques for Adapting Activities

There are many ways to adapt an activity to increase successful participation.

➤ Activity equipment or materials can be replaced by equipment/materials that are easier to see, easier to grip, lighter, larger contact surface, more stable, require less fine motor control, less strength, etc.

➤ Activity rules or procedures can be simplified, fewer rules to remember, fewer decisions to make, more time allowed, removing number concepts, allowing more bounces or extra swings or touches as needed.

➤ Changes can be made in the distance or space typically used for the activity. Decreasing the playing area (distance between bases), reducing the distance to a target, or the height of a basket or net.

➤ "Lead-up" activities are games incorporating a few elements of the original activity in a simplified version. Examples of lead-up games; line soccer, volleyball catch and throw, one base kickball, and there are many others.

Additional means of adapting activities include:

➤ Games/activities that have various "roles", enabling participant to take role most compatible with his/her skills

➤ Games/activities that are highly individualized, allowing participants to work independently at their own pace and with equipment/materials most conducive

➤ Games/activities that are cooperative, requiring all participants to work together towards a single objective

➤ Providing individual staff assistance (one to one) may be an effective way to assure participation, however, the staff member must be careful not to "over assist" and should be looking for ways for the individual to participate without this level of assistance.

Remember:

❖ What makes an activity **fun** has more to do with the social interactions (and staff enthusiasm) than how you play. Focus on the participant's abilities and what they consider to be fun.

Individual behavior support plan. Staff write behavior support plans after they become aware of the environmental influences and social behaviors expected of participants during program experiences. This form of accommodation results when environmental features influence, both positively and negatively, behaviors of consumers, peers, staff or others during the experience. Features of the environment, such as excess noise or sunlight, may contribute to seizure activity or spasticity that interfere with participation: Or the participant may exhibit inattentive or compulsive behaviors with sensory overload. By writing behavior plans staff clarify and define safety protocols and procedures to follow as experiences are implemented. Additionally, behavior plans help managers by identifying training staff might need to manage consumer behaviors. Also, strategies useful with peer interaction are noted and incorporated into peer orientation. Or, prior to experiences, environmental adjustments such as modifying size of the area or relocating experiences to less congested areas are made to decrease interferences.

As noted in the example plan (refer to Figure 4.12, Behavioral Support Plan, Cincinnati Recreation Commission, n.d.), a key accommodation element is to document the need to make adjustments by recording previous incidents and observations and recommendations of staff and caregivers. Also critical is establishing a timeline and evaluation plan with progress notes to measure the effectiveness of the accommodation. Lastly, procedures to monitor and manage future incidents after the accommodation is evaluated are stated.

A behavior plan is filed with a participant's inclusion support plan and shared with team members, peer coaches, leisure buddies, and caregivers. During meetings held to address specific behavioral incidents or prior to actual program participation, the plan is shared with staff, volunteers, and the consumer to orient them to the experience and environmental expectations. Thus, the preparation of a behavior support plan helps develop support staff schedules, observations, meetings with caregivers, and set dates to review inclusion and behavior support plans (refer to Chapter 6 Motivating and Managing Participants for additional details on writing behavior support plans).

Evaluation Information. A final step of the planning phase is preparing evaluation tools and a plan to revise services after they have been evaluated. This includes preparation of documents to 1) record individual consumer progress, and 2) monitor program delivery and results of inclusion experiences. Staff develop documents and a time table to record information and collect input from consumers, caregivers, peers, and general recreation professionals. The intent of an evaluation plan is to document 1) accomplishment of participant goals and objectives, 2) relevance of participant experiences, 3) effectiveness of leadership and management procedures, and 4) appropriateness of accommodation and accessibility strategies. Thus, before the experience is implemented, a formative or process and a summative or product instrument(s) are identified and/or developed. Training sessions are planned to inform staff of data-collection procedures. Lastly, timelines to collect and present results to the inclusion team and revise experiences are specified.

A comprehensive evaluation plan considers formative or on-going experiences and concluding or summative results. Formative evaluation is continuous and enables the planner to adjust services as they occur to enable achievement of participant goals and objectives and appropriateness of accommodations. Thus the focus is on consumer participation and program delivery. Formative tools, like assessments, may be self-administered or designed to use with interviews and observations. To monitor progress toward participant goals and objectives, staff create individual and group goal sheets to use as participants are observed in programs. As shown in the illustrations, goals are organized by functioning areas so staff either 1) check the degree to which behaviors are individually performed (refer to Figure 4.13, Therapeutic Recreation Day Camp Observation Checklist, Cincinnati Recreation Commission, n.d.) or 2) check the goal statement under the functioning area by the listed participant name when he/she demonstrates the behavior during a program (refer to Figure 4.14, Therapeutic Recreation Group Goal Sheet, Cincinnati Recreation Commission, n.d.). A third approach is to write progress notes for each goal and identify activities and interactions used to promote the goal, refer to Figure 4.8, Individual Goal Sheet Progress Notes, Cincinnati Recreation Commission Therapeutic Recreation, (n.d.).

Another formative tool evaluates the delivery of each session (refer to Figure 4.15, Program Planning and Evaluation sheet, Cincinnati Recreation Commission/Therapeutic Recreation, n.d.). This tool documents resources used and accommodations prepared to deliver programs. The document is a recording of information from persons associated with the program. Staff document at the end of each session (refer to Figure 4.16, Post Program Evaluation sheet, Cincinnati Recreation Commission/Therapeutic Recreation, n.d.). At the conclusion of a program season, staff revisit session sheets to assess program accommodation effectiveness to better prepare for the new season.

Figure 4.12

CINCINNATI RECREATION COMMISSION
DIVISION OF THERAPEUTIC RECREATION

BEHAVIORAL SUPPORT PLAN

PLAN DEVELOPMENT DATE _____

Participant _____ Program/Location _____

1. Description of Behavior: Describe specifically the behavior(s) to be addressed. If more than one area of concern, prioritize according to severity or frequency.

   _____

   _____

   _____

2. Documentation of previous incidents (list or attach, include date)

   _____

   _____

   _____

3. Antecedents. (observations/recommendations from the Behavioral Observation Sheet)

   _____

   _____

   _____

4. Based on staff observations and parent/guardian input, what could be the cause of the behavior? What (do we think) participant is communicating or gaining through this behavior? What outcomes may be maintaining this behavior?

   _____

   _____

   _____

Figure 4.12 continued

Figure 4.12 – (continued)

5. Positive Reinforcement. What activities or items are considered rewarding to the participant?

_____

_____

_____

6. Strategies: Identify strategies which may be effective in reducing the negative behavior(s).
Include pro-active strategies intended to prevent behavior(s) from occurring as well as
consequences to apply following behavior(s). (These strategies should incorporate parent/
guardian suggestions as well as school-based plans if available).

_____

_____

_____

_____

7. Timeline. Suggested time frame to review and evaluate plan.

Is the target behavior considered to be a ìdirect threatî (aggressiveness towards others, potentially
harmful to self or others)?

Yes_____No_____

If yes, please indicate the degree of threat as follows (circle number):

1	2	3	4	5	6	7	8	9	10
some potential for slight injury (scratch, bruise)		moderate potential for slight injury		slight potential for more serious injury		moderate potential for more serious injury			high potential for serious injury

What will be the time frame used in determining the effectiveness of the accommodation
(number of program meetings, number of weeks, etc.)?

_____

_____

Figure 4.12 continued

Figure 4.12 – (continued)

What will be the measurement (number of incidents per session, severity of incident, etc.) used in determining the effectiveness of the accommodation (behavior support plan)?

_____

_____

8. Progress Notes: (attach additional notes, incident reports, as needed)

_____

_____

_____

_____

_____

_____

Managers and inclusion specialists observe staff, volunteers, and general recreation staff as inclusion experiences are delivered. When this occurs, recorded information captures the degree to which staff plan and implement relevant inclusive options (refer to Figure 4.17, Program Observation/Evaluation, Cincinnati Recreation Commission, Division of Therapeutic Recreation, n.d.). Formative evaluation results help the manager plan leadership training as well as document appropriateness of accommodations and experiences to achieve consumer outcomes.

Summative evaluation uses information from formative evaluations and data collected when services are concluded to determine program effectiveness. Feedback on each of the four areas—participant objectives, participant experiences, leadership and management, and accommodations and accessibility, follows collection of summative information. Recommendations are made on individual support and behavior plans and transitions and program operations. Examples of summative tools include: staff summaries of individual and program formative tools, caregiver and consumer self-reports, re-administration of initial assessments, management review of budgets, safety audits, and compliance documents, and team member and advisory committee reports.

Each individual inclusion support plan contains sections for evaluations, recommendations, and revisions (refer to Figure 4.6, Part C, Plan for Accommodation on Assessment and Accommodation Request, Cincinnati Recreation Commission, n.d.). The plan is a repository of information from general recreation staff, consumers, caregivers, and support persons. Additionally, agency-generated tools gather information from multiple persons and program sites. As illustrated, triangulated techniques relevant to an inclusive summer day camp offered at a recreation center include: 1) center manager evaluation 2) inclusion support staff evaluation, and 3) participant and/or parent evaluation (refer to Figures 4.18-4.20, Cincinnati Recreation Commission, 2002). Summarized responses are documented on individual support and behavior plans and shared with team members during program evaluation.

After formative and summative evaluation tools are in place, managers assign staff and prepare timelines to collect information. Also, staff are trained to use the tools. Staff arrange to gather information at the least intrusive times and places. Naturalistic processes occur while the program is being delivered, formative evalua-

Figure 4.13

Cincinnati Recreation Commission.

Therapeutic Recreation Day Camp Observation Checklist

Date:_____Program Location:_____

Camper's Name:_____

EVALUATION SYSTEM

0	NOT OBERVED OR EMPLOYED WITH CAMPER
1	PERFORMS WITH PHYSICAL AND VERBAL ASSISTANCE
2	PERFORMS WITH VERBAL ASSISTANCE

PHYSICAL

0 1 2 3 Negotiates Camp Area
0 1 2 3 Manipulates Steps And Inclines
0 1 2 3 Manipulates Path/ Trails/ Sidewalks
0 1 2 3 Walks Daily To Program Sites
0 1 2 3 Maintains Energy Level
0 1 2 3 Fatigues Easily
0 1 2 3 Dances To Music
0 1 2 3 Employs Hand/Body Movement With Music
0 1 2 3 Plays An Instrument
0 1 2 3 Employs A Steady Beat
0 1 2 3 Cuts With Scissors
0 1 2 3 Tears And Folds Paper
0 1 2 3 Applies Glue
0 1 2 3 Paints With Tools/Materials
0 1 2 3 Uses Tools/Materials Correctly
0 1 2 3 Dresses/Undresses Self
0 1 2 3 Washes Hands And Face
0 1 2 3 Brushes Teeth
0 1 2 3 Feeds Self
0 1 2 3 Helps With Clean Up
0 1 2 3 Makes A Name Tag
0 1 2 3 Makes A Sand Project
0 1 2 3 Makes A Nature Collage
0 1 2 3 Constructs A Puppet
0 1 2 3 Throws/Strikes Ball
0 1 2 3 Catches Ball
0 1 2 3 Kicks Ball
0 1 2 3 Plays Volleyball
0 1 2 3 Works Puzzle

COGNITIVE

0 1 2 3 Listens To Music
0 1 2 3 Sings Familiar Songs
0 1 2 3 Sings On Pitch
0 1 2 3 Creates/Contributes Skit Material
0 1 2 3 Imitates During Skit

(over)

0 1 2 3 Selects Own Project
0 1 2 3 Selects Own Colors
0 1 2 3 Demonstrates Creativity
0 1 2 3 Follows Directions/Instructions
0 1 2 3 Follows More Than One Direction At A Time
0 1 2 3 Manages Own Time
0 1 2 3 Completes Tasks
0 1 2 3 Initiates Tasks
0 1 2 3 Works Neatly
0 1 2 3 Completes Project/Follows Sequence
0 1 2 3 Shows Knowledge Of Community Resources
0 1 2 3 Able To Follow A Story
0 1 2 3 Responsible For Personal Belongings

SOCIAL

0 1 2 3 Aware Of Others, Shows Interest
0 1 2 3 Initiates Conversation
0 1 2 3 Cooperates With Others
0 1 2 3 Socializes With Others
0 1 2 3 Assists Others
0 1 2 3 Listens To Others
0 1 2 3 Interacts Appropriately With Peers
0 1 2 3 Interacts Appropriately With Staff
0 1 2 3 Initiates Leadership Of Activities/Group
0 1 2 3 Practices Personal Habits Of Cleanliness
0 1 2 3 Practices Acceptable Eating/Table Habits
0 1 2 3 Makes Eye Contact
0 1 2 3 Expresses Thoughts And Ideas

EMOTIONAL

0 1 2 3 Accepts Challenges
0 1 2 3 Respects Rights/Property Of Others
0 1 2 3 Initiates And Develops Friendships
0 1 2 3 Recognizes Contributions Of Others
0 1 2 3 Communicates Needs/Ideas

Figure 4.13 continued

Figure 4.13 — (continued)

0 1 2 3 Expresses Emotions Appropriately
0 1 2 3 Manages Frustration
0 1 2 3 Asserts Self Appropriately
0 1 2 3 Ignores Negative Comments
0 1 2 3 Deals Appropriately With Competitive Activities
0 1 2 3 Takes Responsibility For Actions
0 1 2 3 Able To Move On After Conflict

Leisure Interests

	EVALUATION SYSTEM
1	No Interest Demonstrated/Expressed
2	Some Interest Demonstrated/Expressed
3	Much Interest Demonstrated/Expressed

Sports/Active Games

1 2 3 Baseball, Softball, T-ball, Kickball
1 2 3 Golf, Putt-putt, Croquet
1 2 3 Bowling
1 2 3 Tennis, Badminton, Volleyball
1 2 3 Basketball
1 2 3 Swimming
1 2 3 Target Games (darts, ring toss, etc)
1 2 3 Hockey, Pillo-pollo
1 2 3 Soccer
1 2 3 Roller Skating
1 2 3 Gymnastics, Tumbling
1 2 3 Football
1 2 3 Fishing
1 2 3 Parachute Games
1 2 3 Other:

_____

_____

_____

Comments:_____

_____

_____

_____

Staff Signature

Crafts/Hobbies

1 2 3 Drawing, Painting
1 2 3 Modeling (clay, playdough)
1 2 3 Wood Work

1 2 3 Latch Hook, Weaving
1 2 3 Ceramics, Pottery
1 2 3 Beads, Jewelry
1 2 3 Model Kits (cars, planes, etc)
1 2 3 Computers/Video Games
1 2 3 Photography/Video Production
1 2 3 Music, Playing/Listening
1 2 3 Collecting (coins, stamps, cards, etc)
1 2 3 Cooking
1 2 3 Other:

_____

_____

_____

Indoor Games

1 2 3 Pool
1 2 3 Ping-pong
1 2 3 Card Games
1 2 3 Checkers, Chess
1 2 3 Board Games
1 2 3 Bingo
1 2 3 Puzzles
1 2 3 Dominoes
1 2 3 Charades
1 2 3 Other:

_____
_

_____
_

Miscellaneous

1 2 3 Drama, Plays, Skits
1 2 3 Music Games, Dance
1 2 3 Sensory Activities (specify activity)
1 2 3 Adventure Activities (climbing, canoeing, etc.)
1 2 3 Nature, Outdoor Ed. (specify behavior)
1 2 3 Other:

___

_____

_____
___

_____

_____

_____

_____

_____

Camp Director Signature

Figure 4.14

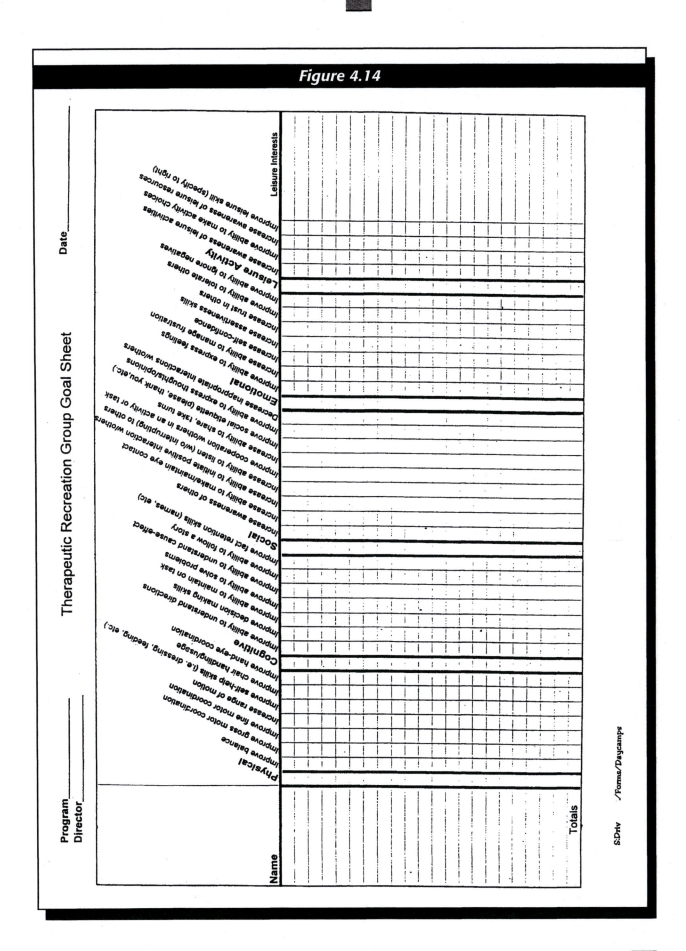

Therapeutic Recreation Group Goal Sheet

Program _____
Director _____

Date _____

Leisure Interests

Leisure Activity
- improve leisure skill (specify to right)
- increase awareness of leisure resources
- increase ability to make activity choices
- improve awareness of leisure activities
- increase awareness of leisure activities

Emotional
- increase ability to ignore negatives
- improve ability to tolerate others
- improve trust in others
- increase assertiveness skills
- increase self-confidence
- increase ability to manage frustration
- increase ability to express feelings
- improve appropriate interactions w/others
- decrease inappropriate interactions w/others

Social
- improve ability to express (thoughts/opinions)
- improve social etiquette (please, thank you, etc.)
- improve ability to share, take turns
- increase ability to listen (w/o interrupting) to others
- increase cooperation w/others in an activity or task
- improve ability to initiate positive interaction w/others
- increase ability to make/maintain eye contact
- increase awareness of others
- increase social skills (names, etc)

Cognitive
- improve fact retention skills
- improve ability to follow a story
- improve ability to understand cause-effect
- improve ability to solve problems
- improve ability to maintain on task
- improve decision making skills
- improve ability to understand directions

Physical
- improve hand-eye coordination
- improve chair handling/usage (i.e. dressing, feeding, etc.)
- improve self-help skills
- improve range of motion
- increase fine motor coordination
- improve gross motor coordination
- improve balance

Name

Totals

S:Drrv   ./Forms/Daycamps

Figure 4.15

**Cincinnati Recreation Commission / Therapeutic Recreation
Program Planning and Evaluation**

Program / Location: _____   Director: _____

Date: _____ Attendance: _____ Absent: _____ Volunteer Hours: _____

from	to	activity / description / participant grouping / location	staff assignments	equip. / supply

transition activities, alternate activities, individualized adaptations:

*Note: Identify activity leader, behavior staff and other assignments

(use additional sheets if needed for planning)

Figure 4.16

Cincinnati Recreation Commission / Therapeutic Recreation
Post Program Evaluation

Program / Location: _____ Date: _____

Please comment on the success of the planned activities (what worked, what did not, what changes should be made)

_____

_____

_____

Were the necessary resources available/adequate for this program session (equipment, supplies, facility, number of staff, etc.)?
Yes_____ No_____ If "No", please explain:

_____

Please comment on any participant issues (complete the **Behavioral Incident Report or Accident to Participant** if required)

_____

_____

Please comment on any pertinent parent/guardian communications:

_____

_____

Additional issues, concerns, comments, successes, etc.

_____

_____

Figure 4.17

Division of Therapeutic Recreation
Program Observation/Evaluation

Program/Location_____ Date_____

Director_____ Staff/Volunteers_____

Number of Participants_____ Number Absent_____ Evaluator:_____

Planning and Preparation

Participant information (complete, accurate, up to date) is readily available	Yes___	No___
All staff are familiar with all participants (names, disabling conditions, etc.)	Yes___	No___
Participant assessment has been completed, reviewed with all staff	Yes___	No___

Written plan for program which includes:

Detailed description of activities with specific time frames	Yes___	No___
Staff/volunteer assignments identified	Yes___	No___
Individualized activities/adaptations identified (as needed)	Yes___	No___
Alternate, back-up activities, transition activities, identified	Yes___	No___

Staff arrive with adequate time to review plan and check assignments	Yes___	No___
Staff arrive with adequate time to set up for activities, prepare materials, etc.	Yes___	No___

Comments: _____

_____

Implementation (introducing/explaining)

Activity is introduced/explained clearly and efficiently	Yes___	No___
Demonstrations (combining verbal with visual) used appropriately	Yes___	No___
Safety issues relating to activity are clarified	Yes___	No___
Leader checks participant understanding	Yes___	No___
Leader motivates group, shows enthusiasm	Yes___	No___
Activity starts on time	Yes___	No___
Late arrivals are added to the activity with little/no disruption	Yes___	No___

Comments:_____

_____

Implementation (directing/controlling)

Adjustments made (as needed) to maximize participation and enjoyment	Yes___	No___
Individual assistance/instruction is provided as needed (not over assisting)	Yes___	No___
Appropriate behavioral interventions (early recognition, redirecting, etc.)	Yes___	No___

Figure 4.17 continued

Figure 4.17 – (continued)

Positive reinforcement for all participants (encouragement/recognition)   Yes___ No___
Staff are alert and pro-active for potential safety concerns   Yes___ No___

Comments:_____

_____

Implementation (concluding/transitioning)

Leader prepares participants in advance for conclusion of activity   Yes___ No___
Leader brings participants together for conclusion   Yes___ No___
Leader gives positive feedback, explains what happens next   Yes___ No___

Comments:_____

_____

Activity Appropriateness and Structure

Activities meet interests, participants enjoy   Yes___ No___
Activities match skill levels, participants can do with minimal assistance   Yes___ No___
Activities promote individual/group objectives   Yes___ No___
Activities are age appropriate based on peers without disabilities   Yes___ No___
Facility, equipment, supplies, materials are sufficient/appropriate   Yes___ No___
Activity sequence is appropriate   Yes___ No___
Activity time allocations are appropriate   Yes___ No___
Staff assignments/ratios are appropriate   Yes___ No___

Comments:_____

_____

Staff Interactions

Staff recognize when and how to assist participant   Yes___ No___
Staff recognize when and how to assist each other   Yes___ No___
Director provides appropriate directions, support and feedback to all staff   Yes___ No___

Comments:_____

_____

Program Communications, Conclusion/Evaluation

Staff meet and greet participants/parents/guardians upon arrival   Yes___ No___
Staff make efforts to thank at conclusion and to provide/receive feedback   Yes___ No___
Staff are prepared with information concerning next program   Yes___ No___
Director/staff available at pick-up for questions, issues, progress, etc.   Yes___ No___
Staff remain to evaluate the program, able to recognize areas for improvement   Yes___ No___
All staff assist in the facility clean up, rearrangement, closing, etc.   Yes___ No___

Comments: _____

_____

Figure 4.18

Inclusion Support Evaluation
Center Evaluation

Summer 2002

Please take the time to complete the evaluation regarding inclusion in your community center.
We will utilize these evaluations to better facilitate inclusion within our community centers.

Do you feel you were adequately prepared to include a child with the disability into your program?

Yes   No

If no, please identify specific areas of concern (i.e. registration, training, etc)_____

_____

_____

Do you feel you were provided with enough support from the Inclusion Specialist (Division of Therapeutic Recreation)?

Excellent   Good   Satisfactory   Fair   Poor

Additional Comments _____

_____

If you were provided with an Inclusion Assistant (1:1), how would you rank the quality of their work?

Excellent   Good   Satisfactory   Fair   Poor

Comments _____

_____

Do you feel the child with the disability was successful in your program?

Extremely Successful   Somewhat Successful   Average Success   Little Success   No Success

Comments_____

_____

Recommendations/ Suggestions _____

_____

_____

_____

We appreciate your feedback on how to better serve individuals with disabilities within our community centers. Please return your evaluation to Steve LeConey (CRC Main Office- Therapeutic Recreation). Thank you!

Cincinnati Recreation Commission

Figure 4.19

Inclusion Support Assistant Evaluation

Summer 2002

Please take the time to complete the evaluation regarding your employment this summer with our organization.
We will utilize these evaluations to better serve individuals with disabilities in an inclusive setting.

What was the disability of the child in which you were providing Inclusion Support?

Do you feel you were adequately prepared to work with the child with the disability in an inclusive setting?

Training	Excellent	Good	Satisfactory	Fair	Poor
Modeling	Excellent	Good	Satisfactory	Fair	Poor
Orientation to Community Center	Excellent	Good	Satisfactory	Fair	Poor
Ongoing Assistance	Excellent	Good	Satisfactory	Fair	Poor

Additional Comments _____

_____

_____

Do you feel you received enough support from the Inclusion Team (Division of Therapeutic Recreation)?

Excellent	Good	Satisfactory	Fair	Poor

Comments _____

_____

_____

Do you feel you were supported enough by the center staff (i.e. willingness to assist)

Excellent	Good	Satisfactory	Fair	Poor

Comments _____

_____

_____

OVER

Figure 4.19 continued

Figure 4.19 — (continued)

Do you feel the child was successful in this inclusive setting?

Excellent   Good   Satisfactory   Fair   Poor

Comments _____

_____

Would you return to the Cincinnati Recreation Commission as an Inclusion Assistant for another program/child?

Yes   No

Would you return to the same community center?

Yes   No

Any particular program? _____

_____

_____

Name:

Address:

City, State:

Phone:

Recommendations/ Suggestions _____

_____

_____

_____

_____

_____

_____

_____

Thanks for a great summer! We appreciate your hard work and dedication to individuals with disabilities. Please return evaluation in the self addressed stamped envelope provided to you.

Cincinnati Recreation Commission

Figure 4.20

Inclusion Support Evaluation
Parent/Guardian

Summer Day Camp 2002

Please take the time to complete this evaluation regarding the inclusion support provided to your child through our summer day camp program. We will utilize these evaluations to better facilitate inclusion within our community centers.

Center:

Name of Participant:

INTAKE PROCESS

Upon registration, do you feel you were adequately prepared/ informed to include your child into a general day camp program?

       Yes   No

If no, please identify specific areas of concern (i.e. registration, accommodation form, info about program, etc)_____

_____

_____

_____

PARTICIPANT SATISFACTION

➡   Appropriateness of Activities

	Excellent	Good	Satisfactory	Fair	Poor

➡   Social Interaction

	Excellent	Good	Satisfactory	Fair	Poor

➡   Safety – Supervision

	Excellent	Good	Satisfactory	Fair	Poor

➡   Structure / Schedule

	Excellent	Good	Satisfactory	Fair	Poor

➡   Area/ Space

	Excellent	Good	Satisfactory	Fair	Poor

➡   Skills Improved/ Maintained

	Excellent	Good	Satisfactory	Fair	Poor

Comments _____

_____

_____

Figure 4.20 continued

Figure 4.20 – (continued)

ACCOMMODATIONS

Were you/ your child given enough Inclusion Support to successfully participate in the program?

Yes   No

If yes, what type of support did your child receive?_____

_____

_____

If you were provided with an Inclusion Assistant (1:1), how would you rank the quality of their work?

Excellent   Good   Satisfactory   Fair   Poor

Comments _____

_____

_____

Do you feel that there was open communication between yourself, the Inclusion Support, and the Camp Director?

Yes   No

Comments_____

_____

_____

How could this program experience be made better for you/ your child:_____

_____

_____

_____

We appreciate your feedback on how to better serve individuals with disabilities within our community centers.

Please return your evaluation to :

Cincinnati Recreation Commission
Division of Therapeutic Recreation
805 Central Avenue, Suite 800
Cincinnati, OH 45202

tion: Summative evaluation takes place after services are concluded. The evaluation plan describes arrangements to consolidate information on individual support and behavior plans and agency-generated tools to share with the inclusion team. Forms allow staff to make recommendations to transition consumers among services and to revise program delivery options.

At the conclusion of the planning phase in the APIE process, individual support and behavior plans and evaluation forms are prepared; and, resources are in place to deliver services. Other tasks completed include personnel training, marketing, preparation of operating documents, and securing resources. Planning is ongoing: As one season concludes, another begins. During the next step in the APIE process, implementation, professionals use documents and resources generated during the planning phase to deliver programs with measurable results and recommended accommodations.

Implementation

During the implementation step in the APIE process, programs are delivered and monitored. Participants attend preplanned structured experiences while professionals and support staff provide leadership, supervision, and document interactions. Professionals use inclusion support plans to prepare program planning and evaluation sheets that outline how experiences are delivered. Second, staff use a variety of strategies to lead and promote inclusive programs. Adaptations and behavioral interventions are implemented to promote accommodations and maintain safe experiences. Finally, during and after program delivery notes are recorded on participant performance, individual plans are reviewed, and revisions are made on accommodation documents. These formative evaluation tasks allow programmers to make immediate program adjustments and plan supplemental skill training with consumers and disability awareness programs with peers (refer to Figure 4.21, implementation includes, Cincinnati Recreation Commission, n.d.).

Structured group experiences appear to be one accepted practice to promote inclusion (Smith, Austin, & Kennedy, 2001). Group experiences tend to promote development of social skills like cooperation, sharing, and taking turns. Also, group experiences support teaching and intervention strategies such as modeling, guiding and vicarious learning as group members mimic others in the group like the paid coach or peer volunteer who may not have disabilities (Shank & Coyle, 2002). Structured experiences facilitate empowerment by fostering choices and decision-making, foundational elements of leisure education and independent functioning. Lastly, as a best practice, group experiences promote friendships and partnerships that support acceptance among peers and caregivers.

Daily Implementation: A plan of supervision, Program Planning and Evaluation sheet in Figure 4.15, is a guideline to deliver each experience. The plan identifies 1) goals and objectives, 2) step-by-step description of participant activities, 3) length of time of each experience in the session, 4) places or locations of experiences, 5) resources used, 6) staff assignments, 7) individual adaptations and alternate or backup experiences, 8) risk management or safety precautions including participant behavioral strategies and rules of conduct, and 9) transitional procedures. Supervisory plans are protocols that relate participant objectives to service outcomes; program standardization or consistency in delivery is promoted (Peterson & Stumbo, 2000). Specific experiences are tied directly to outcomes so regardless of who leads the experience consumers engage in similar experiences.

Leadership Strategies: An ongoing task during implementation is direct leadership. A plan of supervision organizes content and outlines the leader's responsibilities. Whether an experience is a one-on-one, small or large group, the leader provides structure as the experience is 1) introduced 2) managed, and 3) concluded (Jordan, 2001). During this three-step process, specific behavioral interventions and adaptations are used to sustain positive, goal-directed interactions and accommodate participant abilities. Further discussion on interventions is presented under Structuring Effective Intervention Groups in Chapter 6, Motivating and Managing Participants. First, a summary of tasks is listed followed by techniques used in each step.

Figure 4.21

Implementation - Participant begins program, Inclusion Support Plan implemented with recommended accommodations

Includes:

Program/activities prepared and implemented as planned (adaptations as needed)

Program leaders/support staff provide appropriate levels of assistance (intervene and redirect as needed)

Program leaders/support staff implement a variety of strategies to promote inclusion, such as:

Supplemental skill training in specific areas as may be needed (social skills, activity skills, self-help skills, etc.)

Organizing small group activities to add structure to non-structured times

Providing specific behavioral interventions as needed (anger management, frustration tolerance, etc.)

Promoting peer friendships, partnerships for specific activities

Influencing program activity selection towards activities which allow for a wider range in skill levels

Providing disability awareness programs to encourage peer acceptance

Introduction Steps
- Assemble the group or gain the individual's attention
- Give a brief explanation/demonstration with experience purpose
- Ask/observe if participant comprehends desired outcome
- State safety and behavioral expectations
- Move into formation or location of experience

Introduction Techniques and Procedures
- Establish a routine so participant's focus is on leader
- Eliminate distractions, keep equipment out of sight
- Assume a position so everyone sees and hears directions
- State rules positively, "do this" rather than "don't do this"
- Give one- and two-step directions followed by demonstration
- Move participants into experience by giving precise descriptions using visual landmarks

Management Steps
- Maintain verbal and visual supervision, be within hearing and sight distance of consumers
- Observe and reinforce verbal and nonverbal participation
- Intervene and redirect prior to non-goal-directed behaviors
- Monitor safety
- Provide supplemental skill training in social, activity, and self-help skills
- Carry out modifications and adaptations

Management Techniques and Procedures
- Maintain continual visual, voice, or alternative communication interaction presence
- Incorporate opportunities to choose, make decisions, and partner with group members
- Stop experience and redefine outcome rather than experience unsuccessful outcome
- Keep group involved/isolate and remove disruptive behavior
- Enforce rules, protect individual from harm, intervene prior to concern
- Anticipate conditions and behaviors, look for antecedents and rewards
- Prepare backup and alternative plans
- Control pace of experience with adaptations
- Teach skills by repetition/demonstration/modeling/physical assistance

Conclusion and Transition Steps
- Stop experience prior to or at peak, gauge level of excitement/participant energy
- Reassemble or bring participant to initial contact area away from experience site
- Recognize and restate desired outcome(s)
- Seek feedback or responses on experience
- Use transition time to check participant's physical well-being and condition

Conclusion and Transition Techniques and Procedures
- Give participants advance notice that experience is coming to an end
- Follow routine as each experience concludes so participants recognize definitive ending
- Summarize outcomes and describe next experience
- Check appearance/vital signs/general condition of participant allowing time to clean up, calm down and prepare for next interaction
- Recognize winning and losing appropriately so participants gain positive recognition of their talents
- Debrief peers, staff, volunteers, caregivers, and consumers including 1) what happened 2) why did it happen, and 3) what happens next

A leader's personality, style, and professional motif are integral to establishing a helping relationship: And, this relationship is the key to effective implementation during inclusive experiences. Each participant is unique as is each experience. Unanticipated and unplanned outcomes result with even the most prepared professional. Qualities like sensitivity, flexibility, judgment, anticipation, consistency, positive outlook and expectancy, and the ability to walk in the shoes of each participant are assets and instrumental to helping relationships that result in satisfying participant benefits.

Recording Progress and Facilitating Acceptance: Several techniques are used to record formative information, plan transitions to the next experience, and/or make revisions in the experience before participation occurs again. One approach has staff preparing progress notes on each goal then making recommendations for future programs (refer to Figure 4.8, Individual Goal Sheet Progress Notes, Cincinnati Recreation Commission, Therapeutic Recreation n.d.). Another practice is to record inclusion notes as CTRSs observe and consult with recreation staff so immediate adjustments are made in inclusion and behavior plans (refer to Figure, 4.22 Cincinnati Recreation Commission Inclusion Notes, 2002). Participants are included in the process so they become aware of participation benefits and need for supplemental skill training and/or disability awareness sessions, for example.

Photographs, videotapes, and journal writing are also formative methods used to focus participants on experience outcomes, plan transitions to future activities, and apply outcomes to daily functioning (Shank & Coyle, 2002). The inclusion team uses formative information to 1) rewrite individual goals, objectives, support and behavior plans, 2) select new or different experiences and behavioral interventions, and 3) plan alternative accommodations. Peer and caregiver involvement in assessing outcomes relative to their expectations fosters awareness and engagement. Collaboration during implementation creates acceptance and advances inclusion options (Klitzing, 2002).

Figure 4.22

Center: Visit:

Region: Date:

Program:

Cincinnati Recreation Commission
Inclusion Notes

Time Arrived:_____ Participants Name:_____

Observations/Contact:_____

_____

_____

_____

_____

_____

_____

_____

_____

_____

_____

_____

_____

_____

_____

What intervention/ suggestions were discussed with center staff? (ie: Inclusion Plan, Behavior Support Plan, pamphlets, or any information discussed)_____

_____

_____

_____

_____

_____

_____

Other Comments: _____

_____

_____

_____

_____

Time Left Center: _____   Scheduled Next Visit: _____

                                                     ❑   See back side

05/24/02

_____

Inclusion Specialist Signature

Evaluation

The culminating step of program delivery is evaluation. A comprehensive evaluation plan is prepared during the planning phase of program design: Formative and summative documents, timelines, and staff are prepared to collect information. Formative information is gathered during program implementation while summative information is gathered at the conclusion of a program or at pre-set intervals, i.e., monthly, quarterly, semi-annually as determined by the management team. Summative evaluation considers each aspect of the APIE process and program management. Input from the inclusion team, participants/caregivers, direct service providers, and managers is reviewed. Planned and unintended program happenings are considered. Review of summative information results in revisions to agency compliance plans, accommodations, participant plans, staffing, marketing, training, financing, and resource management. The scope of the evaluation and nature of the revisions are dependent upon how inclusion is managed in the agency. Regardless of approach, participant and program evaluations take place. Each phase of the APIE process is examined to determine if individual support and behavior plans and agency programs remain status quo or are modified to better address consumer needs through available agency services and resources (refer to Figure 4.23, evaluation includes, Cincinnati Recreation Commission, n.d.).

Figure 4.23

Evaluation— Inclusion Support Plan is evaluated at pre-determined intervals, revisions made as needed.

Includes: Post program evaluation to determine:
Activities, participation level, skills acquired/needed
Effectiveness of adaptations
Level of social interaction
Behavioral interventions, frequency and effectiveness

Monthly or quarterly evaluation to determine:
Participant objectives being met
Staff development, teamwork, attitudes towards inclusion
Peer acceptance,
Parent/guardian satisfaction
Overall effectiveness of Inclusion Support Plan and recommendations

Summative Evaluation Plan

Evaluation is considered an important element in the success of the inclusion process (Wachter & McGowen, 2002). Common evaluation practices found with inclusion programs include surveying buddies/inclusion aides/companions; interviewing parents/caregivers/leaders/companions/participants; and, daily observation of programs by on-site inclusion coordinators (Wachter & McGowen, 2002). The intent of evaluation is threefold: 1) to assess participant responses to support and behavior plans, 2) to determine program efficacy and efficiency, and 3) to identify the need for revisions (LeConey, et al., 2000).

Participant evaluation provides specific feedback on performance and outcomes as they relate to interventions in individual support and behavior plans (Lee, et al., 2000; Peterson & Stumbo, 2000). Program evaluation provides a reliable method to obtain information on the value of the program to the community, its practical effectiveness, and costs relative to financial needs (LeConey et al., 2000; Smith, et al., 2001). A comprehensive program evaluation determines 1) if programs are appropriate (good and right) for the consumer, 2) if they accomplish what was intended, and 3) if the costs and effort compared to consumer, agency, and community benefits were relatively efficient (Sylvester, et al., 2001).

To illustrate, a comprehensive summative evaluation plan is presented according to participant and program evaluation concerns applicable to each phase of the APIE process.

APIE Tasks	Participant Concerns	Program Concerns
Assessment		
Pt assessment tools	Are pt skills accurately assessed?	Are accommodations accurately assessed?
Teacher input	Are all medical/safety concerns identified?	Are all personnel adequately trained?
Assessment & Accommodation	Are pt social & behavioral needs measured?	Are marketing & financial resources adequate?
Request form	What are caregiver expectations & resources?	What activity resources are needed?
Environmental assessments & ADA compliance documents		
Planning		
Activity adaptations	Do support plans properly identify outcomes?	Are accommodations suited to pt needs?
Support & behavior plans	Are behavior interventions properly documented?	Are agency accommodations reasonable?
Staff training & orientation	Do pts have adequate skills to enter inclusive experiences?	Are personnel aware of impact of disability on experiences?
Peer training & orientation		
Implementation		
Program planning & evaluation forms	Do forms reflect pt goals?	Are supplies & equipment safe & adequate?
Program observation/ evaluation form	What behavioral issues arise?	Are leaders following plans?
	Are pts social, behavioral & functional skills improving?	Are pt to staff ratios OK?
Progress notes & final evaluation	Are pts interacting appropriately with/without disabilities?	Are accommodations adequate/appropriate?
Supplemental Pt skill training	Are pts progressing toward achieving their objectives?	Are personnel making adaptations properly?
Disability awareness training	Are pt management strategies implemented sensitively?	Are finances adequate?
Evaluation		
Center evaluation	Did pts achieve desired goals?	Were program goals met?
Inclusion support	Are outcomes relevant to	How many persons with/

assistant evaluation
Parent/guardian
evaluation
Revision of support &
behavior plans &
accommodations

pt needs/transition plans?
Are pts satisfied with benefits?
What were unanticipated
pt outcomes?
Were behavioral interventions
effective?
Are pts ready to transition
to new services?

without disabilities
participated?
Were accommodations
effective?
Were program outcomes
judged as beneficial and
cost effective?
What additional training, market
ing, and advocacy is needed?
Which programs require
modification?

Participant Evaluation

Participant evaluation provides feedback on achievement of objectives as a consequence of participating in specific experiences. Unanticipated or unexpected outcomes are also documented. Features like family support, behaviors of peers, and weather conditions influence outcomes. Narrative comments on individual support and behavior plans and inclusion notes document the influence of these factors on participant performance. Data collected are compared to needs and behaviors identified in assessments. The intent is to link participant needs to outcomes resulting from specific behavioral interventions, adaptations, and experiences. The cumulative effect of gathering data on each participant has a direct relationship to program evaluation (Peterson & Stumbo, 2000). Leaders, managers and governing boards desire information on program outcomes as they make decisions on which programs satisfy participant needs and which are targeted for modification because consumer benefits are not realized or are achieved to a less than desired degree.

Program Evaluation

Participant evaluation tends to take place immediately following completion of a program session or season; program evaluation is likely to occur at specified intervals, monthly, quarterly, semi-annually or with the end of the fiscal year (FY). Program evaluation considers effectiveness of programs and inclusion support processes in achieving consumer outcomes and program goals. Additional uses of program evaluation results include: 1) providing information to stakeholders 2) developing publicity/advocacy strategies to promote and sell outcomes 3) obtaining information necessary to justify financial support 4) preparing board reports, and 5) developing procedures to transition participants among programs and services in the community (Lee, et al., 2000; Smith, et al., 2001).

Program evaluation in inclusive settings may occur over extended time periods. A disadvantage is the fragmentation of information that results when data are gathered from several programs and program sites. Unless a comprehensive evaluation document is prepared, there is no guarantee all information on a particular consumer is conveniently available (LeConey, et al., 2000). Likewise, without a systematic compilation of outcomes from all programs, overall effectiveness of agency accommodations and inclusion processes remain illusive. A comprehensive report summarizes and organizes information collected on participants and programs for each APIE task. The report includes: 1) agency inclusion (mission) statements 2) definition of leisure options and inclusion approaches 3) narrative and statistical information on participant and program accommodations 4) staffing and resource use 5) costs and revenue streams, and 6) individual participant support and behavior plan and program revisions. A concluding section of the report presents a timeline to implement changes in the agency's inclusion services resulting from the report findings.

Program Revisions

A number of variables influence when and how revisions are made in individual support and behavior plans and agency programs. These include organizational structure, inclusion approaches, fiscal resources, staffing patterns, and clientele composition. Changes are made informally, following formative evaluation in individual support and behavior plans as participants engage in programs. Formal changes result after meetings among inclusion team members who have reviewed summative evaluations. Adjustments are made in the types and levels of support by adapting equipment, using alternative behavior techniques or increasing/decreasing personal assistance. Placement in supplemental skill training sessions prior to program entry illustrates another form of program revision. The inclusion team may recommend additional disability awareness training for all program participants.

Agency program adjustments to enhance support include marketing and registration accommodations, staff training, program relocation, purchase of assistive devices, changing program schedules to accommodate available transportation, and altering the staff-to-participant ratio. Agency program changes coincide with FY directives, board mandates, executive orders, modifications in agency ADA compliance statements, or upon Advisory Committee review of staff-prepared comprehensive evaluation reports.

Evaluation is a continuous process intended to enhance quality and accountability. As a method of quality improvement, evaluation validates inclusion best practices. Evaluation determines if predetermined participant goals and objectives are achieved during systematically designed programs. Managers' decisions are based on cost benefits and cost effectiveness. Evaluations gather information used as managers determine program status and future agency initiatives. Evaluation is the concluding step of the APIE process. Information gathered during formative and summative evaluations is used to revise tasks in each of the other APIE steps. Ultimately, the intent is to document best practices so professionals consistently deliver programs having specific consumer-oriented outcomes.

References

burlingame, j., & Blaschko, T. M. (2002). *Assessment tools for recreational therapy and related fields* (3rd ed.). Ravensdale, WA: Idyll Arbor, Inc.

Bullock, C. C., & Mahon, M. J. (2000). *Introduction to recreation services for people with disabilities: A person-centered approach* (2nd ed.). Champaign, IL: Sagamore Publishing.

Carter, M. J., VanAndel, G. E., & Robb, G. M. (2003). *Therapeutic recreation a practical approach* (3rd ed.). Prospect Heights, IL: Waveland Press, Inc.

Cincinnati Recreation Commission, Division of Therapeutic Recreation. (n.d.).
    Adapting Recreation Activities for Maximum Participation and Enjoyment!
    Assessment and Accommodation Request
    Assessment includes
    Behavior Support Plan
    Dear Teacher
    Evaluation includes
    Implementation includes
    Inclusion Notes
    Inclusion Support Assistant Evaluation, 2002
    Inclusion Support Evaluation Center Evaluation, 2002
    Inclusion Support Evaluation Parent/Guardian, 2002
    Individual Goal Sheet
    Participant Skill Assessment
    Planning includes
    Post Program Evaluation
    Program Observation Evaluation
    Program Planning and Evaluation
    Registration Questions
    Therapeutic Recreation Day Camp Observation Checklist
    Therapeutic Recreation Group Goal Sheet
    Therapeutic Recreation/Inclusion Services Intake Form
(Available from Cincinnati Recreation Commission, Division of Therapeutic Recreation, 805 Central Avenue, Cincinnati, Ohio 45202).

Fox Valley Special Recreation Association. (2002). *Fox Valley special recreation association summer 2002*. [Brochure]. North Aurora, IL: Author.

Jordan, D. J. (2001). *Leadership in leisure services: Making a difference* (2nd ed.). State College, PA: Venture Publishing, Inc.

Klitzing, S. W. (2002). The best practices for successful inclusion. *Parks & Recreation, 37*(5), 60-65.

LeConey, S., Devine, M. A., Bunker, H., & Montgomery, S. (2000). Utilizing the therapeutic recreation process in community settings: The case of Sue. *Parks & Recreation, 35*(5), 70-77.

Lee, Y., McCormick, B., & Perkins, S. (2000). Are you an outcome engineer? Therapeutic recreation in the third millennium. *Parks & Recreation, 35*(5), 64-68.

Peterson, C. A., & Stumbo, N. J. (2000). *Therapeutic recreation program design principles and procedures* (3rd ed.). Boston, MA: Allyn and Bacon.

Schleien, S. J., Green, F. P., & Stone, C. F., (2003). Making friends within inclusive community recreation programs. *American Journal of Recreation Therapy, 2*(1), 7-16.

Schleien, S. J., Ray, M. T., & Green, F. P. (1997). *Community recreation and people with disabilities strategies for inclusion* (2nd ed.). Ravensdale, WA: Idyll Arbor, Inc.

Shank, J., & Coyle, C. (2002). Therapeutic recreation in health promotion and rehabilitation. State College, PA: Venture Publishing, Inc.

Smith, R. W., Austin, D. R., & Kennedy, D. W. (2001). *Inclusive and special recreation opportunities for persons with disabilities* (4th ed.). Boston, MA: McGraw Hill.

Stumbo, N. J. (2002). *Client assessment in therapeutic recreation services*. State College, PA: Venture Publishing, Inc.

Sullivan, A. K., & O'Brien, M. B. (2001). Inclusive programming at summer camp. *Parks & Recreation, 36*(5), 66-72.

Sylvester, C., Voelkl, J. E., & Ellis, G. D., (2001). *Therapeutic recreation programming: Theory and practice*. State College, PA: Venture Publishing, Inc.

Wachter, C. J., & McGowen, A. L. (2002). Inclusion practices of special recreation agencies in Illinois. *Therapeutic Recreation Journal, 36*(2), 172-185.

CHAPTER 5

Individuals with Disabilities

Autism

Who are individuals with autism?

A child with autism has a pervasive developmental disorder characterized by impairments in the development of reciprocal social interactions, verbal and nonverbal communication skills, and in imaginative play (APA, 2000). Every individual has a unique combination of characteristics and behaviors that may change with age and the social environment (Sherrill, 1998). The word autism is derived from the Greek word "autos" meaning "self" and is interpreted to mean withdrawn and self-absorbed. Autism is usually manifest prior to 30 months of age; and is characterized by developmental deviations in speech, language, and cognitive capacities; unusual responses to sensory stimuli (covering the ears, for example); inability to relate to people, events or objects (indiscriminately will accept an extended hand while perseverating on an object held in the other hand); repetitive or stereotyped motor behaviors like turning or spinning; and inappropriate play skills as displayed by fixation on a spinning wheel or preoccupation with ordering the play objects. The cause of autism is unknown and there is no known cure. Autism is believed to be present in two to 20 of every 10,000 births, with boys being affected four to five times more frequently than girls (APA, 2000). With intensive structured early intervention and intermittent life-long support, varying degrees of independence result (Sherrill, 1998).

What medical and health care needs are considered?

Seizure activity may be present or may develop in adolescence. Individuals may be oblivious to real danger, such as the height of a tree during a climbing escapade. Participants may be undersensitive to pain and temperature, yet oversensitive to touch, i.e., place their hand on a hot craft object while withdrawing from the leader's hand as the street is crossed. Aimless wandering, darting or running triggered by hearing a siren, for example, may take the participant into the street or a program area without supervision. Presence of functional deafness (appears to not hear noises and speech) may result in no response to a potentially harmful experience, i.e., riding a bicycle into the path of oncoming bikers. A participant's lack of eye contact affects the ability to exchange safety information and to use modeling as a leadership strategy. Medications to control seizures (anticonvulsant drugs) and aggressive behaviors (neuroleptic drugs) have side effects such as extreme drowsiness or dizziness that impede participation.

Why and how is the therapeutic recreation process (APIE) implemented?

Lifelong interdisciplinary interventions focus on the development of interactive social and communication skills, functional skill development enabling self-care and independent community living, and safe, appropriate use of free time (Hawkins, 2001). Observations rather than written techniques are used to assess and evaluate change and progress. Audio and video recordings and photos may also capture improvements. Planning with teachers, social workers, family physicians, and caregivers facilitates year-round transitions. Consistency, structure, routine, and predictability are key implementation strategies as is ongoing in-home training with parents and caregivers, since skill transitions and generalizations require continuous supervision. Consumers' strengths in nonlanguage areas such as music, assembly-type activities, or mechanical skills like computers are avenues through which communication skills are developed and social interaction commences. Physical guidance is used with discretion as consumers resist touch. Inclusive experiences like walking on the sidewalk near a busy street or bicycle riding with friends and family expose consumers to appropriate behaviors and responses to real-life occurrences. Coping behaviors like retreating to a corner or running away are replaced with hiding under a tent and jogging on the track around the football field. Cues, contingencies, alternative communication techniques (sign language, communication boards), prompting, fading, and other behavioral interventions are used to manage self-stimulatory behaviors while teaching new skills.

Where are there available resources?

American Psychiatric Association, www.psych.org
   1400 K St., NW, Washington, D.C., 20005, 202-682-6000
Autism Society of America, www.autism-society.org
   7910 Woodmont Ave., Suite 300, Bethesda, MD 20814, 1-800-3AUTISM
National Information Center for Children and Youth with Disabilities (NICHCY), www.NICHCY.org
   Box 1492, Washington, D.C., 1-800-695-0285

When sensitivity and awareness are experienced: Training Experiences

With your finger, draw a letter on the bare sole of a friend's foot and have the person try to guess it. Now repeat the process rubbing with a terry-cloth towel—tactile sensitivity (Getskow & Konczal, 1996).

Sit quietly by yourself inside a building, using all of your senses, visual, auditory, tactile, kinesthetic, olfactory, and gustatory, record all of the sensations experienced for at least two minutes; repeat the experience outside; how much sensory stimulation was experienced?

Mental Retardation

Who are individuals with mental retardation?

Mental retardation is a developmental disability influenced by interaction between the social environment, expectations, supports and resources available, and individual characteristics. The American Association on Mental Retardation (www.aamr.org) defines mental retardation in terms of what an individual is capable of doing when appropriate supports are present. The features of their definition include: 1) substantial limitations in certain personal capabilities, 2) significant subaverage intellectual functioning, 3) concurrence with related disabilities in two or more adaptive skill areas (self-care, social skills, community use, leisure), and 4) commencement prior to age 18 (Carter, VanAndel, & Robb, 2003; Sherrill, 1998). This interpretation of mental retardation considers the supports (resources and strategies) needed at different life stages to address environmental demands, enhance well-being, and foster social inclusion. Thus, a person with mental retardation may require: 1) no support, 2) minimal/intermittent/pre-arranged support such as transportation, 3) extensive/regular/ongoing support in an adaptive area such as self-care, and 4) pervasive/24-hour support to sustain his/her health (Bullock & Mahon, 2000). There is no one cause for mental retardation since it may occur at any time during an 18-year period and is influenced by interaction between the consumer, environment and supports used. Likewise, there is no cure, per se. Three percent of the newborn population may be diagnosed as mentally retarded at some point in their life (Mobily & MacNeil, 2002). Of the individuals who are mentally retarded, the overwhelming majority are considered to be mildly impaired and more like their peers than different. In general, persons with mental retardation experience slower learning rates, lower levels of fitness, deficits in communication, social-emotional immaturity, and have difficulty meeting the personal independence and responsibility expected of persons in their chronological age group.

With the exception of unique syndromes, the majority of individuals with mental retardation do not appear different than their peers without mental retardation (Smith, Austin, & Kennedy, 2001). Persons with lower cognitive functioning tend to display motor deficits, have additional disabilities and exhibit physical differences; consequently requiring increased levels of support.

One of the more commonly occurring (five to six percent of all persons diagnosed with mental retardation) identifiable syndromes is Down Syndrome (Mobily & MacNeil, 2002). Specific physical characteristics tend to distinguish a person with Down Syndrome. Commonly apparent characteristics include: upward slanting eyes, a protruding pointed tongue, square flat hands with short fingers and a single crease across the palm of one or both hands, broad short necks with loose skin on the sides and back of the neck, a flat bridge on the nose, short, low-set ears, excessive ability to extend the joints, and a stocky appearance because the arms and legs are short in relation to the trunk. People with Down Syndrome tend to experience premature aging and brain changes associated with Alzheimer's disease. Information on this syndrome is available from the National Down Syndrome Congress (www.carol.net/~ndsc) and Down Syndrome Society (www.ndss.org).

What medical and health care needs are considered?

Persons with Down Syndrome may experience atlantoaxial instability: Muscles and ligaments around the joint of the two cervical vertebrae, the atlas and the axis, are lax, allowing the vertebrae to slip out of alignment, which could occur in activities like swimming and gymnastics and result in injury to the spinal cord. Thus, service providers may require an X-ray of the spinal column prior to participation. Because participants have difficulty understanding cause-and-effect relationships, making decisions, and solving problems or making judgments, safety during activities is of utmost importance and requires the supervisor to carefully assess situations and set boundaries prior to beginning the experience. Individuals may use assistive devices including wheelchairs or communication boards; this too requires attention to ensure the devices are not damaged nor the consumer is placed at a disadvantage if the device is or is not used during the activity. Secondary dysfunction like heart and lung abnormalities may contribute to breathing difficulties; and the presence of unique syndromes like Fragile X or Prader-Willi, which may or may not be accompanied by mental retardation, may necessitate implementation of behavioral strategies to ensure personal safety.

Why and how is the therapeutic recreation process (APIE) implemented?

Therapeutic recreation interventions facilitate skill acquisition, decision making, selection of leisure experiences, participation in age-appropriate experiences, inclusion within the community, development of functional skills, physical well-being, self-care, and communication (Carter, et al., 2003). A comprehensive approach to service provision includes social service and education personnel, rehabilitation personnel with expertise in assistive technology and supportive living and employment, caregivers, consumers, and recreation and therapeutic recreation specialists. Assessment considers individual preferences, constraints, supports, and expectations and transitions within the environment. Planning includes a review of the consumers individual education plan (IEP) and/or individual care/rehabilitation plan (IRP) to ascertain expected educational or rehabilitation outcomes and identified supports. Use of behavioral techniques like positive reinforcement, task analysis, skill sequencing, chaining, shaping, prompting, and skill demonstration promote concrete, step-by-step instruction. Skill development is enhanced when implementation occurs in a structured environment, limiting distractions and maintaining routines, and when repetition of directions and hands-on experiences are incorporated into programs. Although adult consumers may respond positively to conversation and activities used with children, age-appropriate communication and social responsibility is encouraged when the supervisor realizes consumers bring to the experience a life repertoire of activity and a level of understanding that may be greater than their capabilities to associate meanings with words or to communicate. Evaluation of outcomes takes into consideration transitions between living, learning, and leisure settings, as skill generalization may not be automatic. Evaluation also considers benefits to caregivers and their interactions with consumers, i.e., sometimes consumers experience limited opportunities or heighten challenges due to caregiver overprotection, frustration, unrealistic expectations, and/or denial/rejection of the consumer's actual abilities.

Where are there available resources?

The Arc of the United States, www.thearc.org
   500 East Border Street, Suite 300, Arlington, TX 76010, 817-261-6003
American Association on Mental Retardation (AAMR), www.aamr.org
   444 North Capitol Street, NW, Suite 846, Washington, D.C., 20001, 1-800-424-3688

Special Olympics International, www.specialolympics.org
1325 G. Street, NW, Suite 500, Washington, D.C. 20005, 202-628-3630

When sensitivity and awareness are experienced: Training Experiences

Participate with assistive technology items like switches that control objects, joysticks and trackballs that control the cursor on a computer screen, or speech synthesizers that produce audio and taped conversations.

Review consumer magazines like *Exceptional Parent,* 605 Commonwealth Avenue, Boston, MA 02215, 617-536-8961; Mainstream, 2973 Beech Street, San Diego, CA 92102, 619-234-3138.

Acquire catalogs with adaptive play equipment like Crestwood Co., 6625, North Sydney Place, Milwaukee, WI 53209, 414-352-5678.

Learning Disabilities

Who are individuals with learning disabilities?

The term learning disabilities is used to describe a heterogeneous group of disorders resulting from difficulties in acquiring and using academic skills. Specific learning disorders are identified when an individual's achievement on standardized tests in reading, math, or written expression is below that expected for age, schooling, and level of intelligence (APA, 2000). A number of learning, motor skills, communication, and attention-deficit and disruptive behavior disorders are identified for educational purposes. To illustrate, a reading disorder, dyslexia, indicates impaired ability to recognize words and to comprehend what is read, while a communication disorder, expressive or receptive aphasia, indicates impairment in expressive or receptive language development. Impaired development in motor coordination is referred to as dyspraxia. A number of specific behavior disorders are identified by the American Psychiatric Association (2000); ADD (attention deficit disorder) and ADHD (attention deficit hyperactive disorder) are presented as unique disorders (pattern of inattention and/or persistent hyperactivity) yet may also appear with other learning disorders. A learning disability is not visually apparent to the casual observer; upon closer scrutiny, an individual with a learning disability might appear awkward, impulsive, hypo- or hyperactive; become easily distracted; experience perceptual-motor difficulties; lack self-regulation skills; and display low frustration levels or quick loss of temper: Persons with the same specific learning disability may not necessarily display the same behavioral traits. A characteristic with adults is lack of social skills and difficulty in inclusionary activities. Nearly one-half of the children who receive special education services are identified as having specific learning disabilities with boys having a higher rate than girls. A number of factors are believed to contribute to learning disabilities, including brain damage, biochemical imbalance, environmental factors, and genetics. Learning disabilities are lifelong yet somewhat less apparent when the focus is not on academic performance or achievement results during the school years.

What medical and health care needs are considered?

Safety and communication are considered as services are planned and delivered. To illustrate, knowing that a person is dyslexic (reading impairment), enables the leader to use verbal or graphic directions rather than written materials; or knowledge that a person is dysgraphic (writing impairment) allows the leader to modify the written registration process to include oral reporting of information. Children with specific learning disabilities may be on prescribed medications such as Ritalin, Dexedrine, Benzedrine, Methedrine and Cylert (Dunn, 1997) to improve attention and compliant behavior and reduce impulsive and disruptive behavior. The side effects of stimulants like these are increased irritability and daydreaming; as a consequence, the leader carefully monitors interaction to ensure consumer safety and responsiveness to group members and fast-moving objects, for example. To ensure safety, the supervisor sets expectations and boundaries with consequences prior to participation.

Why and how is the therapeutic recreation process (APIE) implemented?

The therapeutic recreation process is used to assess and promote the acquisition of skills supportive of academic, motor, social-emotional functioning, inclusion, and community involvement as well as to prevent disruptive behaviors and the display of inappropriate interactions (Litner & Ostiguy, 2000; Sitlington, 1996).

Modifications in assessment processes consider discrepancies between potential and actual performance, for example, reading directions, comprehending oral commands, and/or completing a motor pattern or sequence, by using alternative communication techniques. Planning experiences include organizing the area, so excess distractions (noise, colors, people) are not present and extra equipment is out of sight. The leader plans to use various reinforcement measures like task analysis, sequencing, chaining, fading, and cuing to promote natural consequences and consumer motivation. When experiences are implemented, consistency, structure, routine, repetition, hands-on practice and over-learning techniques are employed to encourage independence and acquisition of behaviors. Relaxation and debriefing following experiences allow the consumer to regain composure and adapt to the changes anticipated with the next activity while leaders evaluate the experience.

Where are there available resources?

Attention Deficit Disorder Association (ADDA), www.add.org
P.O. Box 972, Mentor, OH 44061, 1-800-487-2282
Children and Adults with Attention Deficit Disorders (CHADD), www.chadd.org
499 NW 70th Avenue, Suite 101, Plantation, FL 33317, 1-800-233-4050
Learning Disabilities Association of America (LDA), www.ldanatl.org
4156 Liberty Road, Pittsburgh, PA 15234, 1-888-300-6710
National Center for Learning Disabilities (NCLD)
381 Park Avenue South, Suite 1401, New York, NY 10016, 1-888-575-7373

When sensitivity and awareness are experienced: Training Experiences

Write your name on a piece of paper looking only in a mirror.
Use your nondominant hand to cut out and glue stars on a piece of paper.
Mirror activity: Use your nondominant hand to outline the Star of David (refer to Figure 5.1).

Head Injury (Traumatic Brain Injury—TBI)

Who are individuals with head injuries?

Injury to the brain results from trauma to the head or brain, often resulting from motor vehicle accidents. In a closed head injury there is little or no visually apparent evidence of the trauma while in an open head injury there is visible evidence of the accident, gunshot wound or brain surgery to remove the tumor. Each person with a head injury is affected in a different way (Bullock & Mahon, 2000). The area of the brain injured determines specific impairments. Personal awareness of the extent of one's disabilities may be lacking for a number of years post-injury. Difficulties in memory and thought, movement and sensation, social interactions, emotional and affective responses, care of self, and inappropriate behavior may continue for months or years after the injury. A person who has sustained injury to the left cerebral hemisphere of the brain displays language and comprehension difficulties; is somewhat anxious, disorganized and responds slowly to new situations; and may exhibit right hemiplegia (paralysis on the right side of the body). With right cerebral hemisphere injury, judgment and visuo-perceptual functions are affected; persons may experience left hemiplegia (paralysis on the left side of the body); and the individual may tend to be self-centered, overestimate his abilities, and be somewhat insensitive to the needs of others (Carter, Dolan, & LeConey, 1994).

The prognosis for children who sustain the same injury as an adult is usually better since the developing brain compensates for the impact (Carter, et al., 2003). There is no cure, only prevention, and younger males tend to experience more head injuries than other age cohort groups (Dattilo, 1994).

What medical and health care needs are considered?

A person who has experienced a TBI may neither exhibit readily apparent signs nor be insightful into their deficits. As a consequence, the consumer and the observer may both experience difficulties during initial interactions. Persons who have sustained a head injury may experience seizures, aggressive behavior, depression, and exhibit volatility in their moods. Consequently, a number of medications may be taken. Some of these medications have side effects including drowsiness, hyperactivity, dizziness, and nervousness that require monitoring and the taking of additional medications to offset specific side effects. Planning is a deficit area that also

Figure 5.1

EXERCISE TO ILLUSTRATE EFFECTS OF A LEARNING DISABILITY

Place paper on a flat surface. Place a mirror on the horizontal line facing the reader at a 45-degree angle. Using the nondominant hand and looking at the mirror, trace the star as you see it through the mirror, attempting to stay within the lines. Notice how many times the outside line is touched. The difficulty experienced during this activity simulates the difficulty experienced by a person with a learning disability.

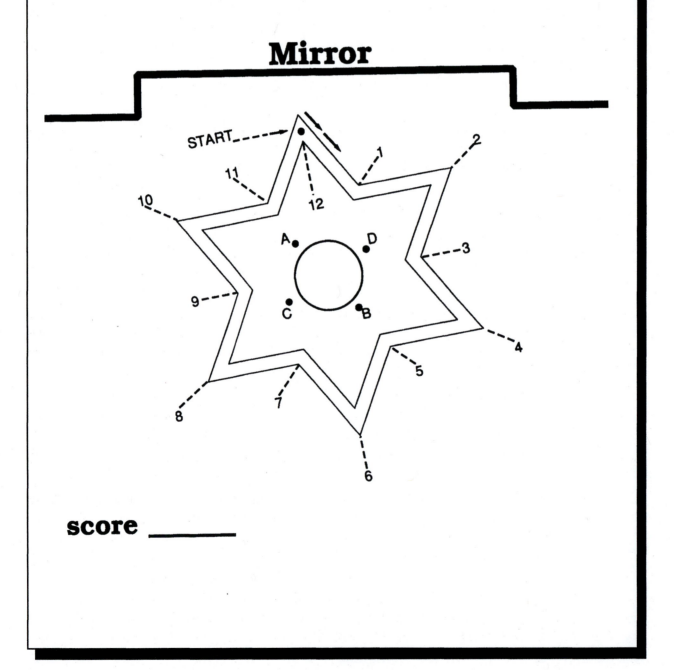

score _____

requires careful supervision and the use of reminders to assure that daily routines, safety, and personal care tasks are performed. Variation in energy levels is helped by including opportunities for resting and relaxation. Inappropriate behaviors such as the use of socially unacceptable terms and references to, for example, private body parts are controlled through adherence to behavior management techniques such as contracts, privileging systems, and positive reinforcement. Review of rules prior to participation also is an appropriate safety precaution. Improvements in affective responses and social skills may be slow and return to "the way it use to be" may never happen. Professionals may have their patience tested as consumers and family members adjust their respective lifestyles.

Why and how is the therapeutic recreation process (APIE) implemented?

Assessment information considers supports and resources from within the family and the community, the level of cognitive functioning, and premorbid behaviors of the consumer (prior to the injury), especially coping skills, motivation, and assets in order to anticipate the consumer's response to intervention and potential to regain skills and assume past roles. Also, patterns like competitiveness or interest in sports displayed prior to the injury may be intensified as a result of the injury. Planning allows for repetition, sequencing, concreteness, visual and verbal cues, physical guidance (when consumers do not display tactile defensiveness), modeling, one- and two-step directions, and self-reinforcing outcomes. When programs are implemented, the supervisor also is observant to wandering, inappropriate use of objects like pencils or weights, excessive laughing or crying, increasing spasticity attributed to tension, distractibility, impulsiveness, and gait impairments. Computer games and technological advancements facilitate communication, cognitive retraining and community integration. Evaluation takes into consideration the uneven rate of return and the ebb and flow of skill development as memory, for example, may allow counting out correct change one day, yet not the next.

Where are there available resources?

Brain Injury Association, www.biausa.org
105 N. Alfred St., Alexandria, VA 22314, 1-800-444-6443

When sensitivity and awareness are experienced: Training Experiences

Which side do you use: Reach for a pencil or ball someone else is holding, which hand do you use? Kick a stationary ball, which foot do you use?

Place a number of recreation objects in front of the group, allow them to look at the objects for a few minutes, then remove the objects, ask them to recall as many as possible. Repeat the activity, the second time asking participants to recall the objects after a considerable time lapse, more than an hour or portion of a day.

Cut out stars already drawn on a piece of paper, glue them to a plain sheet of paper; cut out one set with your dominant hand then repeat the star cutting with the nondominant hand.

Spinal Cord Injuries (SCI)

Who are individuals with spinal cord injuries?

When the spinal cord and/or vertebrae are damaged through sudden traumatic injuries or disease, an individual may be paralyzed below the level of the injury and may experience impairment in sensations and functioning (Bullock & Mahon, 2000). The extent of the paralysis and loss of sensation and functioning is determined by the level at which the damage occurs and the severity of damage to the spinal cord. If the nerve fiber cells are completely destroyed, no recovery of sensation or function below the level of the damage will occur. A partial or incomplete lesion results from bruised, torn, or crushed nerve tissue in the spinal column and causes only partial damage to functions and loss of sensation below the injury level with some recovery possible.

The spine consists of 30 vertebrae surrounding the spinal cord that also may be injured (fractures, hyperextension or compression). Each vertebrae and nerve pair (31) are numbered and identified by the region of the body: Thus, injuries to the vertebrae and nerve tissue are referred to by letter and number according to the region of the body; C1-C8, cervical (7 vertebrae 8 nerves) (neck and shoulders), T1-T12 thoracic (chest and trunk to top of pelvis), L1-L5 lumbar (lower back, top, and posterior of the pelvis), and S1-S5 sacral (pelvic floor, bladder, anal sphincter, and external genitals) (Dunn, 1997; Levine, 2001) refer to Figure 5.2. The higher the

Figure 5.2

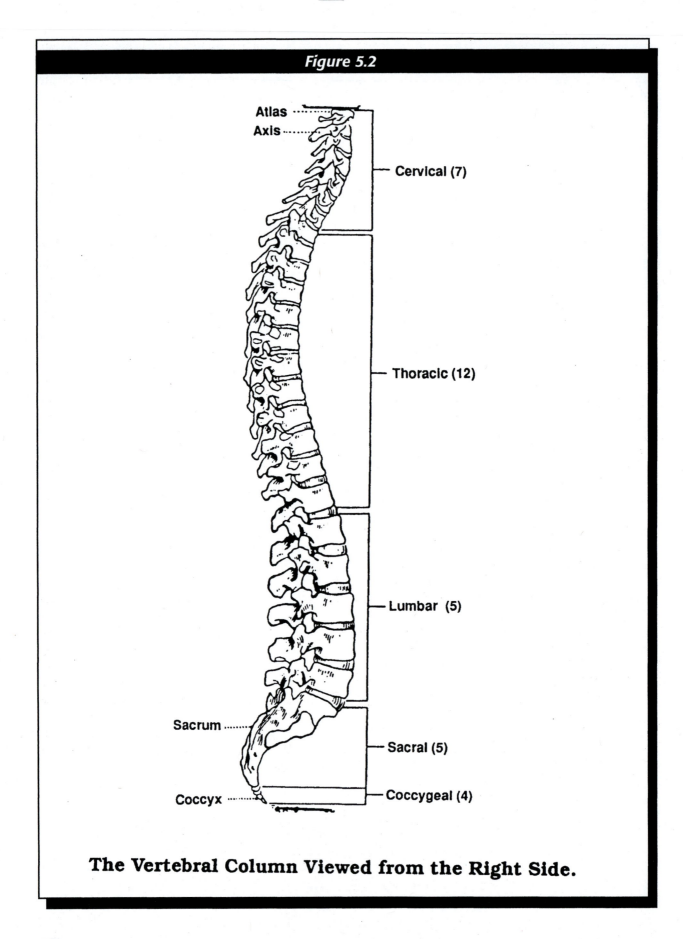

The Vertebral Column Viewed from the Right Side.

level of the damage or injury, the more movement, sensation and function are impaired. Thus, when injury occurs in the C1 through T1 region, the person experiences quadriplegia, four limbs are affected; and, when the injury occurs at T2 or below paraplegia results, involvement of the lower trunk and legs occurs (refer to Figure 5.3.), SCI causes loss of sensation and/or function, because the brain is not able to send messages through the nerves in the spinal cord to the injury site; cognition is not affected (Bullock & Mahon, 2000). The most common injury is quadriplegia and males between 16 and 30 years of age tend to sustain the majority of the injuries (Sherrill, 1998).

What medical and health care needs are considered?

An individual with SCI may sustain a number of secondary complications impacting their emotional, physical and social well-being. Because the incident may be sudden and unexpected and affects work and family roles, the person may experience frustration, denial, and even depression as adjustments in personal care and social roles must take place. Mobility is facilitated by the use of wheelchairs and, as a result, persons may experience lowered fitness levels as well as barriers attributed to accessibility issues. The skin is prone to developing decubitus ulcers that can become infected and result in the immobilization of the person for extended periods of time while the bed sores heal. Urinary tract infections are a health care concern, so the use and care of external collection devices and catheters are closely monitored. Spasticity, more evident with incomplete injuries, causes pain and contractures that limit full range of movement. Hyperreflexia or exaggerated reflexes resulting from trauma to the spinal cord causes profuse sweating, hypertension and excruciating headaches that may require medication and/or relaxation strategies to manage. Reduction in the ability of the abdominal muscles to function properly affects respiration and the ability to regulate body temperature, blood pressure, and heart rate. Consequently, persons with SCI may experience pneumonia, difficulty coughing and breathing, and cardiac arrhythmia. Weight control problems result from weak abdominal muscles and lowered levels of expended energy that may be, in part, attributed to using a wheelchair for ambulation. One affected area, sexual functioning, is interrelated with self-image and social roles, and as a consequence, may be addressed with family members during interdisciplinary planning.

Why and how is the therapeutic recreation process (APIE) implemented?

Although acute care services have improved the likelihood of surviving traumatic injuries, the challenge of minimizing disability and improving health and independence remains for persons who have sustained SCIs (Sable, Craig & Lee, 2000). Professionals address the issues that prevent consumers from fully participating in their communities after hospitalization. Thus, assessment focuses on identifying residual skills and adjustments needed to gain a comfortable level of independent functioning with an altered lifestyle. Relaxation, fitness exercises, especially deep breathing, stretching, and strengthening, prevent contractures and promote respiration and wheelchair mobility. During participation, precautions are taken to ensure that participants do not dehydrate and that their temperature does not rise too high, as they tend not to perspire below the lesion level. Leisure resource awareness sessions address the use of assistive devices to create accessible options. Family members participate during activities so they become comfortable with using, for example, respirators and electric chairs, during transport and while engaged in the activity. Participation in competitive events with Wheelchair Sports, USA, for example, promotes altitudinal adjustments and adds to the quality of life by providing meaningful use of increased amounts of free time. Professionals encourage hope and a sense of future well-being when they promote the development of assertiveness skills and incorporate inclusive experiences like aquatics or theater clubs. Evaluation measures improvements in life satisfaction and adjustment to environmental barriers as well as skill acquisition and the health of a consumer's support system.

Where are there available resources?

Wheelchair Sports, USA, www.wsusa.org

   3595 E. Fountain Blvd., Suite L-1, Colorado Springs, CO, 80910, 719-574-1150

National Spinal Cord Injury Association, www.spinalcord.org

   8300 Colesville Road, Suite 551, Silver Spring, MD, 20910, 1-800-962-9629

Paralyzed Veterans of America, www.pva.org

   801 18th Street, NW, Washington, D.C. 20006, 1-800-424-8200

Figure 5.3

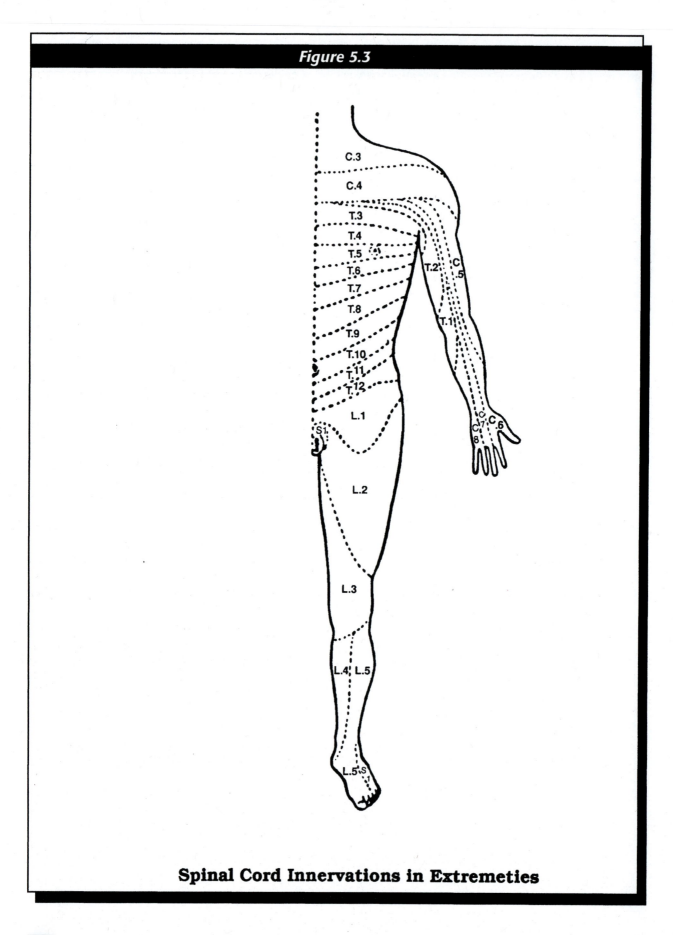

Spinal Cord Innervations in Extremeties

When sensitivity and awareness are experienced: Training Experiences

Check license plates, stores, parking spaces/lots, building entrances, rest rooms, elevators, and water fountains, for the universal access symbol, where is the symbol used, is it the same for every state, what are the advantages and disadvantages of using this symbol (refer to Figure 1.2)?

How accessible is your workplace, office, or program area? Using the ADA guidelines, measure walkways, corridors, aisles, rest room stalls, doorways and entrances, phones, water fountains, fire alarms, parking spaces (size and number), and accessible routes to and from activity areas. What are the actual measurements and are there differences between ADA guidelines and the measurements taken (refer to Figure 1.1)?

Visit a vendor who sells/services electric wheelchairs, ask him/her to demonstrate the use of various sport chairs and electric chairs; participate in a walk or activity in a sport chair and electric chair; record and/or discuss your feelings and perceived and real environmental barriers.

Seizure or Convulsion and Epilepsy

Who are individuals with seizures (convulsions) and epilepsy?

The term seizure or convulsion refers to an electrical disturbance in the brain that causes an involuntary spasm or contraction of the muscles and results in a sudden change in consciousness or behavior (Dattilo, 2002; James & Crawford, 2001). A seizure may be a one-time occurrence like those that occur during alcohol or drug withdrawal, or accompany other disorders such as brain injuries, mental retardation and cerebral palsy. A person who is identified as having epilepsy experiences repeated seizures as a result of disturbed brain functioning; thus seizures are not always caused by epilepsy, but an individual who has more than one, regardless of when it occurs, night or day, is said to experience epilepsy (Getskow & Konczal, 1996). Persons who experience seizures may or may not lose consciousness and/or be aware of where they are or what they are doing; thus, it is important for professionals to recognize and describe seizure types to give feedback to appropriate medical personnel and caregivers. Partial seizures begin in one specific body site and travel through the limb, affecting all of the limb's muscles and may or may not result in loss of consciousness: A simple partial seizure or "Jacksonian" seizure is characterized by jerky muscle contractures without impaired consciousness, while a complex partial seizure or "psychomotor" seizure is characterized by altered consciousness and periods of automatic behavior like rubbing movements, sleepwalking, striking, or talking. When a person experiences seizures that affect more than one site or progress from one site to entire body areas, they have one of the forms of generalized seizures. One of the more common types, absence seizure, is evident when a person abruptly blinks or stops talking, then continues as if nothing has happened; this person experiences no change in muscle tone or consciousness and the seizure generally lasts between five and 30 seconds (James & Crawford, 2001). A number of generalized seizures are characterized by display of tonic (rigid or tension) and clonic (jerky or relaxed) movements with loss of consciousness and definitive behavior sequences described in safety publications on seizure management (refer to Figure 5.4).

The age of onset varies from prior to age 10 to after age 40 and the cause for nearly half are unknown since, in many situations, only those that are uncontrolled are brought to the attention of physicians. Birth trauma, head injuries, sleep deprivation, blood alkalinity, tumors, strokes, drug intoxication, and flashing or flickering (strobe) lights or certain shapes like stripes or checks may either cause or trigger seizure behavior.

What medical and health care needs are considered?

A number of anticonvulsant medications control the presence of seizures: Dilantin, phenobarbital, tegretol, and depakene are used to prevent future seizures and have side effects such as reduced coordination and concentration, drowsiness, dizziness, fatigue, slurred speech, unsteady gait, and emotional irritability. Consumers may carry these medications with them during activities, so professionals need to follow pre-established protocols to administer them at scheduled times during program operation and to be keenly observant of any behaviors that may affect participant safety when side effects do result. Activities that could result in a direct blow to the head such as bicycling and rock climbing, require safety precautions, e.g., wearing helmets. When consumers have noted the presence of a seizure disorder on registration and/or medical forms, staff are alerted to behaviors or auras that serve as a warning of an impending seizure. An aura is usually reported as hearing, seeing, or smelling something or having an unusual taste or sensation on his/her tongue. This sensation is

---

Figure 5.4

LEADERSHIP PROCEDURES WITH SEIZURE

1. Remain calm and stay with the participant.
2. Anticipate an "aura" or sign, such as a stare, head jerk, or report of "seeing stars" or "hearing a sound."
3. Permit the seizure to run its course which may be a few seconds to a few minutes.
4. Do not restrain or move, only protect, the participant; prevent injury by removing objects and people.
5. Do not force a blunt object between the teeth.
6. Loosen restrictive clothing around the neck, arms, and waist.
7. Turn the head to the side for release of saliva or vomitus; protect limbs that may be hitting hard surfaces.
8. Remember that during the seizure the participant hears those activities and voices in the immediate environment.
9. Allow the participant to rest after the seizure; confusion may be present for a while and thus the participant should be monitored until rational behavior returns.
10. Repeat directions and instructions since a blank stare may indicate that the person has had a seizure, causing the person to miss the directions.

---

unique to each individual and presents the leader with the opportunity to prepare to manage the impending seizure in a socially inclusive manner. If a fall does result from a seizure or occurs during a seizure, like dropping to one's knees as a result of the loss of muscle tone, staff are called upon to apply fundamental first-aid skills. Medical personnel and caregivers may be helped by staff recording the length (time) of the seizure and the nature of the behaviors during and following the seizure so appropriate medication adjustments or changes in routine are made. Changed activity levels may influence the routine times at which medication is taken. One strategy to promote inclusion is to explain to participants the sequence they may observe as a seizure occurs and to indicate consumers actually hear what is being said around them as they experience the seizure.

Why and how is the therapeutic recreation process (APIE) implemented?

Assessment considers the nature of the seizure disorder and the side effects, if any, experienced with medications. Also considered as planning takes place is the social environment and lifestyle of the consumer. To illustrate, with whom does recreation occur and are they sensitive to the behaviors that occur during a seizure and the side effects that may result from taking anticonvulsant medications? And, are there specific behaviors, such as alcohol or drug consumption, or skateboarding, that might result in seizure activity or head trauma? Planners consider the environmental stimuli that might trigger seizure activity and foster negative responses from other participants if a seizure were to occur during participation. Programs are implemented by staff prepared in first aid and seizure management. Staff also are prepared to discuss the impact of perceptions about seizures on social interactions and self-efficacy. It is important for staff to help consumers with seizures to self-assess and monitor their behaviors and participation levels so medication routines are adhered to or adjusted to compensate for energy consumption. Consumers are encouraged to evaluate the benefits of specific experiences on their well-being.

Where are there resources available?

Epilepsy Foundation of America, www.efa.org
  4351 Garden City Drive, Landover, MD 20785-4941, 1-800-332-1000

When sensitivity and awareness are experienced: Training Experiences

Role play the leadership procedures recommended when a consumer has a seizure on a ropes course or in or near the pool.

Ask professionals from the nearest office of the Epilepsy Foundation of America to attend an inservice and provide information and sources on seizure management.

Spina Bifida

Who are individuals with spina bifida?

Spina bifida means cleft spine and results when, prior to birth, the vertebral arches fail to close completely around the spinal cord. There are three forms that describe the nature of the impairment: Spina bifida occulta occurs when the lumbar or sacral vertebrae remain open at the spinous processes; the spinal cord is unaffected and the only external sign of the impairment might be a mole, tuft of hair, or a dimple in the skin above the vertebrae. Spina bifida with meningocele is the protrusion (cele means tumor) of the covering (meningo) of the spinal cord (myelo) in a sac through the vertebrae; this is a more serious form and requires surgical closure to prevent infection. Spina bifida with myelomeningocele or MM is the most serious and common form and occurs when the spinal cord itself protrudes in the sac through the vertebral and is visually apparent through the back. Usually within the first 48 hours of life, surgery is done to close the opening and drain spinal fluid to protect against hydrocephalus (an enlarged head caused by the accumulation of spinal fluid in the cranial vault). If hydrocephalus is present, a shunt is inserted behind the right ear to drain the fluid into the right atrium of the heart. Even with surgery soon after birth, some children might experience brain damage that limits their intellectual abilities or gives rise to seizure disorders or learning disabilities. The degree of impairment is determined by the level of the lesion on the spine. Sacral lesions cause weakness in the feet while lumbar-thoracic (lower back) lesions cause partial paralysis (paresis) or paraplegia and the need for training to manage bladder and bowel functions. Spina bifida is the second most common impairment in school-age children (cerebral palsy is the most prevalent), with one of very 1,000 infants born with spina bifida (Getskow & Konczal, 1996); yet many Americans, perhaps 40 percent, have spina bifida occulta and are unaware they are affected because they experience little or no limitations (Bullock & Mahon, 2000; Dattilo, 2002).

What medical and health care needs are considered?

Below the level of the lesion, there is a lack of sensation, the individual does not sweat and is susceptible to bruises, burns, cuts and cold because as the incident occurs nothing is felt. Wearing a wrinkled sock or putting wet feet in dry shoes may cause a blister that could lead to a slow-healing bed sore (decubitus ulcer). Urinary tract infections are very serious, so if urination requires the use of a catheter or tube that is inserted through the urethra into the bladder to drain urine at controlled intervals, precautions are taken to ensure cleanliness as the procedure occurs. If an individual has had a shunt inserted, care is taken to avoid impact or trauma to the area as this could trigger imbalance in the circulation of spinal fluids through the spinal cavity and result in the need for immediate surgical repair of the shunt. Children and adults may wear braces or use crutches or wheelchairs for mobility: When this occurs, care is taken to ensure that their skin does not rub against the assistive device, because the open sore created could bleed without their knowledge or become easily infected.

Why and how is the therapeutic recreation process (APIE) implemented?

Individuals with spina bifida may need to build and/or maintain their upper-body strength, postural alignment, and manage their weight. When MM is present, for example, there is also a need to prevent secondary contractures and adapt to the energy expenditures that result from the use of wheelchairs and orthopedic aids for mobility. Consequently, participation includes exercises like chair aerobics and swimming that encourage muscle strengthening, endurance and proper posture. Assessment of the physical accessibility of recreation areas and facilities like wellness centers and aquatic facilities helps participants become aware of how to use these types of resources during their leisure.

Where are there available resources?
Spina Bifida Association of America, www.infohiway.com/spinabifida
4590 MacArthur Boulevard, NW, Suite 250, Washington, D.C., 20007-4226, 1-800-621-3141

When sensitivity and awareness are experienced: Training Exercises

Visit a chiropractic office and discuss the importance of proper posture.

Wear a heavy pair of gloves that easily show the markings of wear and tear. Use a wheelchair to ambulate throughout the recreation facility and outdoor program areas. Observe the damage that occurs to the gloves as a result of this use; this represents the damage that can occur to the skin without the person being aware of the injury to his/her skin.

Cerebral Palsy

Who are individuals with cerebral palsy?

An individual who experiences cerebral palsy has a lifetime disability that originates prior to, during, and/or after birth or early in life as a result of damage to the brain. No two people with cerebral palsy appear or act alike as the term is used to describe a group of conditions characterized by an inability to fully control motor behaviors, including postural movement. The most prevalent form of cerebral palsy, spastic cerebral palsy, is characterized by increased muscle tone and contraction when affected muscles are stretched (Dattilo, 2002). Individuals appear to have jerky movements with flexed joint muscles and their walk is characterized by a scissors gait; they also may have difficulty swallowing. Athetosis is a form of cerebral palsy that is characterized by wavelike uncoordinated movements that become less evident upon relaxation (Levine, 2001). Individuals with ataxia have difficulties with balance and their sense of direction. Their gait is poorly coordinated and they experience difficulty with tasks requiring fine hand movements (Bullock & Mahon, 2000). Rigidity is the most severe form of cerebral palsy, and it is characterized by stiffness, hyperextension, and may be accompanied by intellectual difficulties. When a person experiences tremors, an involuntary movement with a regular rhythm occurs as movement is initiated or when there was no intent to move, for example, a hand or arm. Some individuals experience more than one form of cerebral palsy. When this occurs, they are identified as having a "mixed" form as evidenced with persons who have both spasticity and athetosis. These forms of cerebral palsy may affect one or more of an individual's extremities, so terms that describe affected limbs are also used: Monoplegia affects one limb, hemiplegia affects both limbs on one side of the body, diplegia affects the legs with limited arm involvement, triplegia affects three limbs, paraplegia refers to leg involvement, and quadriplegia refers to involvement of all four extremities. Persons may also have seizures, curvature of the spine, and problems with vision, hearing, and speech. Early intervention and therapeutic management help the child develop fundamental skills important to mobility and self-care as an adult while preventing atrophy and reduced range of motion.

What medical and health care needs are considered?

In some instances, participants wear braces to reinforce a muscle group, take medications to help reduce muscle tension and/or seizures, and use assistive devices to improve their ability to communicate or to increase their mobility. Excitement, tension, cold water or air or a sudden loud noise may cause the participant to become more "spastic" or "rigid", lose their balance or overstep or overreach their intended target. Swallowing difficulties may necessitate that food intake is monitored or foods are blended to avoid choking. Persons may also wear neck scarfs to help manage drooling. The person with cerebral palsy may retain abnormal reflexes like the hand grasp reflex or the asymmetrical tonic neck reflex, and as a consequence, when staff are assisting the person from a wheelchair into the pool they are alert to an unexpected movement like an arm that automatically moves upward when the would-be swimmer turns his/her head.

Why and how is the therapeutic recreation process (APIE) implemented?

Assessment considers the impact of movement and retention of reflexes on recreation experiences and successful completion of daily activities. Also considered is the use of wheelchairs, assistive and orthopedic devices like AFOs—ankle-foot-orthoses, on the physical stamina of the user and the participant's access to inclusionary experiences. Programs are planned to improve tolerance and fitness levels, reduce tension caused by muscle contractures, develop overall strength, and promote participation in social and competitive events like those sponsored by the United States Cerebral Palsy Athletic Association (USCPAA). When programs are implemented, flexion-oriented activities like weight lifting or kicking that may limit range of motion are discouraged. Experiences completed from a stationary position like bowling and that promote parallel movements like hand-crank bicycles foster the development of balance and perceptual-motor improvements. Staff adapt activities like grasping a sponge rather than a paint brush or wrapping hand grips around eating utensils so experiences are equalized. Program accessibility is planned for by taking into consideration environmental conditions: For example, staff have extra towels ready as consumers exit the pool so the effects of the cool air are minimized or sports chairs are substituted for personal chairs during events to increase participant mobility (if appropriate). Staff encourage community resource awareness and the development of friendships and social networks through leisure education.

Where are there available resources?

United Cerebral Palsy Association, www.ucpa.org

1660 L St., NW, Suite 700, Washington, D.C., 20036, 1-800-872-5827

United States Cerebral Palsy Athletic Association, www.uscpaa.org

25 W. Independence Way, Kingston, RI 20881, 401-874-7465

When sensitivity and awareness are experienced: Training Experiences

Participate in a sporting event like basketball or bowling using a wheelchair and adaptive devices like a bowling ramp.

Visit with participants in their homes about the adaptations made to their living area.

Restrict movement in your arms or legs as you explore physical accessibility in your environment to experience the challenge faced by consumers with various forms of cerebral palsy.

Muscular Dystrophy

Who are individuals with muscular dystrophy?

Individuals with muscular dystrophy (MD) experience one of several conditions that cause the muscles to progressively weaken and atrophy. Muscle tissue wastes away and is replaced by fat or connective tissue resulting in difficulty climbing stairs, sucking through a straw or rising from a recumbent position (Levine, 2001). Eventually, the effects on the respiratory and cardiac systems may cause death prior to the third decade (Bullock & Mahon, 2000). These diseases vary with the age of onset, the initial muscles attacked, and the rate of progression. Early onset MDs such as Duchenne or Friedrick's ataxia manifest themselves during childhood or adolescence, attack the muscles of the shoulders and spine, and progress rapidly with most children using wheelchairs by age 10 (Levine, 2001). Those MDs that manifest themselves during adulthood e.g., limb girdle, fascioscapular-humeral or amyotrophic lateral sclerosis (ALS—known as Lou Gehrig's Disease), attack specific muscle groups in the shoulders, hips, and/or face, and vary in their rate of progression: ALS progresses rapidly and is always fatal, while limb girdle progresses slowly, may be arrested at any time, and has a prognosis of a near normal life span. Individuals do not experience loss of intellectual ability yet as the disease progresses, lowered tolerance levels are noticed, range of motion and strength decline, posture is affected, breathing becomes labored, and self-care becomes increasingly difficult.

What medical and health care needs are considered?

Persons with MD may rely on wheelchairs for mobility. As the disease progresses, contractures causing severe pain may develop; if the legs are affected, foot-drop results and fall precautions are necessary; postural difficulties are evident with spinal curvatures; obesity results from lack of activity and muscle degeneration; and, the weakened thoracic muscles increase susceptibility to respiratory infections and pneumonia. Children may experience intermittent hospital stays to manage infections and fit assistive and orthopedic devices causing missed school time and the social interaction that occurs during the school years. When the muscles of the shoulder and hip girdle are weak, lifting, transferring, and carrying of participants is done with caution and becomes difficult due to the excess weight or bulk. Support groups help participants and caregivers mourn the loss of abilities and family members as the cause of the disease is genetic and may affect more than one male child in the family (Mobily & MacNeil, 2002).

Why and how is the therapeutic recreation process (APIE) implemented?

If the progression is slow, as in adult onset, individuals participate in community activities and may require assistance in maintaining their range of motion, strength, and respiratory capacity. With early onset, assessments consider caregiver issues like physical accessibility; sustaining regular school attendance; maintaining independence—a parent may tend to overprotect a child who experiences decreasing degrees of physical health and stamina; and adjustments necessary to maintain ambulation—some finger control may be retained even in the most severe situations allowing the use of light touch equipment e.g., electric wheelchairs, computers and video games (Bullock & Mahon, 2000). The effects of atrophy are countered by introducing activities that exercise specific muscle groups in the arms and legs such as throwing and kicking while stretching and flexion-extension counter the effects of contractures in the same muscle groups. Planning and implementation of exercises includes the use of Yoga breathing—diaphragmmatic breathing—to maximize lung volume and sustaining correct posture in seated positions to minimize spinal curvatures. Social networks are maintained through the Internet, while keeping an electronic journal creates a legacy and facilitates evaluation of life quality. Professionals carefully plan with consumers how to transfer from vehicles, complete rapid movements like turning to track moving objects, and how to include rest periods after prolonged physical activity.

Where are there available resources?

Muscular Dystrophy Association, www.mdausa.org
   3300 East Sunrise Drive, Tucson, AZ 85718-3208, 1-800-572-1717

When sensitivity and awareness are experienced: Training Experiences

Experience transfers from an automobile to a wheelchair using a sliding or lap board and having two or three individuals perform a lift-carry. Also, exit from a van/bus in a wheelchair using a lift or ramp. Discuss with others your feelings and concerns.

Visit with a pastor, child psychologist, about how children and family members cope with death of a child or sibling.

Participate from a wheelchair using a light-touch device to play computer/video games.

Multiple Sclerosis (MS)

Who are individuals with multiple sclerosis (MS)?

Individuals who experience MS are usually young adults or adults with varied and unpredictable symptoms resulting from the replacement of myelin that coats and insulates the nerve cells in the spinal cord and brain by scar tissue that forms plaques that interrupt the transmission of impulses to and from the brain (Carter, et al., 2003; Levine, 2001). Persons experience periods of exacerbation, increased severity of the symptoms and decreased motor ability; and remission, relief of symptoms and increased motor proficiency. MS might be mistaken for other disorders, because symptoms are so varied and the course of the disease waxes and wanes for unpredictable time periods. Symptoms persons experience include: rapid eye movement, double or blurred vision; slower, slurred, staccato speech; staggered gait, numbness, weakness, loss of balance, dizziness, and stiffness or paralysis in their legs; facial muscle weakness; progressively more intense tremors; swallowing problems; lack of coordination, and poor control of bowel and bladder. As a consequence of the disorder, persons experience depression, pneumonia, and infection caused by pressure sores. After an exacerbation, more than 75 percent of the individuals improve without treatment: And, over two-thirds remain ambulatory with or without assistance 20 years following diagnosis (Center for Neurological Diseases/Rocky Mountain Multiple Sclerosis Center, 1998). In early phases of the disease, some symptoms disappear during remission while they become more prominent in later periods when remission occurs less frequently. Throughout the course of the disease, fatigability and thermal sensitivity are common and over-heating caused by physical exertion may worsen symptoms or result in new symptoms developing.

What medical and health care needs are considered?

Persons with MS may rely on wheelchairs or electric scooters for mobility. The symptoms of MS become more evident with exposure to heat, so air conditioning and natural shade are used during hot weather. Also swimming in cool water (71-75 degrees Fahrenheit) reduces symptoms and improves range of motion. Medications are used to relax rigid muscles and reduce joint inflammation, yet have side effects like drowsiness and flu-like effects, so leaders adjust accordingly. Regular stretching and exercise relieve tension and reduce stress, but leaders must monitor participants so they do not become tired or exhausted.

Why and how is the therapeutic recreation process (APIE) implemented?

Persons remain active yet continually assess their adaptation to the varying symptoms and unknown course of the disability. Balance, endurance, stamina, flexibility, and the maintenance of routine social interactions are important planning goals. Activities like walking, aquatic therapy, relaxation training, and yoga promote relaxation and participation with family members. Awareness of the variability of the disease helps the professional make accommodations that promote participation with others. As the disease progresses over a number of years, persons may attend day programs with specific therapeutic interventions, yet for many, participation with family and friends in community and day therapeutic experiences continues throughout the course of the disease. The use of computers aids communication yet becomes difficult with visual impairments. Participants may relocate to temperate climates to avoid exposure to very high or low temperatures.

Where are there available resources?

The National Multiple Sclerosis Society, www.nmss.org

733 3rd Avenue, New York, NY 10017, 1-800-fight-ms

Multiple Sclerosis Association of America, www.msaa.com

706 Haddonfield Road, Cherry Hill, NJ 08002, 1-800-LEARN-MS

Multiple Sclerosis Foundation, INC., www.msfacts.org

6350 North Andrews Avenue, Fort Lauderdale, FL 33309

When sensitivity and awareness are experienced: Training Experiences

Visit with a sales representative for a company marketing electric wheelchairs and scooters. Use ambulatory aids that have padded/protected seats, backs, to cushion against pressure sores. Investigate costs of the equipment and adjustments that are made as sensation and mobility become more impaired.

Experiment with font size and contrasting colors for text on computers to judge how visual acuity is influenced by shapes, moving objects on the screen, size of the script, and contrast between background and lettering.

Arthritis

Who are individuals with arthritis?

Arthritis is a term that describes joint inflammation in individuals of all ages. Over 100 types of the disease cause pain, swelling, stiffness, discoloration, loss of mobility, decreased range of motion, aching, and loss of work time and claims for disability benefits (Bullock & Mahon, 2000). The most common form of arthritis is osteoarthritis. The joints in the hands, knees, hips, feet and ankles swell, and with weight bearing or standing for lengthy time periods, the swelling worsens. Rheumatoid arthritis is a chronic, progressive disease that may be characterized by a series of remissions and exacerbations, so symptoms worsen, and the joints as well as organs and tissues like the heart and muscles are affected. When children have this form of arthritis, it is referred to as juvenile rheumatoid arthritis. Arthritis is not infectious nor contagious, yet it is unpredictable, sometimes invisible, and may cause a person to feel "sick all over".

What medical and health care needs are considered?

The effects of arthritis may cause some individuals to have difficulty walking long distances, climbing stairs, standing for lengthy time periods, grasping objects, carrying heavy loads, and rising from seated positions. Children and adults with rheumatoid arthritis may experience extended periods of bed rest and as a consequence be at risk for cardiovascular issues. Cold and wet weather may trigger pain and stiffness. If steroids like cortisone are used, normal growth patterns are interrupted: When anti-inflammatory drugs, like aspirin, are used for prolonged time periods, persons might experience mild stomach irritations. Adjusting to pain, deformity, and the uncertainty of disease progression affects youth and adults emotionally and may impair their access to social activities.

Why and how is the therapeutic recreation process (APIE) implemented?

Persons with arthritis may continue to participate in customary activities with the aid of adaptations like velcro straps, card holders, or the option to complete the activity from a seated position or following a brief rest period. Assessments identify exercise routines to promote flexibility. Through the Arthritis Foundation, persons may be trained to implement a number of aquatic and "chair aerobics" programs. Precaution is taken to avoid unnecessary impact to the joints. Activities like cycling that move the joints through a full range of motion encourage mobility and reduction of swelling. The knee is one of the most commonly affected joints. Bed rest and relaxation are prescribed, along with heat applications and range of motion exercises. Programmers carefully evaluate exercise intensity and duration and air and water temperatures to avoid joint stress and overheating. If the person is in remission, participation may be unaffected.

Where are there available resources?

Arthritis Foundation, www.arthritis.org
1330 West Peachtree Street, Atlanta, GA 30309, 404-872-7100

When sensitivity and awareness are experienced: Training Experiences

Contact the Arthritis Foundation to acquire the instructional manuals and guidelines for swim programs; observe an aquatics program with individuals having arthritis. Participate in an exercise program designed to accommodate individuals with arthritis.

Amputations

Who are individuals with amputations?

An individual who is born without a limb or portion of a limb experiences a congenital amputation, while a person who experiences the loss of a limb or portion of a limb as a result of trauma, injury, disease (cancer or diabetes), or surgery is said to have an acquired amputation. Lower limb amputations are more commonly experienced than are upper limb amputations. The location of the loss is labeled as AK or BK, above or below the knee or AE or BE, above or below the elbow. A prosthesis is an artificial or substitute limb, like a Flex-Foot, and is designed to compensate for the functional loss of the missing limb. A cosmetic prosthesis is designed for appearance, and as a consequence may not be capable of replicating all of the movements of the missing limb. Computer design and the use of electric or battery-driven devices have enabled the re-creation of joint motion and customary movement patterns. Prostheses are fitted as early as possible, within the first one or two years of life, and as a child grows are periodically replaced. When an adult experiences limb loss, prosthetic fitting also occurs as soon as possible to aid in the psychological adjustment to limb loss.

What medical and health care needs are considered?

A person's balance is affected more by bilateral (both sides) than unilateral (one side of the body) amputations. When a limb is lost, the body tends to compensate for the weight loss by realigning so weight is more evenly distributed over the remaining limbs, which may result in poor posture or back pain. Damage to a prosthesis is caused by excessive force or not drying a limb that has become wet. Persons who have experienced the loss of a limb monitor carefully the stump's surface as blood circulation in the area is poor and, for example, bed sores or blisters caused by a prosthesis rubbing become easily infected. Also, the muscles around the stump or lost limb tend to atrophy and contract, which is painful and reduces the participant's range of motion.

Why and how is the therapeutic recreation process (APIE) implemented?

Individuals with prostheses may need assistance protecting their artificial limbs while participating in recreation; for example, near a pool, the limb should be kept in a dry place away from the sun. Some participants may choose to use a wheelchair or other motorized device to enhance their mobility during activity. Assessment of balance, range of motion, strength, posture, body alignment, flexibility, and agility identifies appropriate remedial exercises and adaptations to maintain recreation activities of choice. Professionals may assist persons as they participate in sport competitions governed by the International Sports for the Disabled and Disabled Sport/USA. For events like basketball, participants are given classifications according to the nature of their amputation(s) in order to equalize competition. During participation, if recreation equipment is used (racket, backpack), the participant may need to adjust weight distribution so balance is maintained. Also, energy expenditure is increased during participation with the use of prostheses and the person may perspire more heavily. In this situation, care is taken to keep the sock and stump dry.

Where are there available resources?

Disabled Sports/USA, www.dsusa.org

451 Hungerford Drive, Suite 100, Rockville, MD 20850, 301-217-0960

When sensitivity and awareness are experienced: Training Exercises

Use only one arm/hand or one leg to participate in your favorite leisure activity. What adaptations were made and how do you feel about the experience?

Poliomyelitis and Post Polio Syndrome (Sequelae)

Who are individuals with polio and post polio syndrome (sequelae)?

Individuals of any age may experience poliomyelitis, an acute infection in the central nervous system caused by a virus that attacks the nerves controlling movement: The result is temporary and permanent paralysis in the upper and/or lower extremities. Post polio syndrome (sequelae) describes a number of returning symptoms affecting those who have had polio. Fatigue, weakness, joint pain, difficulty breathing, and intolerance to cold (Bullock & Mahon, 2000; Sherrill, 1998) affect about 25 percent of the people who have had polio. Polio does not grow worse or progress, although people may die as a result of complications from polio, there is no known treatment, only a vaccine to prevent polio. The degree of physical impairment with polio varies; for example, some persons may walk with a limp, while others require a respirator and are paralyzed in all four limbs. Some forms of polio are remittent, yet between attacks weakened and contracted muscles do not regain their functional capacity (Carter, et al., 2003). With post polio, persons may experience muscle weakness that progresses over a number of years.

What medical and health care needs are considered?

The use of braces and wheelchairs requires adapting movements, yet the adjustment to intermittent joint pain may have significant psychological impacts. Temperature extremes during participation are avoided as is strenuous physical exercise, to the point of overwork or exhaustion. High-protein diets also are promoted.

Why and how is the therapeutic recreation process (APIE) implemented?

With physical accessibility adaptations, participation in recreation activities of choice is likely. Support groups provide emotional support to the participant and caregivers and assist in leisure resource awareness.

Where are there available resources?

The Post Polio Task Force Information Center, www.post-polio.org

When sensitivity and awareness are experienced: Training Experiences

Visit with adults who have had polio and are experiencing symptoms of post polio. What types of daily adjustments do they make and how is their recreation participation impacted? What other disabilities have some of the same symptoms?

Thermal Injuries

Who are individuals with thermal injuries?

Thermal injuries, burns, result from prolonged exposure to extreme heat and cold caused by flames, chemicals, electricity, and the sun. Persons between 20 and 30 years old receive the highest number of burns (Sherrill, 1998). Most thermal injuries occur in the home and may result in long hospitalizations, disfigurement, mobility impairments, chronic pain, and amputations. When a burn does occur, the individual may be isolated and immobilized to protect against infection and to permit the growth and repair of skin.

What medical and health care needs are considered?

Children and youth are familiar with fire and hot stoves, yet the concept of "stop, drop, and roll" is one that might be practiced along with, for example, weather emergency procedures, when programs include activities that use open flames (camp setting) (Getskow & Konczal, 1996). As the burn wound heals, scar tissue causes contractures that limit range of motion. The replacement of this scar tissue is very painful and causes physical disfigurement. Itching and skin sensitivity to sunlight and chlorine require that participants wear protective clothing.

Why and how is the therapeutic recreation process (APIE) implemented?

Individuals who have experienced burns may spend lengthy time periods at home or receiving outpatient services to regain mobility and repair burned tissues. Once rehabilitation is completed, the physical features of the person may not resemble the pre-burn appearance. Professionals help family and friends as they include participants in social activities and physical exercises that promote acceptance of the new self-image and improved range of motion.

Where are there available resources?

American Medical Association, www.ama-assn.org
The Association for the Care of Children's Health (ACCH), http://look.net/acch
National Information Center for Children and Youth with Disabilities, www.nichcy.org

When sensitivity and awareness are experienced: Training Experiences

Visit with a dermatologist or guest speaker from a burn center and view splints and braces used to apply pressure and immobilize limbs during rehabilitation.

Cerebrovascular Accident (CVA) or Stroke

Who are individuals who experience a CVA?

An individual who experiences a stroke is usually male and 60 years old or older; yet, persons any age may experience a stroke. In general, the younger the person and the less damaged the brain tissue, the better the prognosis. When a portion of the brain is deprived of blood, a stroke or CVA occurs. A small or mini stroke, referred to as a transient ischemic attack (TIA), may forewarn of an impending stroke. A TIA causes sudden weakness or numbness on one side of the body in the face, hand, arm or leg; sudden dizziness; visual loss; or loss of clear speech or understanding of speech (Dattilo, 2002). The most apparent sign of a stroke is hemiplegia—paralysis or paresis—weakness. If the right side of the brain is damaged, the left side of the body experiences hemiplegia or paresis and when the left side of the brain is damaged, the right side of the body experiences hemiplegia or paresis. Right cerebral damage results in depth perception problems, difficulty interpreting visual information, inappropriate reflex crying, laughter or anger; and in some instances, a lack of awareness of one's deficits. Left cerebral damage results in memory loss, speech and language problems and cautious behaviors; yet, consumers are aware of what is said to them (Dattilo, 2002). Persons who have had a stroke have varying degrees of visual neglect or a lack of visual awareness on the side of the body opposite the brain damage which results in, for example, ignoring people standing on the affected side. Aphasia also affects communication, as the person may either no longer understand what is said or be unable to respond even though the message is understood. Persons may also experience what appears to be a dropped shoulder with the arm held at a 45-degree angle and the hand forming a fist. Persons also may experience difficulty swallowing.

What medical and health care needs are considered?

If the consumer does not accurately estimate his/her capabilities, the professional is cautious to monitor impulsivity and compliance. Participants also may experience seizures, so professionals determine if this is the case and respond according to the guidelines presented under leadership for seizure behavior, refer to Figure 5.4. A number of medications are used with individuals having heart conditions, e.g., high blood pressure is a frequent contributor to CVAs. Consequently, professionals are aware of the medications a consumer might be taking and the side effects attributed to the medication(s). Professionals are also careful to monitor the effect of visual neglect as the consumer may completely ignore approaching entryways, people, or moving objects.

Why and how is the therapeutic recreation process (APIE) implemented?

The professional determines whether the person has experienced right or left cerebral damage as this helps identify how to communicate and interact with the participant. When the participant is a left hemiplegic (right cerebral damage), the professional requests the person to demonstrate a skill, because there is a tendency to overestimate capabilities: If the person is a right hemiplegic (left cerebral damage), the professional uses short concrete statements, demonstration and modeling to involve the participant. Professionals encourage the person to develop strength, endurance, and cardiorespiratory fitness. A stroke may suddenly alter every aspect of the participant's life. Consequently, professionals aid participants and caregivers through support groups, information referral, and by facilitating social contacts and community resource awareness.

Where are there available resources?

American Heart Association, www.americanheart.org

National Center, 7272 Greenville Avenue, Dallas, TX 75231-4596, 1-800-242-8721

When sensitivity and awareness are experienced: Training Experiences

Place a blindfold or patch over one eye to simulate visual neglect. Practice eating or walking through rotating doors to experience the absence of visual field on one side. In a pool, use life jackets to create the sensation of buoyancy on one side of the body, then simulate a side stroke to swim; and, use a hydraulic lift to enter and exit the water to experience the sensation of assistive devices guiding transfer from one surface or position to another.

Heart Conditions

Who are individuals who experience heart conditions?

There are a number of heart conditions or cardiovascular diseases (CVD); the most apparent are heart attacks or myocardial infractions (MI) and strokes (CVA) (McGuire, Young & Goodwin, 2001). Heart diseases are caused by either congenital or acquired conditions: Congenital diseases occur as the heart develops in the first month or two of pregnancy and result in structural defects in the heart walls and valves; thus, most heart problems in children are present at birth (Getskow & Konczal, 1996). Acquired diseases like coronary heart disease (CHD) and high blood pressure or hypertension develop after birth and primarily affect the arteries that supply oxygenated blood to the heart and brain. Some diseases like rheumatic fever, unusual complications from strep throat, or diabetes result in acquired heart conditions that originate during childhood yet persist into adulthood. Coronary heart disease results when the arteries that supply blood to the heart—coronary arteries—narrow and the blood supply to the heart muscle is decreased resulting in damage or death (heart attack) to an area of the heart muscle. When the heart is forced to pump harder because arteries are constricted due to loss of elasticity or thickening of the walls (arteriosclerosis) or accumulation of fatty deposits along artery walls (atherosclerosis), hypertensive heart disease and increased blood pressure, may result in a heart attack. Another acquired condition, congestive heart failure, occurs when progressive weakness of the heart causes accumulation of fluid in the body's tissues like the lungs, legs and feet; this condition is seen among individuals who, for whatever reason, remain in bed or do not sit upright regularly. A person may experience severe chest pain, angina pectoris, when the heart muscle does not receive a sufficient blood supply to perform a task like walking or riding a bicycle or when the person is under emotional stress. Electrical impulses cause the heart to beat. If the beat is fast, slow or irregular (dysrthythmia), the amount of blood pumped to body organs varies, and the abnormality is referred to as cardiac arrhythmia. An inherited blood disorder, hemophilia, may cause prolonged internal and external bleeding after an injury. Anemia, reduced oxygen carrying capacity of the blood, affects persons of all ages: A person may experience anemia with other diseases like cancer.

What medical and health care needs are considered?

A person who experiences heart conditions may also experience "hidden" symptoms like chronic pain and fear of impending heart failure as well as apparent signs, such as shortness of breath, bluish skin tone (cyanosis), swelling (edema) in the feet, dizziness, double vision, and fatigue. Functional ability may vary from no limitations or symptoms even though heart disease is present to extreme discomfort with any physical activity. Children may tire easily, feel weak, and lack the stamina characteristic of their peers. The presence of risk factors such as inactivity, stress, smoking, excessive body weight, and/or high cholesterol, require lifestyle adjustments. Professionals aware of medications (beta blockers, digitalis, blood thinners) used by persons experiencing heart conditions are alert to side effects like lowered heart rates, reduced blood pressure, dizziness (vertigo), and diminished clotting capability.

Why and how is the therapeutic recreation process (APIE) implemented?

Professionals assess the risk factors and environmental influences such as humidity levels and high or low temperatures that inhibit a participant's capacity to benefit from active participation. Participation considers the intensity, frequency, and duration of activity. If the participant is or has been in cardiac rehabilitation or had recent cardiac surgery, professionals monitor exertion rates, caloric intake, stress levels, and energy expenditures; with children, professionals adjust the length of time for active recreation and take precautions to prevent accidents that might cause bleeding (hemophilia). Professionals may cooperate with the American Heart Association, YMCAs, and employee assistance programs to sponsor fitness and lifestyle management courses. Professionals may also assist participants as they learn to monitor heart rate and blood pressure before and after participation. A MET or metabolic unit measures the energy cost or exertion level during any exercise or activity. One MET is equivalent to expending the amount of oxygen required to sit quietly; while, for example, 16 METS may be expended during golf or bicycling (Sherrill, 1998). Professionals assist persons as they plan the types of experiences that promote appropriate levels of energy expenditure. Leaders must develop a sense of when to "push" participants and when to have them reduce their energy levels. One of the initial signs of nearing maximum energy output is bluish lips; yet some individuals experience this occurrence regardless of activity level.

Where are there available resources?

American Heart Association, www.americanheart.org
National Center, 7272 Greenville Avenue, Dallas, TX 75231-4596, 1-800-242-8721
National Information Center for Children and Youth with Disabilities (NICHCY), www.NICHCY.org
    Box 1492, Washington, D.C., 1-800-695-0285

When sensitivity and awareness are experienced: Training Experiences

Contact a local American Heart Association and request information on their functional classification of activity levels. Review the chart to identify the types of limitations experienced as a result of the degree of heart damage. Obtain a copy of the Borg rating scale of perceived exertion; examine the points assigned to various exercise levels then for one of your planned activities estimate the number of METS expended.

Respiratory Impairments

Who are individuals who experience respiratory impairments?

Children and adults may experience a variety of impairments that prevent the lungs from properly ventilating. The phrase COPD, or chronic obstructive pulmonary diseases, includes disorders like bronchitis and emphysema and is the most common chronic lung disease in the United States (American Lung Association, 1998). "Asthma is the leading cause of chronic illness in children" (Getskow & Konczal, 1996, p.138). Hay fever, cystic fibrosis, and tuberculosis are also respiratory disorders that affect children and adults. Bronchitis is the inflammation of the lining of the bronchial tubes that may accompany a cold (acute bronchitis): chronic bronchitis is often associated with smoking, and the characteristic cough is referred to as a smoker's cough. Emphysema affects the air sacs in the lungs and results in difficulty expelling air from the lungs. "Asthma is a chronic condition in which breathing becomes difficult because of mucus in the air sacs of the lungs and tightening of the bronchial tubes" (Getskow & Konczal, 1996, p. 138). Asthma symptoms vary from mild to severe and include shortness of breath, coughing, wheezing (whistling sounds during breathing), and tightness in the chest. Some people experience seasonal asthma, others have the symptoms daily, and, for some, the symptoms develop suddenly—an asthma attack. Many children with asthma have allergies to pollens, mold, and animal dander. An asthma attack may be caused by viral respiratory infections, cigarette smoke, paint fumes, stress, medications, hormonal changes, cold air, and exercise (exercise-induced asthma-EIA). Hay fever is an allergy to a common substance (certain foods like milk) that may accompany or be a precursor to asthma. Cystic fibrosis or CF is the most common fatal inherited disease in the United States. The disease causes certain glands, exocrine glands, to fail to function normally. The usual thin slippery secretions (mucus, sweat, tears, saliva) are replaced by thick, sticky secretions that plug the ducts in the lungs and intestines and interfere with breathing and digestion. Children experience varying symptoms, including recurrent wheezing or pneumonia, persistent coughing, excessive appetite but poor weight gain, high levels of salt in their perspiration, and clubbing (enlargement of the fingertips and toes) (Getskow & Konczal, 1996). The disease is not contagious. Tuberculosis or TB is believed to be on the increase as a result of, for example, substance abuse and HIV/AIDS. Normal body defenses usually prevent the infection from becoming active; however, extensive lung damage does result if the disease is manifest.

What medical and health care needs are considered?

Children and adults with COPD, asthma, and CF generally experience time at home or in the hospital recovering from attacks complicated by colds, flu, and respiratory illnesses. Treatments include postural drainage (chest physical therapy), nebulizer breathing therapy, oxygen therapy, daily enzyme supplements, and medications like bronchodilators, anti-inflammatories, and antibiotics. Graded or reconditioning exercises may be prescribed. Also, physicians recommend the avoidance of triggers like house dust, strong odors, tobacco smoke, and environmental conditions like cold, dry air, high humidity, dramatic weather changes or conditions that cause changes in body temperature. Side effects of medications may cause dizziness, and seizures; long-term effects include hypertension, diabetes, and interference with children's growth. Fear of an asthma attack may cause inactivity that eventually results in fatigue, weight gain and general feelings of ill health.

Why and how is the therapeutic recreation process (APIE) implemented?

Assessment of the extent of lung damage or lung capacity determines the types of activities a child or adult is able to tolerate without excessive fatigue. Planning includes ways to improve the functioning of respiratory muscles while maintaining physical capacity and adjusting to a chronic illness. Implemented activities incorporate diaphragmatic breathing exercises, relaxation, aerobic exercises, and activities like golf and weight training that strengthen abdominal and shoulder muscles. Appropriate warm-up activities and taking medications before exercising may help prevent breathing difficulties. Professionals constantly evaluate the environment for the presence of pollens, strong odors like chlorine in the pool, and weather conditions that might precipitate an attack or exacerbate symptoms.

Where are there available resources?

American Lung Association, www.lungusa.org
> 1740 Broadway, New York, NY 10019

Cystic Fibrosis Foundation, www.cff.org
> 6931 Arlington Road, No. 200, Bethesda, MD 20814, 1-800-344-4823

When sensitivity and awareness are experienced: Training Experiences

Have an individual familiar with a nebulizer demonstrate what it does for a person with asthma.

Visit with a physical therapist, dietician, and exercise specialist to discuss proper breathing, nutrition, and exercise and to become familiar with postural drainage routines and the use of aspirators, inhalers, and oxygen tanks.

Diabetes Mellitus or Diabetes

Who are individuals who experience diabetes mellitus or diabetes?

Diabetes mellitus, called diabetes, is a high-incidence chronic inherited disease of unknown origin that affects infants and individuals through adulthood. It is a general term used to describe conditions characterized by excessive urination (Sherrill, 1998). An individual with diabetes has an insufficient supply of insulin, a hormone that converts carbohydrates into energy; resulting in the accumulation of sugar in the body that is eliminated upon urination. There are two types of diabetes. Type I, juvenile diabetes or insulin-dependent diabetes mellitus (IDDM), appears at any age, is life-long, develops abruptly, and is usually identified after an individual experiences sudden weight loss accompanied by higher than normal sugar levels in the blood and urine. Type II, maturity on-set or non-insulin dependent diabetes mellitus (NIDDM), usually develops in the middle or later years, occurring mainly in overweight adults (Sherrill, 1998), and may be present for some time without detection as it tends to develop slowly. With Type I, individuals take daily insulin injections since the pancreas does not manufacture enough insulin; and, for Type II, insulin is produced but not properly, so diet and exercise may be used along with oral medication or insulin to control diabetes. Individuals who experience diabetes are at higher risk of blindness, coronary heart disease, and amputations.

What medical and health care needs are considered?

Diabetes control is a constant balancing of food, exercise, and insulin (Getskow & Konczal, 1996). Glucose or sugar levels rise after eating and fall with exercise and insulin. Individuals monitor their blood sugar levels several times daily using a glucometer. If blood sugar levels are too low (blood contains too much insulin) insulin shock (reaction) or hypoglycemia results, and sugar (fruit juice, candy, non-diet cola, glucose tablets) is necessary. The onset of insulin shock is rapid and may occur after skipped or delayed meals and prolonged strenuous physical activity. Symptoms include confusion, irritability, paleness, perspiring, shakiness, headaches, nausea, raised pulse rate and double vision. Without administration of glucose, loss of consciousness and death may result. High blood glucose levels, diabetic coma, or hyperglycemia, cause excessive thirst and urination, weight loss, leg cramps, fatigue, and vomiting that are evident several days before loss of consciousness or a coma develop. A diabetic coma may result from unregulated or improper doses of insulin, stress, stroke, heart attack, surgery, overeating, and excessive alcohol consumption: Death may result if proper doses of insulin are not taken. Individuals with diabetes carefully monitor cleanliness, foot care, and skin break down at injection sites. They also may monitor blood sugar levels before, during, and after participation.

Why and how is the therapeutic recreation process (APIE) implemented?

Unless diabetes is associated with another disability or presents secondary complications like blindness or heart conditions, persons have exercise and participation needs like their nondiabetic peers. Professionals may assist participants as they monitor heart and blood pressure rates and self-administer medications in socially discrete ways. Professionals may also have a ready supply of fast-acting sugars (orange juice, non-diet cola, glucose tablets) available and may have snacks like popcorn, fresh vegetables or cheese on-hand to help control sugar intake. Professionals may introduce stress management techniques like relaxation and journaling to help participants monitor participation intensity and insulin regimen. They are also sensitive to mood swings and are comfortable approaching participants when symptoms of hypo- or hyperglycemia are evident.

Where are there available resources?

American Diabetes Association, www.diabetes.org

P.O. Box 25757, 1660 Duke Street, Alexandria, VA 22314, 1-800-232-3472

When sensitivity and awareness are experienced: Training Experiences

Read ingredient labels to identify sugar content then design a list of healthy vs. caloric snacks. Monitor glucose levels before, during, and after exercise and eating, to experience the impact of activity and diet on sugar levels.

Cancer

Who are individuals with cancer?

Cancer is a group of diseases characterized by uncontrolled growth and spread of abnormal cells that affect any body system. For youth, cancer is second only to accidents as a cause of death (Sherrill, 1998); while for adults in middle and old age, only heart disease exceeds cancer as the leading cause of death. Cancer is caused by multiple mutations in the genes that control cell division. A normal cell grows and divides in a coordinated manner, while a cancer cell multiplies out of control, destroying adjacent normal tissue as it spreads to other body parts. The names given a cancerous growth are determined by the primary organ involved and the site of origin of the growth: Skin cancer—epithelioma; glandular cancer—carcinoma; muscle, tendon, bone cancer—sarcoma; lymph tissue—lymphoma; and, white blood cell cancer (highest incidence in childhood)—leukemia.

What medical and health care needs are considered?

Cancer treatments include surgery, radiation therapy, and chemotherapy. With each type of treatment, the individual may experience temporary or permanent changes, hospitalization, and varying side effects. With surgery, an individual may have a complete organ removed (cancer of the larynx) and experience the loss of a particular function (speaking). Radiation is used with surgery and chemotherapy to control symptoms of recurrent cancers and to relieve pain; side effects may include nausea, vomiting, allergic reactions, fatigue, and loss of hair, appetite and weight. The side effects of chemotherapy are similar and include depressed red and white blood cell and platelet production that may result in anemia, susceptibility to infections, bleeding episodes, and periodic need for blood transfusions. Children and adults may change in their physical appearance. Also, each individual's emotional response to the fear of rejection by others and recurrence or death will vary and may trigger uncertain reactions to discussions or activities on "future" events.

Why and how is the therapeutic recreation process (APIE) implemented?

It is important to see that the quality of life is maintained (Getskow & Konczal, 1996). The temptation to overprotect a child or enable "dependent" relationships effects, for example, discipline and the freedom participants have to choose (self-determination) alternative recreation opportunities. Continuation of peer activities is important to maintain psychological benefits of physical exercise and social relationships. Professionals help participants assess their physical tolerance and adjustment to the side effects of treatments in order to anticipate questions and create a supportive emotional environment. Professionals plan diversionary activities like expressive arts and outdoor events to help participants relax and cope with pain while family and friends remain involved and supportive. When activities are implemented, professionals are prepared to handle emergencies like bruises or cuts that could lead to uncontrolled bleeding and the need for blood transfusions. Continual evaluation considers fatigability, lethargy, periodic bouts of depression or sadness, and blood cell counts. Professionals communicate with family and friends to make supportive adaptations and encourage their participation.

Where are there available resources?

American Cancer Society Inc., www.cancer.org

1599 Clifton Road, NE, Atlanta, GA 30329-4251, 1-800-ACS-2345, 404-320-3333

When sensitivity and awareness are experienced: Training Experiences

Contact the American Cancer Society Inc., request and review publications like *A Resource Guide for Parents of Children with Cancer* or *Cancer Facts and Figures*. Visit with a member of a treatment team on an oncology unit to discuss treatments and side effects experienced by patients.

Hearing Losses

Who are individuals with hearing losses?

Persons who experience hearing losses have one of the most common disabilities the United States (Bullock & Mahon, 2000; Oliva & Simonsen, 2000). "Hearing impairments affect two out of every 100 school children" (Getskow & Konczal, 1996, p. 100). Noise is measured in several ways: Sound intensity, loudness and softness, is measured in decibels (db) with a sound of 0 barely audible while sounds over 85 are painful and harmful. Sound frequency, high or low pitch, is measured in units of Hertz (Hz)—20-20,000 Hz frequencies are heard by humans, some individuals may hear-low pitched sounds better than high-pitched sounds like the letters d, h, s, t, and z. Spectrum or timbre is the attribute of sound that makes one tone or series of tones distinguishable from another, so spectrum ranges from pure tone or single frequency to complex tones that occur during speech, vowel and vowel combinations are more easily distinguished tones than consonants (Sherrill, 1998). An audiologist or speech and hearing specialist using an audiometer conducts hearing tests. Actual hearing losses are measured by the degree of speech heard per decibel level, so persons who experience losses of 70 db or more in the better ear are said to experience deafness, while those with less than a 70 db loss in the better ear are referred to as hard of hearing. A factor that affects how well a person is able to speak is the age of onset of a hearing loss. A congenital loss refers to a hearing loss present at birth while a prelingual loss occurs prior to the development of spoken language; a postlingual or acquired loss occurs after language development or later in life. When a hearing loss occurs after the age of three, the individual has a language foundation upon which to develop spoken communication. Throughout life, hearing losses may occur. Infants with middle ear or sinus infections or children with impacted wax in their external ears may develop conductive losses because the sound waves are not reaching the inner ear. Older individuals who acquire high tone nerve deafness are experiencing a sensorineural hearing loss caused by damage to cells or nerve fibers in the inner ear that convert sound waves to neural impulses. When young children experience a sensorineural loss, residual hearing is distorted so learning to speak becomes a challenge. This type of hearing loss also affects the person's balance, so this explains why older persons may develop a fear of falling or the young child has difficulty learning to coordinate movements.

What medical and health care needs are considered?

Individuals with hearing losses vary in their ability to access audible environmental information such as sirens, auto horns, and background sounds. And, they vary in their ability to benefit from the amplification of hearing aids—individuals with conductive losses experience more success than individuals with sensorineural losses. Hearing aids are worn behind the ear, in the ear, on the chest, or with eyeglasses. They all are powered by batteries and have control devices so the person may increase or decrease the volume; hearing aids selectively amplify sounds so participants must learn to distinguish essential sounds from background noises. Individuals may exhibit shuffling gaits or unusual head tilts or rotations because they have balance problems or are attempting to discern/avoid certain sounds. Individuals who experience hearing losses develop various ways to speak and communicate: Speech-reading or lip-reading is used when a person looks at the speaker's lips and mouth and identifies words by the shape and position of the lips and tongue (Bullock & Mahon, 2000); cued speech involves the use of spoken words supplemented by hand signs near the face; American Sign Language or ASL is a language like Spanish with its own grammar and syntax; signed English is using signs (finger spelling—using hand shapes to create a predefined symbol for each letter in the alphabet) in the order of spoken English; and, Pidgin sign combines finger spelling in English with ASL. Persons may begin to learn sign language by finger spelling their name, address, and the alphabet. Interpreters are trained professionals who are paid to transmit information from English to ASL or vice versa. Computers and electronics have been used to create a number of assistive listening devices and communication systems: Individuals use augmentative or alternative communication (AAC) devices like phone relay systems (TDD—telecommunication device for the deaf) or text telephones (TTY), communication books, computerized voices, and communication boards to expand their verbal interactions.

Why and how is the therapeutic recreation process implemented (APIE)?

Many recreation experiences do not preclude participation by individuals with hearing losses (Bullock & Mahon, 2000). The most common accommodation is to incorporate visual cues into the activity so the participant does not have to respond only to verbal cues. Additionally, the leader must remember to enunciate, face the participants, eliminate background movements and distractions, and place themselves in the participant's direct line of vision. To protect hearing devices, they may need to be removed during activities that involve either fast movements, moving objects or water. Leaders consider safety arrangements to ensure that alternative systems, flashing lights as well as audible alarms, are in place to warn of danger. Also, leaders and participants may need to be made aware of and practice responding to dangerous situations that arise unexpectedly like "flying objects" or weather changes. Leaders assess a participant's degree of balance, rhythm and perceptual motor development to determine the need to include experiences that improve or enhance skill in these areas. Adaptations like adjusting swimming strokes so participants' heads are not completely under the water as they swim helps build comfort and confidence. When programs are implemented, the addition of flags, hand signals or lights to cue participants helps maintain the activity momentum without interrupting the experience. The leader continually evaluates each participant's residual hearing ability and adjusts to the participant's preferred communication methods. When interpreters are present, the leader talks directly to the participant in first-person language and positions him/herself so the participant can clearly see the interpreter and the instructor. Repetition of words or writing down directions may assist participants as they become comfortable with the environmental sounds and distractions in the activity setting. Refer to Chapter 6 for additional participant management information.

Where are there available resources?

Alexander Graham Bell Association for the Deaf, www.agbell.org

3417 Volta Place, N.W., Washington, D.C. 20007-2778, 202-337-5220 voice and TTY

National Information Center on Deafness (NICD), www.gallaudet.edu/~nicd/index.html

Gallaudet University, 800 Florida Ave. NE, Washington, D.C. 20002-3695, 202-651-5051 or TTY 202-651-5052

When sensitivity and awareness are experienced: Training Experiences

Develop bingo cards using fingerspelling, alphabet letters, and play bingo to experience an activity using sign language and to learn to sign the alphabet. Participate in an activity wearing earplugs; repeat the activity without the earplugs—discuss your feelings and adaptations. Learn how to sign the lyrics to a popular song. Rent a captioned video, view and discuss your reactions. Use a TDD or TTY to carry on a conversation—what adaptations occurred? Take an ASL class and practice communicating using sign language during lunch, staff meetings, and with colleagues.

Visual Impairments

Who are individuals with visual impairments?

"Vision is the richest and most stimulating of our senses. Two-thirds of our information about the outside world comes to us through our eyes" (Getskow & Konczal, 1996, p. 119). With the exception of school children who are deaf-blind, visual impairments affect fewer children than any other disability; blindness and visual impairments are largely associated with older adults (Sherrill, 1998). A person who is legally blind, with corrective lenses, sees at 20 feet what a sighted person sees at 200 feet in the better eye or 20/200 (20/20 is a visual acuity measurement that refers to the ability to see at 20 feet what a person with perfect vision sees at 20 feet). These individuals may be able to distinguish light from dark and read large print (Getskow & Konczal, 1996). A person who is totally blind often may be able to distinguish light and discern large forms (Getskow & Konczal, 1996). A person who possesses visual acuity of at least 20/200 but no greater than 20/70 in the better eye after correction is also considered to have a visual impairment. Visual field is a second visual measurement. A person with perfect vision who looks straight ahead sees objects in a visual arc of 180 degrees (visual field) while a person who is legally blind is limited to an angle of 20 degrees (visual field), or less. A person with tunnel vision only sees straight ahead and does not have peripheral vision while a person with peripheral vision only sees to the sides and does not have central vision. Other types of visual impairments include difficulty in the perception of colors, extreme sensitivity or insensitivity to light, and conditions like retinal detachment, cataracts, glaucoma, retinitis pigmentosa, and diabetic retinopathy. Refractive errors (blurred visual images due to improper focus of light rays) and muscle imbalance (muscles surrounding the eyes are not synchronized) may result in individuals of any age wearing corrective lens or contacts or having laser surgery to correct the impairment. A child may be born with a visual impairment (congenital) or through an accident (retinal detachment) or disease (diabetic retinopathy) develop a visual impairment (adventitious impairment).

What medical and health care needs are considered?

People with visual impairments rely on memory and the senses of touch, smell, hearing, and perception of movement to gain information from the environment. "The attendant effects of a visual impairment are determined by the individual's age at the onset of the loss and the degree of vision that remains" (Carter, et al., 2003, p.289). Vision loss prior to or at birth leaves the child without the opportunity to acquire information from observation, while loss after age seven, when language and motor skills have been developed, leaves the child with skills to adjust to his/her environment. Likewise, a person with a visual impairment has the ability to perceive travel, motion, and light, while a person who is legally blind has limited access to environmental information. Professionals help create accessible environments by using a variety of tactile, kinesthetic, and auditory sensations and special equipment like closed-circuit television, reading aids and Optacons (convert print into tactile images that a person feels). Orientation and mobility training (O and M) techniques are used to help participants become aware of objects in the environment, location of entry and exits, distances and relationships between destinations and travel routes, and natural pathways and potential hazards. Brailling is the term used to describe the tactile inspection of objects in the environment. The use of braille to read is limited to less than 10 percent of the individuals with low vision (Bullock & Mahon, 2000). Professionals may also have participants that use Hoover canes, guide dogs or assistive animals, and sighted guides to increase access.

Why and how is the therapeutic recreation process implemented?

Professionals rely on nonvisual information to deliver recreation experiences. Before an activity commences, a communication system (guideline, audible signs, sighted guide), including emergency procedures are planned and practiced. The leader then orients each participant to the area, to the objects in the area, and to the location of the other participants. Providing color and surface contrasts encourages independent activity as does the use of sighted partners, audible balls, and tactile guides: Beep baseball, goal ball, and track and field events are sports that use these adaptations. Other helpful approaches incorporate demonstration with guided discovery, whole-part-whole teaching, marked boundaries, large print, audio cassette systems, pairing haptic (touch) with auditory senses, and placement of the participant's hands on the leader's body as activities are modeled or role played. It is important to ask if the participant wants to accept an offer of assistance; if so, the participant grasps the leader's elbow (bent at 45 degrees and held close to the body) with the opposite hand and travels approximately one-half step behind the leader. When programs are implemented, the pace of an activity may be slowed to accommodate mobility aids. Wearing a hat or sunglasses may help control glare and shadows. Echo and sound detection help discern distances among objects while light variations (natural and artificial) and odors (chlorine smell) help participants distinguish and remember locations. Unnecessary noises and distractions are eliminated and objects are stored in the same place. The leader verbally identifies him/herself upon entry or exit to avoid surprises. The face of a clock or compass is used to describe the locations of objects in the area in relationship to entry and exit locations (the door is at noon while the computer desk is at nine o'clock). Letters of the alphabet are used to describe the entry-exit route and relationship between destinations (to access the pool from the parking lot a leader might draw the letter "L" in the palm of the participant's hand). Other health and safety considerations are to anticipate the direction a door opens and the presence of stairs, curbs, ramps, and natural hazards. Emergency procedures incorporate how to evacuate participants with visual impairments. Refer to Chapter 6 for additional participant management information.

Where are there available resources?

American Foundation for the Blind, www.afb.org

11 Penn Plaza, Suite 300, New York, NY, 10011, 1-800-232-5463

American Printing House for the Blind, 1-800-572-0844

1839 Frankfort Avenue, P. O. Box 6085, Louisville, KY 40206-0085

When sensitivity and awareness are experienced: Training Experiences

Role play activities with a sighted guide and an individual with a visual impairment like eating a meal, exploring an inside activity area, hiking, tandem bike riding, walking/running with a lead rope, and escaping from an encroaching weather condition. Discuss the types of adaptations that enhanced communication and participation.

Explore physical accessibility of a building and natural area; how effective is the use of braille signage and audible emergency systems?

Aging Process

Who are individuals affected by the aging process?

More and more people are expected to live longer than ever before. By the middle of the 21st century, those over age 65 are expected to constitute 20 percent of the population (presently less than five percent) while those in the 85-and-over age cohort group are expected to continue to increase faster than the 65-age cohort group. Older adults with lifelong, adult-onset, and traumatic illnesses or disabilities are also living longer and are expected to continue increasing in number. Less than five percent of the population over age 65 resides in long-term care centers. In the future, a more diverse older population will be living in the community. A lifelong condition affecting older adults is developmental disabilities; adult-onset illnesses affecting the aging population are arthritis, heart conditions (strokes and high blood pressure), and hearing losses; and, a disability with an incidence that tends to increase with age is dementia of the Alzheimer's type. Alzheimer's disease may appear while a person is in his/her forties (early onset) but is more common in persons over age 65 (late onset). It is a progressive, irreversible disability that results in complete loss of cognitive functioning, followed by loss of all physical abilities: Each individual's rate of progression and losses is unique and may extend over six or more years (Carter, et al., 2003). Depression and alcoholism (lifelong or adult onset) are also concerns with older adults. Aging persons have nearly the same potential to recover from an illness as they did when they were younger, yet secondary impairments such as infections (pneumonia), malnutrition, and perceived and real fear of accidents and falls are more evident. Also, aging persons tend to show fewer signs of illness (changes in body temperature, pulse rate and coloration), have a higher tolerance for pain, and tend to limit their reporting of discomfort. The aging process is primarily a physiological phenomenon unique to each individual. "In general, age-related physical changes result in a decrease in the body's capacity to resist illness and disability, recover from physical exercise, and interact efficiently with others and the environment" (Carter, et al., 2003, p. 486).

What medical and health care needs are considered?

The aging person experiences a longer adjustment period before returning to a state of homeostasis following activity. Pulse rate, oxygen consumption, and the ability to resume normal respiration following activity vary more greatly with age. "Advanced age is usually accompanied by decreased visual acuity, some hearing loss (especially of higher pitched sounds), and decreased motor performances" (Smith, et al., 2001, p. 59). Persons with arthritis and strokes may limit their movement due to pain or the use of assistive devices for ambulation while some (individuals with Alzheimer's) may be less purposeful in their mobility. Decreased sensory awareness and reaction time affect the rate of decision-making and affective responses and require precaution with cold and hot sensitivity. Another general concern is the need to urinate more frequently, caused by decreased muscular activity and reduction of fluids in the gastrointestinal tract. Fear of crime and falling may also limit participation and inclusion in community events, especially during evening hours. With mobility and life-expectancy increasing, more older adults are less likely to live near family; consequently, accessible transportation and companionship become programming considerations. As the shield of health care benefits continues to decline and co-payments and health care costs increase, expenditures for personal care will increase and may cause financial concerns among older adults. Professionals are alert to side effects of medications like Aricept that treat the symptoms of Alzheimer's or antidepressants that might cause fatigue, heat intolerance, or photo-sensitivity.

Why and how is the therapeutic recreation process (APIE) implemented?

Programs and services offer health-related benefits as well as social and recreational participation. Experiences promote healthy behaviors, optimal physical and cognitive functioning, and serve as avenues to access information, resources, social support and caregiver assistance. Programs address particular needs, arthritis swim; encourage competition, Senior Games; and, allow for lifelong learning, Elderhostel. Environmental assessments consider the noise level, temperature and light controls, and accessibility to parking, restrooms, and rest areas. Planning considerations incorporate daily routines, weather conditions, traffic flow and patterns, amount of remaining daylight, accessibility and availability of transportation, costs to participants, nutritional value of foods (sugar-free desserts), facility appearance (muscle-bound environments are not attractive to individuals beginning exercise programs), and availability of companionship. During program implementation, the leader considers voice clarity, tone, and how the participant is addressed (Mr. or Doctor...); rest intervals are incorporated; incidental conversation, food, and opportunities to assume leadership roles recognize talents and motivate participation; auditory stimulation enhances memory; intergenerational experiences enable the assumption of meaningful roles; and the inclusion of spiritual activities are a means to boast morale and cope with age-related changes and losses. Program evaluation like a follow-up phone call or e-mail takes into account ongoing physical and socio-economic changes and encourages contact among caregivers, service providers, and health care resources.

Where are there available resources?

American Association of Retired Persons, www.aarp.org
   601 E St., NW, Washington, D.C. 20049, 1-800-424-3410
The National Council On The Aging, Inc.
   409 Third Street SW, Washington, D.C. 20024, 202-479-1200
Administration on Aging (AOA), or Area Agencies on Aging (AAA), www.aoa.dhhs.gov
Creative Forecasting, Inc., P.O. Box 7789, Colorado, Springs, CO 80933-7789, 719-633-3174

When sensitivity and awareness are experienced: Training Experiences

Visit an arthritis swim, Senior Games competition, or Elderhostel program to observe participant skills and program adaptations.

Review the contents of publications like *Creative Forecasting* to gain activity ideas.

Interview a gerontologist to gain information on research and aging.

Do internet searches of AOA to identify information on programs like the Foster Grandparent Program or National Family Caregiver Support Program.

Multiple Impairments

Who are individuals with multiple impairments?

There is no one explicit definition that describes a person with multiple or severe impairments. A number of characteristics are used to describe individuals of any age who require ongoing support in one or more life activities like toileting, feeding, and ambulation to engage in meaningful social experiences. Persons experience difficulties with communication, mobility, behavior, sensory responses, and completing ADL—activities of daily living tasks. A person with cerebral palsy tends to show the greatest variety of multiple impairments, while persons who are mentally retarded also display physical disabilities. A person who is dually diagnosed has at least two major impairments such as affective or emotional disorders and alcoholism or mental retardation. The same impairment may appear to have different effects on different individuals, and when an individual has two impairments, for example, there is no definitive relationship between the impairments; that is, the person with cerebral palsy or a severe emotional disorder may be intelligent yet unable to express him- or herself so the impression is that the person is also severely mentally disabled, which is not accurate. Each impairment tends to impact development or behaviors in the other areas of growth and life functioning.

What medical and health care needs are considered?

Persons with multiple impairments may require regular administration of medications to manage, for example, seizures or behavioral outbursts. Also, the use of behavioral management techniques to encourage responsiveness requires consistency and routine in day-to-day activities. Consequently, an interdisciplinary or team approach is used to support lifelong interactions. Safety is an important consideration, as participants may not respond to their name or recognition of a hazard identified by the leader. Thus, it is important to develop a communication system and procedures to use during emergency situations. Team members may use various forms of sign language or assistive technology and computers to communicate with participants.

Why and how is the therapeutic recreation process (APIE) implemented?

Participation in recreation experiences helps participants become more independent by improving functional skills like movement, developing leisure skills and options, creating supportive networks among caregivers and professionals, and acquiring individualized adaptations that encourage social interaction. Individual assessments and evaluations note gains in one area such as range of motion or compliance with leader directives that may not be readily apparent because of delays or deficits in other areas such as ambulation or verbal expression. Special efforts may be necessary to help participants identify preferences and friendship opportunities. Planning and implementation of programs includes the use of the kinesthetic approach, relaxation techniques, and behavioral interventions. The leader is using a kinesthetic approach when he/she moves the arm or leg, for example, of the participant through the skill or moves the participant's body so he/she is able to see the group or recreation object (toy). Relaxation techniques like massage are used to reduce muscle tension so participants gain flexibility or range of motion. Behavioral interventions like reinforcement, cues, and sequencing, are used to develop specific leisure and social skills. For instance, rewards are given when proper requests are made by the participant. Physical cues like pointing guide participants to select one of two choices. And, tasks are broken down into the steps to be displayed in order to successfully throw a ball or use a switch or remote control to turn electronic devices on or off. A number of participants may use orthopedic and prosthetic devices so program planning and implementation also considers physical accessibility and, perhaps, the additional time needed to transition from one service area to another.

Where are there available resources?

Association for Persons with Severe Handicaps, www.tash.org
29 W. Susquehanna Ave., Suite 210, Baltimore, MD 21204, 1-800-482-8274

When sensitivity and awareness are experienced: Training Experiences

Role play a person having more than one physical disability by using a wheelchair or electric mobility device while blindfolded or with your hearing reduced (cotton in your ears) and ambulate through a mall or along a street. What are the reactions of others and what obstacles are experienced?

Attend a meeting without the use of sight, sound, or ability to talk. What adaptations are made so you receive information from others at the meeting or share your thoughts with others in attendance?

Disorders of the Affective Domain

Who are individuals that experience disorders of the Affective Domain?

Disorders associated with the affective domain fall under the broad label of mental illness and include: anxiety-based, affective, psychotic, personality, and substance abuse and addictive disorders and behavior disturbances of youth (Mobily & MacNeil, 2002). The common characteristic is manifestation of behavior away from the norm. One in five Americans may be affected in a given year; many experience substance-related disorders while others with diagnosable mental disorders do not seek help (Mobily & MacNeil, 2002). Some causes are known, like brain damage or alcoholism, while others result from various environmental or unknown conditions. These disorders may result in permanent and lifelong issues or temporary situations such as depression or mood changes evident with extreme stress or a series of losses (family deaths and unemployment). Some disorders are associated more with children and youth, eating, conduct or oppositional defiant disorders, while others are more evident in adulthood, dementia of the Alzheimer's type and substance-related disorders. In some instances, persons do not accurately experience reality and report the presence of delusions or hallucinations while others recognize that they are experiencing depression or anxiety more intensely or for a longer period of time than usually occurs following a trauma. A leader may notice participants display sudden or unexpected mood swings, have difficulty focusing or attending, are easily distracted or agitated, exhibit unusual eating habits or weight loss/gain, report strange noises or belief systems, display poor coping skills, defy or oppose leader-initiated requests, disrupt group activities, or appear disinterested or lethargic over lengthy time periods. These disorders are treated and managed with medications, behavioral interventions, and social-emotional support from trained school counselors and professional therapists. Persons experience discrimination as a result of others' apprehensions, perceptions, and responses toward their inconsistent and unusual behaviors.

What medical and health care needs are considered?

Some children and adults take prescription drugs such as thorazine, haldol, zoloft, prozac, or valium that have side effects (involuntary motor movements, lethargy, drowsiness, photosensitivity, dry mouth, weight gain) evident to the leader and other participants. Other individuals may experience "acting out", self-injurious, or withdrawal behaviors that necessitate monitoring to prevent injury to the participant or others in the program. Still others, without supervision, may inappropriately spend their money or report incidents inaccurately. Persons with long-standing disorders experience declines in physical well-being that may result in the need for medical attention.

Why and how is the therapeutic recreation process (APIE) implemented?

Recreation promotes opportunities to improve self-esteem, resiliency, physical health, social and leisure skills, and inclusion in community events. Assessment takes into consideration such environmental features as parental and social expectations, support systems and positive/negative role models, presence/absence of illegal substances, compliance with medication regimens, history of brain injury, and length of time the reported disorder has interfered with interactions at work, home, school or during recreation. Leaders incorporate behavior strategies such as performance levels, contracts, and rewards in recreation programs. Implemented programs include physical exercise, relaxation, leisure education, and opportunities for expression, decision making, goal-setting, and social involvement. Evaluation considers not only improvements in participants' physical and emotional well-being but also acceptance by others in the home and community.

Where are there available resources?

American Psychiatric Association, www.psych.org
   1400 K St., NW, Washington, D.C., 20005, 202-682-6000
National Mental Health Association, www.nmha.org
   1021 Prince Street, Alexandria, VA 22314-2971, 703-684-7722

When sensitivity and awareness are experienced: Training Experiences

Invite a professionally trained counselor or therapist to a staff meeting and request them to discuss how to observe, document and report behaviors indicative of the need for professional help.

Include a behavior specialist in staff training to assist in the design of interventions like contracts, applying restraints, structuring for success, and nonviolent crises interventions.

Visit community mental health centers to discuss with professionals programming strategies, medications/side effects, and precautions to take as services are delivered.

References

American Lung Association. (1998). *Facts about emphysema.* Denver, CO: Author.

American Psychiatric Association. (2000). *Diagnostic and statistical manual of mental disorders* (4th ed., text revision). Washington, D.C.: Author.

Bullock, C. C., & Mahon, M. J. (2000). *Introduction to recreation services for people with disabilities a person-centered approach* (2nd ed.). Champaign, IL: Sagamore Publishing.

Carter, M. J., Dolan, M. A., & LeConey, S. P. (1994). *Designing instructional swim programs for individuals with disabilities.* Reston, VA: American Association for Leisure and Recreation.

Carter, M. J., VanAndel, G. E., & Robb, G. M. (2003). *Therapeutic recreation a practical approach* (3rd ed.). Prospect Heights, IL: Waveland Press, Inc.

Center for Neurological Diseases/Rocky Mountain Multiple Sclerosis Center. (1998). *Multiple sclerosis handbook.* Englewood, CO: Author.

Dattilo, J. (2002). *Inclusive leisure services responding to the rights of people with disabilities* (2nd ed.). State College, PA: Venture Publishing, Inc.

Dunn, J. M. (1997). *Special physical education adapted, individualized, developmental* (7th ed.). Madison, WI: Brown & Benchmark Publishers.

Getskow, V., & Konczal, D. (1996). *Kids with special needs information and activities to promote awareness and understanding.* Santa Barbara, CA: The Learning Works, Inc.

Hawkins, B. A. (2001). Autism. In D. R. Austin, & M. E. Crawford (Eds.), *Therapeutic recreation: An introduction* (3rd ed., pp. 113-129). Boston, MA: Allyn and Bacon.

James, M. R., & Crawford, M. E. (2001). Convulsive disorders. In D. R. Austin, & M. E. Crawford (Eds.), *Therapeutic recreation: An introduction* (3rd ed., pp. 280-296). Boston, MA: Allyn and Bacon.

Levine, G. R. (2001). Neurological disorders. In D. R. Austin, & M. E. Crawford (Eds.), *Therapeutic recreation: An introduction* (3rd ed., pp. 190-219). Boston, MA: Allyn and Bacon.

Litner, B., & Ostiguy, L. (2000). Understanding attention deficit hyperactivity disorder: Strategies and consideration for inclusion of youth in leisure services. *Journal of Leisurability, 27*(2), 11-18.

McGuire, F. A., Young, J., & Goodwin, L. (2001). Cardiac rehabilitation. In D. R. Austin, & M. E. Crawford (Eds.), *Therapeutic recreation: An introduction* (3rd ed., pp. 269-279). Boston, MA: Allyn and Bacon.

Mobily, K. E., & MacNeil, R. D. (2002). *Therapeutic recreation and the nature of disabilities.* State College, PA: Venture Publishing.

Oliva, G. A., & Simonsen, A. (2000). Rethinking leisure services for deaf and hard of hearing persons: A new paradigm. *Parks & Recreation, 35*(5), 78-85.

Sable, J., Craig, P., & Lee, D. (2000). Promoting health and wellness: A research-based case report. *Therapeutic Recreation Journal, 34*(3), 348-361.

Sherrill, C. (1998). *Adapted physical activity, recreation and sport crossdisciplinary and lifespan* (5th ed.). Boston, MA: WCB/McGraw-Hill.

Sitlington, P. L. (1996). Transition to living: The neglected component of transition programming for individuals with learning disabilities. *Journal of Learning Disabilities, 29*(1), 31-39, 52.

Smith, R. W., Austin, D. R., & Kennedy, D. W. (2001). *Inclusive and special recreation opportunities for persons with disabilities* (4th ed.). Boston, MA: McGraw-Hill Higher Education.

CHAPTER 6

Motivating and Managing Participants

eaders create an atmosphere that nurtures participant motivations (Jordan, 2001). The leader's enthusiasm sets a positive tone for learning and growth (Shank & Coyle, 2002). Leaders enforce rules as they manage participant actions and environmental stimuli so relationships are positive and expectations are realized. Behavior management, like motivation, is critical throughout intervention. The intent of both is to foster participant behavior that is socially acceptable (Jordan, 2001).

Effective interventions rely on clear, purposeful communication (Shank & Coyle, 2002). Each experience presents an opportunity for participants to express themselves and staff to respond therapeutically through verbal, nonverbal or kinesthetic feedback. Communicating expectations, requests, and acceptable behavior parameters establishes the framework for participant success and a positive program environment. Effective communication exchanges are influenced by a number of factors, including sensitivity, cultural awareness, the use of alternative communication forms and the ability of both staff and participants to comprehend and express their needs and wants.

During program implementation, participants may require individual assistance to successfully manage their behaviors, interact with others in the group or monitor and use personal items such as wheelchairs or medications that influence their functioning. Each behavior plan, developed during the planning phase, outlines behavior strategies used during program implementation to reduce negative behaviors and promote cooperation and positive participation. A number of behavior management principles guide staff as specific techniques are chosen to maintain safe, acceptable participant behaviors. The ultimate goal of managing behavior is to facilitate the participant's own self-discipline. At times, this may necessitate staff use of positive discipline strategies like a buddy or follow the leader. Incident and observation forms are used to record root causes of behavior, antecedents, detrimental behaviors and consequential actions of staff. These actions and strategies to modify inappropriate behaviors are recorded in behavior plans so staff are aware of consumer needs and efforts are made to implement consistent expectations across programs.

Compliance with ADA requires that staff assess factors influencing essential eligibility requirements (Dattilo, 2002). To meet essential eligibility requirements (refer to list in Chapter 1 on Defining the Service: Assessing the Community and Agency), participants with a reasonable accommodation are not considered to be a direct threat. A direct threat results in: 1) significant risk to the health and safety of others, and 2) with adjustments in policies, practices or procedures or use of auxiliary aids or services, this threat cannot be eliminated (Equal Employment Opportunity Commission & U.S. Department of Justice, 1991). To determine if a direct threat is present, staff: 1) complete an individual assessment that identifies the frequency, intensity, duration and severity of the risk, 2) determine the probability that a potential injury will actually occur and 3) establish whether reasonable accommodations will be effective in reducing the behavior and mitigating the risk. The burden of proof lies with the agency to document a legitimate risk that cannot be eliminated through the provision of accommodations. Disruptive behavior or other behavior not considered to be a direct threat may not justify participant removal from a program. Prior to removing a participant staff must document 1) an individualized assessment was conducted, 2) accommodations included strategies to eliminate the direct threat, and 3) the direct threat continued despite the implementation of accommodations over a period of time. Thus, reasonable accommodations might be modifying rules, providing aids, conducting in-services, or supplying additional staff if this action does not impose undue economic or administrative burden on the resources of the entire agency. If these accommodations have been implemented and documented and have not resulted in the elimination of the direct threat, then the inclusion team may consider if the participant is to be excluded from programs and services.

This section considers motivation and management that create positive program environments and encourage participants to abide by reasonable conduct rules and safety practices. Individual assistance suggestions cover communication techniques, prevention and management of inappropriate behaviors, and assistance with persons using wheelchairs or having hearing and/or visual impairments. Structuring effective group interventions may involve manipulating the environment so behaviors change resulting in acceptable participation consequences and satisfying outcomes.

Creating a Positive Program Environment

Because motivation is a degree of readiness to change, staff are able to motivate participants to change their behaviors (Austin, 2004). This is accomplished through manipulation of the environment (Jordan, 2001). Staff use a number of strategies to facilitate behavioral change and guide participants to adhere to reasonable accommodation standards such as staying with the group and limiting inappropriate interactions with others in the group.

During the assessment phase, environmental scans are completed. These processes reveal unique needs of each consumer as well as environmental features that contribute to certain behaviors. Participants are unmotivated, act out, or are unwilling to change their behaviors for a number of reasons. To illustrate, unmet needs, physical discomfort, low self-confidence, limited social skills, medication side effects, communication deficits, over- or understimulation, fear, skill deficiencies, and family conflicts may be antecedents to inappropriate behaviors. During individual assessments, it is incumbent upon staff to differentiate between behaviors characteristic of a disability such as darting about or unusual hand gestures displayed by children with autism and intentional behavior like sudden running from the group to gain the leader's attention. Assessment reveals personal needs, accommodating behaviors associated with a disability, and motivators. Motivators include recognition, reward, appropriate challenge levels, safety, feelings of belonging, satisfaction of basic needs, feelings of competence gained from participation, acknowledgment of activity preferences, staff feedback, praise, and clear expectations. Thus, revisiting information collected from assessments and collecting new information as participants enter programs are helpful steps in creating a positive program environment, and if appropriate, writing behavioral plans.

Through assessment, participants' preferred communication methods are identified. This includes participants' abilities to comprehend and process information, respond to feedback, and interact with others in group situations. Communication occurs through verbal, nonverbal, and augmentative or alternative communication systems like ASL (American Sign Language), PCS (picture communication systems), or Boardmaker software. Participants comprehend through oral, visual and didactic sensations. Awareness of participant communication processes demonstrates respect for diversity and a sensitivity to reasonable accommodations.

A number of methods are used by professionals to define participant options and describe expectations. These techniques involve active listening skills (Austin, 2004; Shank & Coyle, 2002). Active listening occurs as the manager or leader attends to verbal and nonverbal messages and the affective qualities displayed by the participant and then responds in a nonjudgmental manner. Active listening techniques include the ability to:

- Reflect—identify participant emotions: "I see you are happy."
- Paraphrase—repeat the participant message: "I heard you say you liked camp today."
- Clarify—elaborate on a specific point: "I am confused, could you tell me why you are upset."
- Summarize—tie together several pieces of conversation: "I believe you have several concerns about the program; the number of participants in each group, participant safety, and location of the activities."

- Question—encourage participants to express thoughts and feelings: Closed-ended questions like "Do you want to walk?" elicit yes or no responses, while open-ended questions like "What do you want to do?" encourage elaboration and explanation.
- Confront—challenges discrepancies between what participants do and what they say: "I see you damaging the toys, yet you wanted to play this game."

A number of verbal and nonverbal cues and requests foster acceptable behaviors and are used to create positive participation environments (Fairfax County Community and Recreation Services, Therapeutic Recreation Services, n.d.; Maryland-National Capital Park and Planning Commission, Prince George's County, Department of Parks and Recreation Inclusion Services Staff, 2000).

Nonverbal Cues
Laugh with participant
High Fives
Smile
Head nod
Handshake
Wink
Pat on the back
Approval gesture
Recognition glance

Verbal Cues
I need your help...
Your choices are...
What I think you are saying is...
Is this acceptable behavior?
Its okay to be angry.
Thank you for following directions.
How can we make this better?
I like you, but I don't like your behavior right now.

Requests
Do you want to put the games away now or after swimming?
Let's see how clean we can make this room. I know you can do it.
I'll start again as soon as I know you are attending.
I'll listen as soon as your voice is as calm as mine.
Praise participants so everyone hears: You have a great stroke, I like the way you...
Model behaviors: The bases are marked, can you put the sandbags for each base where they belong?
Recognize behaviors: You completed this skill very well a few minutes ago, I'm sure you can do even better now.

These active listening skills and communication techniques are used to create a motivating and safe environment. Selection of specific strategies is influenced by the interaction among the participant(s), environment, and leaders. Consequently, each situation is unique and staff rely on trial and error to determine which skills and techniques motivate and manage positive interactions.

Structuring Effective Intervention Groups

Activities are the core of therapeutic recreation practice and are used to help participants gain knowledge, skills and abilities (Shank & Coyle, 2002). Functional skills groups are efficient and practical means to enhance skills and provide opportunities for participant interactions. Structuring group interventions creates consistency in delivery, promotes accomplishment of individual participant outcomes, and fosters compliance with safety practices and rules of conduct. An activity or experience is implemented in three leadership steps: introduction, management, conclusion (refer to implementation in Chapter 4 Direct Services). Staff structure or organize their responsibilities to carry out each of these steps; for convenience, staff structure experiences through: 1) preparation, 2) introduction, 3) management, and 4) conclusion tasks (Maryland-National Capital Park and Planning Commission, Prince George's County, Department of Parks and Recreation Inclusion Services Staff, 2000; Shank & Coyle, 2002).

1. *Preparation for the Experience*
- Emphasize benefits of positive participation, establish positive rules to clarify expected behaviors, i.e., respect equipment, follow directions, respect others, take turns.

- Prepare consequences associated with each rule, i.e., if equipment breaks we won't be able to play the game until it is repaired, or if you do not follow directions, I will ask another group member to go first.
- Prepare materials, equipment, and adaptations prior to participant arrival, ensuring that the session goals encompass participant objectives and that each staff person understands his or her assignments.
- Environmental factors such as wind, noise, bees, temperature, playing surface, lighting, number of consumers present, and interactions among consumers are assessed to identify any behavioral triggers or antecedents.
- Experiences allow participants opportunities to make choices, participate cooperatively without long waiting periods, organize into formations conducive to individual "touch" or "spacing" tolerance levels, and experience minimal waiting in line and equipment distractions.
- Experiences like competitive events that can produce negative consequences and emotions are avoided, while low-organized, down or free time is kept to a minimum.
- Experiences are arranged to accommodate high and low energy levels of participants that might follow, for example, highly active or physically inactive experiences, or result from having a meal or medications prior to the experience.

2. *Introduction of the Experience*
- Welcome or greet participants by name and attend to their personal belongings, making sure each participant is aware of where their personal items are secured.
- Safety rules governing play and rules of conduct are reviewed, including behavioral consequences.
- Arrange the group so each participant is in the leader's visual field and their attention is gained and maintained throughout the introduction of the activity.
- As the routine or schedule is reviewed with participants, adapt to their eye level by sitting or kneeling if appropriate.
- Ask the participants to either repeat, demonstrate or model directions for successful activity completion.
- Plan activities to match functioning abilities of participants; so in one session a number of different experiences may be necessary to satisfy the range of participant abilities.

3. *Management of the Experience*
- Activities that use all group members and require behaviors from each domain promote attention.
- Praise positive interaction, re-state desired behavior when unacceptable behaviors occur, i.e., you are safe when you stay with the group.
- Set and keep a predictable routine.
- Reduce waiting and down time by using transition activities, i.e., follow the leader, or tell me an important fact about today, or if I had $100.00 I would...
- Re-direct inappropriate behavior in a matter-of-fact tone of voice rather than a demeaning manner.
- Be firm, yet respectful, avoid making demands, follow through consistently.
- Ignore behaviors that are not harmful or disruptive to the group.
- Maintain proximity using verbal and nonverbal cues to reinforce sportsmanship, sharing, or progress toward individual goals (for example).
- Remain alert to signs of frustration and introduce modifications so participant is successful.
- Isolate and remove disruptive behavior with minimal impact on those participating successfully.
- Address negative behavior consistently and fairly by setting limits as behaviors occur following a five-step process, i.e., prevention prior to escalation:
  1. Identify inappropriate behavior
  2. Explain why the behavior (cause and effect) is inappropriate
  3. Present reasonable choices or consequences
  4. Allow participant time to choose alternative(s)—if possible
  5. Follow-through or enforce the consequence(s)

4. Conclusion of an Experience
- Allow for "decompression or composure" time by telling participants either the time remaining, the next activity, or what is to occur during the next session, i.e., build interest in next experience.
- Reinforce cooperative and successful interactions to summarize outcomes.
- Debrief by using questions: What happened during the experience? Was the experience successful? Did the experience satisfy your goals? What should we do the next session?
- Reward and recognize skill achievements and compliance with rules and safety practices
- Document progress and revisit behavior support plans (refer to Figure 4.12) to update "A-B-Cs" (antecedents, behaviors, consequences).
- Bring participants together prior to transitioning to the next experience stating "check out" procedures and observing physical and emotional behaviors of each participant to assure their safety and well-being and the safety and security of their personal belongings.

Through close supervision and early intervention, behavioral issues are prevented or "de-fused" so they don't interfere with the experience or result in harm to the participant. Staff create a communication system among themselves regarding their assignments, physical positions, and participant contacts during experiences. A team effort facilitates consistency in the routine and monitoring of participant expectations. Staff are alert to each other's positions and remain close enough to intervene and support one another. Staff anticipate and "read" behaviors among themselves and their participants. Each is aware of each other's behavioral triggers or antecedents. The use of a self-assessment form facilitates awareness of the degree to which staff communicate and create structure as programs are delivered, (refer to Figure 6.1, Cincinnati Recreation Commission, Evaluating Program Structure: How Does Your Camp Measure Up? n.d.).

Providing Individual Assistance

Staff provide individual assistance to help participants manage their own behaviors, interact with others in a group, and meet personal needs during experiences. In this section, general behavior principles are introduced followed by specific techniques to manage inappropriate behaviors. Effective discipline solutions are considered. A number of record-keeping documents support the use of individual behavior plans and aid staff as they provide reasonable accommodations. There are as many reasons for acting out and noncompliance as there are individual participants. Consequently, one solution may not be effective every time, so staff accustomed to trial-and-error practices explore alternative management solutions with each participant and situation.

One approach is to prepare and publicize an agency-wide statement on behavioral interventions and expectations. This statement is presented to caregivers and participants as they inquire about or register for programs (refer to Figure 1.6, Guidelines for Parents and Guardians in Chapter 1 Defining the Service: Assessing the Community and Agency). Policies in staff handbooks outline ADA compliance statements and may include a statement on severe behavior and management procedures (refer to Figure 6.2, Behavioral Guidelines and Disciplinary Measures, Cincinnati Recreation Commission, n.d.). An agency-wide approach brings consistency to program delivery and standardizes consequences when behavioral transgressions occur. Even with an agency-wide statement, participants may require accommodations to abide by the guidelines. Uniform approaches are maintained as participants transition from one setting to another and enroll in various programs. Training that includes caregivers and consumers, helps to facilitate awareness of expectations and consequences and eliminates surprises when staff follow agency protocol.

Management Principles and Techniques

Prevention and early intervention curtail acting out and catch the participant in a frame of mind that may accept corrective feedback: Recognition and attention to positive participation reduces negative attention seeking behaviors. The benefits of desirable behavior are reinforced. Verbal and nonverbal cues either interrupt or redirect behaviors to another activity. Sometimes planned ignoral is effective, because the participant does not receive the desired attention so the behavior ceases. Role modeling active listening skills encourages participants to respond positively.

Figure 6.1

Evaluating Program Structure
How Does Your Camp Measure Up?

For many children, moving from the relative structure of a classroom to a loose, sometimes chaotic day camp can be an overwhelming experience. It is no wonder that the first few days of the program are usually the most behavior intensive. To smooth the transition from school to camp and to minimize behavior causing factors, staff should work to add structure to their program. Take a look at your daily program plan/ schedule and see if it passes the structure test.

Rating Scale: 1 = not considered
 2 = considered, but no specific plans to address
 3 = considered with specific plans to address

Participant Arrival (daily routine)

___ Participants welcomed/greeted by staff. Parent/guardians greeted, staff available to talk with parents at drop-off time.

___ Participant's personal belongings attended to. Staff guide participants to first area/activity.

___ Participants assembled. Day's schedule reviewed.

___ Rules of conduct/expectations for behavior are reviewed

___ Bathroom usage procedures, etc., reviewed.

___ Process for handling late arrivals.

Activity Planning/Preparation

___ Leadership assignments determined.

Activity planning includes:
___ Activity choices/options for varying interests/skill levels

___ Plan for introducing/starting activities

___ Alternate/back-up activities prepared

___ Modifications/adaptations to simplify (if necessary)

___ Behavior management strategies identified

___ Plan for concluding activities, transition activities prepared

___ Activity area set-up, materials/supplies prepared in advance

(over)

Figure 6.1 continued

Figure 6.1 — (continued)

___ Safety/supervision factors identified, risk management plan in place

___ Strategies to manage "free" time (adding structure/supervision for those
    needing)

___ Plan for moving (in an organized manner) from one activity area to
    another (swimming pool, etc.)

Program Ending/Participant Departure

Daily wrap-up routine which includes:
___ Assembling participants for recognitions, feedback on day's activities,
reminders about next day, etc.

___ Procedures for checking out participants, assuring all belongings are
gathered, speaking with parents, reminders about upcoming events, etc.

___ Staff meeting to evaluate day, make adjustments for next day

Scoring: 51-60   Highly organized, you should have a great summer!
                40-50   May need some fine- tuning
                20-39   Good luck! (you're going to need it)

Figure 6.2

Cincinnati Recreation Commission
Behavioral Guidelines
And
Disciplinary Measures

Introduction:

The Cincinnati Recreation Commission is dedicated to providing programs and services which meet the needs and interests of all citizens. It is very important for these programs/services to be conducted in a manner which maximizes the enjoyment for all participants. Negative behaviors, which take away from the enjoyment of these programs by others, will not be tolerated. It is the duty of the Cincinnati Recreation Commission to clarify behavioral expectations and to fairly administer discipline appropriate to the situation.

These behavioral guidelines and disciplinary measures were developed to establish clear expectations for participation in Cincinnati Recreation Commission programs and to standardize the consequences for violations.

(In order to promote continuity from school to center, these guidelines are similar in design to those used in the Cincinnati Public Schools)

The following is a partial listing of behaviors considered to be unacceptable in Cincinnati Recreation Commission programs and services (additional behaviors may be identified and included)

Category I: In-center discipline (time-out, loss of privilege, note to parent, etc.)

Unruly/disorderly conduct (guidelines may vary according to program/activity)
Disobedience, disregarding staff directive
Use of profanity
Running in areas where running is not permitted
Intentional, inappropriate touching of others (or their property)
Excessive physical roughness towards others (pushing, shoving, etc.)
Unauthorized leaving of group/program location
Taunting, verbal teasing, bullying or disrespect of others
Violation of van/bus rules of conduct
Inappropriate dress
Intentionally providing false information

• An accumulation of Category I offenses may constitute a Category II offense

Figure 6.2 continued

Figure 6.2 – (continued)

Category II: Parent called/ participant picked up, meeting with parent, possible suspension from all CRC facilities

Physically fighting with another person (self defense may be taken into account)
Stealing, possession of stolen property
Violent disorderly conduct (throwing objects, etc.)
Intimidation or threat of violence towards another person
Intentional damage, destruction or defacement of property
Breaking and entry
Gang activity

* An accumulation of Category II offenses may constitute a Category III offense

Category III: Mandatory suspension, possible expulsion from all CRC facilities

Sexual misconduct, harassment, intimidation
False fire alarms, bomb reports, tampering with alarms, extinguishers
Possession of dangerous weapons
Possession or use of alcohol/drugs
Possession or use of fireworks
Robbery or extortion
Physical assault, sexual assault

A team approach is used to assess, target, and manage behaviors. With help from the participant, family, school personnel, and social workers, staff agree upon what behaviors will be accepted and what will not be tolerated. Staff consult with others to assess environmental features that may support unacceptable behaviors. Staff and management agree upon the sequence of consequences to be used with each participant.

Observation is one practice used to assess, target, and manage unacceptable behaviors. Through observation, questions are addressed that reveal the circumstances surrounding the display of specific behaviors, (refer to Figure 6.3, the Behavioral Observation Sheet, Cincinnati Recreation Commission, Therapeutic Recreation, n.d.). These questions target the antecedents, behaviors, and consequences (ABCs) to be identified prior to the development of a behavior plan. Ideally, a behavior plan is written during the planning phase as individual support plans are developed (refer to Individual Behavior Support Plan Chapter 4: Direct Services in Figure 4.12). Realistically, behavior plans are written during any phase of program delivery as an alternative or reasonable accommodation for reducing or eliminating challenging behaviors. These plans may accompany other accommodations such as modification of rules or procedures, staff in-services, additional staff support, and disciplinary actions. The ABC process is used to determine what may be driving the display of the behavior and how to reduce, eliminate, or replace the less desirable behavior with one that is appropriate to the situation. As a consequence of using this process, positive reinforcement techniques are incorporated into behavior plans, and measures are set-up to note participant progress.

Figure 6.3

Cincinnati Recreation Commission
Therapeutic Recreation

BEHAVIORAL OBSERVATION SHEET

Participant _____ Program/Location_____

Target Behavior(s)_____Date_____

A. Situational Variables:

Observations

Is there any circumstance under which the
behavior does NOT occur?

_____

Is there any circumstance under which the
behavior ALWAYS occurs?

_____

Does it occur at certain times of the day?

_____

Does the behavior occur only with certain
people?

_____

B. Operant Variables

Observations

Does the participant engage in the behavior
to gain attention? Is it peers or staff?

_____

Does the participant engage in the behavior
to escape the activity?

_____

Does the participant engage in the behavior
out of boredom or lack of challenging
activities?

_____

Does the behavior occur prior to or along
with any other behavior?

_____

Could the behavior be related to any
social or activity skill deficit?

_____

Figure 6.3 continued

Figure 6.3 – (continued)

C. **Physiological Variables**   **Observations**

Could the behavior be signalling some
emotional problem?   _____

Could the behavior be a side-effect
of medication (tired, headache, upset
stomach, etc.)?   _____

Does the participant engage in the behavior
as a self-stimulation activity?   _____

Could the behavior be related to
environmental factors (noise levels,
heat/humidity, lighting, over stimulation, etc.)?   _____

D. **Other Considerations**   **Observations**

Is the behavior dangerous to self or others?   _____

Does the behavior disrupt activities?   _____

Does the behavior cause the participant
to be socially excluded by peers?   _____

Recommendations:_____

_____

_____

_____

_____

(This information is used in developing the Behavioral Support Plan)

Staff member completing this document:_____

Adapted from Bailey and Pyles, 1989 in L. K. Koegel, R. L. Koegel & G. Dunlap (Eds.), Positive Behavioral
Support (1996, p. 212). Baltimore, MD: Paul H. Brookes Publishing Co.

A—antecedent behaviors are the circumstances that precede display of unacceptable behavior such as fighting or leaving the group without permission. Observations that answer questions like the following may reveal a stimulus that triggers the behavior response: Does the behavior occur at a certain time each day? Does the participant engage in the behavior to escape the activity? Or, could the behavior be a side effect of medication? In some instances the behaviors may result from one or more stimuli or the accumulation of a repeated stimulus such as flickering lights or inability to gain the leader's attention.

B—action or inaction that is detrimental to the program or individual like "running" or throwing objects. The exact behavior is isolated and defined with a brief explanation of why the behavior is inappropriate.

C—consequence is the immediate positive or negative response to the participant's behavior. Negative reinforcement or consequences are meant to extinguish behaviors. Consequences may involve giving participants reasonable choices. Or, some consequences are logical or natural, i.e., if the bat is thrown and breaks as a result of a toss, participation in the game ends. When consequences are presented with alternatives, the leader allows the participant a brief time period to make a decision, avoiding an ensuing power struggle. Consequences may be thought of as setting limits: So, the limits are set from least to most severe, i.e., a five-minute loss of swim time precedes a 10-minute or more wait. When limits are set, behavioral expectations are clarified and results or consequences of non-compliance are presented. To have desired effects, consequences must be meaningful to participants. Through observation, staff become aware of positive reinforcers that meet participant needs. For some participants, a handshake or leader acknowledgment are effective while, for others, sticker stars or a brief cool-down or time-out period is meaningful; also, for some, immediate recognition is required while others respond to delayed consequences. A behavior plan documents the ABCs and permits staff to record the degree to which positive reinforcers are effective.

A number of positive reinforcement processes may be instituted to bring about behavioral change. Direct service staff use gestures, cues, and environmental manipulation to eliminate or reduce circumstances contributing to escalation of participant behaviors. Positive reinforcement techniques include:
- Stating rules positively
- Establishing routines
- Praising liberally
- Providing choices
- Using "I" messages rather than "you" messages
- Anticipating schedule changes and preparing participants
- Focusing on positive behaviors first—catching the right behaviors and giving immediate feedback
- Using questions rather than directives
- Using an expression of care and concern for participant's well-being and behavior such as "I see you are giving it your all, you're really working hard."
- Using reinforcing actions like a hand on the shoulder or a pat on the back
- Moving toward or away from the activity or participant, in some instances, is enough to reduce the behavior
- Using a gesture, cue or "stare" may send a "stop" message
- Making sure the basic needs of the participant have been met
- Moving the activity to another less stimulating area
- Using a cooling-off period or a time-out from the activity by allowing, for example, running, talking, playing a game, or personal quiet time, before resuming the activity
- Using secondary reinforcers like points, stickers, daily recognition, or a preferred activity may promote compliance
- Using simple negotiation like if you do this...then this will happen...
- Verbal or written social contracts may curtail inappropriate behaviors

Behavior plans outline positive reinforcers and procedures to monitor progress toward compliance and display of appropriate behaviors. When behaviors are displayed that create a potentially dangerous or harmful situation, a Behavioral Incident Report form (refer to Figure 6.4, Cincinnati Recreation Commission, Therapeutic Recreation, n.d.) is used to document the outcome and manner in which unacceptable behaviors are handled, i.e., participant behavior and staff response. When these reports are filed, the team re-assesses the circumstances to identify antecedents, isolate behaviors, and document consequences. The behavioral plan is modified

Figure 6.4

**CINCINNATI RECREATION COMMISSION
THERAPEUTIC RECREATION**

BEHAVIORAL INCIDENT REPORT

Participant_____ Date_____

Program/Location_____ Area_____

Staff completing this form_____

Describe the behavioral incident_____

_____

_____

_____

_____

Did the behavior result in an injury? Yes____No___ If yes, you must complete and submit the Report of Accident to Participant form or the Supervisor's Investigation of Employee Injury form.

Time and duration of the behavior. Start time_____ End time_____

Which staff were present when the incident occurred?_____

_____

Which staff (if any) was the behavior directed towards?_____

_____

What type of activity was occurring at the time of the incident?_____

_____

Did the participant make any type of complaint or give any other indication of a problem prior to the incident? Yes____No_____ If yes, what/how?_____

_____

_____

(over)

Figure 6.4 continued

Figure 6.4 – (continued)

Did another participant say or do something that might have set off the incident? Yes____No____ If yes, what/how?_____

_____

Did a staff member give a direction or make a request prior to the incident?
Yes____No____ If yes, what/how?_____

_____

How did staff manage the incident? What were the consequences for the participant's behavior?

_____

_____

_____

Was the participant's parent/guardian notified? Yes____No____ If yes, what was their response to the report of this incident?

_____

_____

Resolution: What measures will be taken to avoid future incidents with this participant? What changes, if any, will be made in how staff intervene with participant during (or prior to) an incident? Any other comments or observations regarding this incident?

_____

_____

_____

_____

_____

to incorporate additional reinforcers, or perhaps, introduce specific discipline techniques. An agency policy may identify, administrative consequences, like program suspension for zero-tolerance behavior, after a certain number of these reports are filed and all alternative accommodations are implemented and documented.

The use of discipline implies control by someone to enforce compliance with rules of conduct or safety procedures. One approach is to use techniques that encourage the participant to regain control or move toward self-management (Jordan, 2001). Positive discipline or positive behavioral support may include positive reinforcers from the behavior plan, personal contracts, cool-down breaks or brief time-outs. Other techniques include using secondary reinforcers like certificates, awards, and recognition systems. Buddy systems, follow the leader, and peer coaches may also help participants regain control of their behaviors. These techniques are preferred as they tend to minimize the power struggle that could ensue when professionals "tell" or "demand" behavioral changes. Positive discipline tends to remind the participant of the expectations: To illustrate, posting consequences when the rules are stated is one way to remind participants of expected behaviors. One strategy is to have alternative measures in mind as the same behavior may be triggered by more than one antecedent, and at a particular time, different consequences are more reasonable forms of accommodation than are others, i.e., a five-minute time-out is OK during a scheduled program yet unsafe while on a walk through an historic downtown area.

There are a number of behaviors for which discipline might seem a logical consequence. Behaviors that accompany opposition, anger, impulsiveness, distractibility, short attention spans, and the tendency to bolt or run as a reaction to environmental stimuli create unsafe situations. Behaviors evident with these emotions and actions may be associated with a particular disability like ADHD or autism and, therefore, require accommodations. The process of identifying reasonable accommodations may be repeated with each new experience or program setting. General positive behavioral supports as well as the suggested reinforcers and discipline techniques include:

- Reassure the participant that the behavior is legitimate
- Reaffirm that the participant is OK even when displaying the behavior
- Help the participant anticipate and identify the trigger, i.e., "Tommy, the whistle is going to blow very loudly at noon."
- Remain with the participant, i.e., running beside him/her as the behavior is displayed
- Set clear boundaries and let the participant know ahead of time which behaviors will result in disciplinary action, i.e., "If you run into the street, I will stop you, and redirect you to a safer running place."
- Re-evaluate the situation, i.e., Does the participant want to be removed because of fear of failure? Do I need to increase the frequency of reinforcement or change the nature of the reinforcers used by staff?

Disruptive behavior may escalate to a level that becomes dangerous to the participant or others in the group. Out-of-control behavior may be triggered by something in the immediate environment or be a carry-over from events prior to the present situation. A number of professional training programs are available on the management of disruptive and assaultive behaviors (http://www.crisisprevention.com—Crisis Prevention Institute, Inc., http://www.pcma.co—Professional Crisis Management). These programs introduce verbal and physical interventions to use when anxiety turns into acting-out behaviors directed at the self or others.

Physical intervention or non-violent physical crisis intervention is used as a last resort and only if permitted by agency policy. When the welfare and safety of participants and others are endangered, intervention may commence with supportive nonjudgmental verbal intervention followed by limit setting or "take charge" role by the leader. If escalation continues, staff may use physical techniques if permitted by agency policy to avoid hair pulling, biting, grabbing or kicking. As a last resort, some form of physical control like a "bear hug," places a participant in a secure hold so tension is reduced and staff regain rapport with the participant. Techniques used in crisis intervention require special training, a team approach, careful documentation, and pre-set agency protocols.

Managing Persons Using Wheelchairs

For some participants to interact with other group members, assistance with wheelchairs or other assistive devices is necessary. A few general operating principles help participants maximize their independence. Wheelchairs and orthopedic equipment are considered "personal items" and are custom designed to meet individual needs. Thus, when staff interact with participants, contact with an assistive device, whether it is with a chair, cane, or prosthetic limb, is like making physical contact with the participant's body. Therefore, before initiating assistance, staff should ask participants if help is desired and how to proceed. When assistive devices are not in use, i.e., the participant may prefer to transfer to a stadium seat, they are placed in close proximity to the participant and moved upon consent of the participant. In some instances when participants ambulate without the use of a wheelchair, they may prefer to use a chair during an activity to increase participation options. A review of general wheelchair operating guidelines may help staff judge how and when to assist participants (refer to Figure 6.5, Guidelines for Wheelchair Operation and Assistance, Cincinnati Recreation Commission, n.d.).

Managing Persons with Visual Impairments

Several techniques are used to facilitate participation when persons experience visual impairments, additional information is found in Chapter 5, Individuals with Disabilities under Visual Impairments:

Staff orient participants to the area by standing in the entryway and describing locations of objects in the area according to the numbers or directions on the face of a clock or compass, i.e., the exit is at 6 o'clock and the supply cabinet is on your right 90 degrees east.

Staff walk around the perimeter of the area, returning along the same path, identifying objects such as the light switches, inclines, and permanent objects in the travel path.

The travel route to and from one area to another or within the area is described as the letter in the alphabet, i.e., from the restroom to the pool is like the letter "L," which is traced on the palm of the participant's hand.

A sighted guide holds his/her elbow at a 45-degree angle close to his/her side and walks about one-half a step in front of the participant: The participant is asked to grasp the guide's elbow with his/her hand so the palm and thumb face away from the guide's body. The guide identifies the direction doors open (in or out) and whether approaching stairs ascend or descend.

When participants use assist dogs, the animals are "on duty," and contact is avoided unless approved by the participant. If a Hoover Cane (red-tipped) is used, assistance is given on the opposite side if requested.

Establishing a communication system is a first priority. Staff introduce themselves as they approach the participant and encourage others in the group to do the same. A buddy may be assigned so participants are never left alone in an open area and as activities occur, the buddy gives verbal directions and cues to the participant. When skills are demonstrated, participants feel the staff as each movement in the action is described, kinesthetic approach. Instructors use whole-part-whole instruction and manual or guided discovery.

With each experience participants practice emergency procedures and commit warning signals to memory. Staff are alert to distractions like visual glare, improperly placed equipment and variations in echo and sound detection from playing surfaces and indoor-outdoor areas. Adaptations like texture variation identify boundaries: Audible goals and equipment locate targets and moving objects (refer to Figure 4.10, Adapting Recreational Experiences in Chapter 4 Direct Services for additional suggestions).

Managing Persons with Hearing Impairments

Various sensory and environmental cues are used during experiences with participants having hearing impairments, additional information is found in Chapter 5, Individuals with Disabilities under Hearing Losses.

When an interpreter is used, leaders face the participant and continue speaking to the participant rather than the interpreter.

As with visual impairments, establishing a communication system is of utmost importance. Visual aids and diagrams may be used if persons do not have interpreters or assistive devices. Thus, visual cues are designated to start and stop an activity and gain participant attention.

Facial expressions and gestures are important to clarify directions, since subtle voice changes are not heard by the participant. One approach is to use brief sentences requesting verbal feedback or demonstration to affirm the participant's understanding of the activity protocol.

Figure 6.5

Guidelines for Wheelchair Operation and Assistance

There are many different types of wheelchairs with features designed to meet the needs of each specific individual. It is always a good idea to ask the participant (or parent) if there are any special procedures or precautions relating to the chair.

The following points are applicable to most wheelchairs:

Whenever a wheelchair is meant to be stationary, the wheel locks should be set. Be sure to set locks when lifting/transferring someone out of or into their chair. Power wheelchairs should be **turned off** when transferring. Power settings should be turned to low in certain areas (pool deck, crowded rooms, etc.)

Most wheelchairs have some form (or combination) of seat belt or harness. These serve a very important purpose and should be securely fastened whenever the individual is in their chair.

When transferring an individual into or out of their chair it is helpful to remove an arm rest and rotate the foot rests out of the way.

When pushing a wheelchair through doorways, around corners, etc., be sure all parts of the chair (and the participant) avoid contacting walls, doors, door frame, etc.

If you must take a wheelchair down a ramp or slope, it is sometimes better to turn the chair backwards (with pusher walking backwards, supporting the chair). This provides a measure of safety in that the pusher is less likely to lose control of the chair and the participant is kept in more of an upright position.

Front wheels can catch on even a slight change in elevation, causing the participant to lunge forward. When negotiating an elevation change (step, curb), pull the wheelchair backwards over the curb/step.

Anti-tip bars are very important and should be in place before any activity.

If any part of the wheelchair is missing or defective (tire pressure, loose brake, etc.) be sure to notify the parent/guardian as soon as possible.

A hearing aid is custom fitted and may actually intensify background noises, causing confusing communication signals during an activity. If it becomes wet from perspiration or falling into the water, the damage may be irreparable. Likewise, a direct hit from a flying ball may permanently damage the earmold or hearing aid. A participant may choose to participate without wearing a hearing aid to protect the device, e.g., while swimming. Staff may ask the participant to turn an aid up or down to diffuse the background noises or prevent a shrill sound emanating from the aid.

Experiences are planned with regard to background noises and distractions, and pre-arranged visual signals are used to cue participants when to start-stop (in the pool). Leaders use task analysis to sequence the steps required to perform a skill so participants organize the performance expectations from the initial to final step (refer to Figure 4.9, Therapeutic Use of Activities in Chapter 4 Direct Services). Leaders stand in the direct line of a participant's vision, avoiding excessive back lighting.

Buddies model desired behaviors. Guided discovery and manual guidance along with the opportunity to observe others perform movements help participants acquire movement patterns.

Words that have more than one meaning, such as fast, slow, in or out, are demonstrated so participants discriminate the movement patterns with multiple interpretations. Repetition is helpful as new skills are acquired. Practice of emergency procedures alleviates concern among all participants when quick changes in the nature of an activity are required.

References

Austin, D. R. (2004). *Therapeutic recreation processes and techniques* (5th ed.). Champaign, IL: Sagamore Publishing.

Cincinnati Recreation Commission. (n.d.).
  Behavioral Guidelines and Disciplinary Measures
  Behavioral Incident Report
  Behavioral Observation Sheet
  Evaluating Program Structure: How Does Your Camp Measure Up?
  Guidelines for Wheelchair Operations and Assistance
(Available from Cincinnati Recreation Commission, Division of Therapeutic Recreation, 805 Central Avenue, Cincinnati, Ohio 45202).

Dattilo, J. (2002). *Inclusive leisure services responding to the rights of people with disabilities* (2nd ed.). State College, PA: Venture Publishing, Inc.

Equal Employment Opportunity Commission & U.S. Department of Justice. (1991). *Americans with Disabilities Handbook*. Washington, D.C.: U.S. Government Printing Office.

Fairfax County Community and Recreation Services, Therapeutic Recreation Services. (n.d.). *Staff training manual for community recreation integration*. Fairfax County, MD: Author.

Jordan, D. J. (2001). *Leadership in leisure services: Making a difference* (2nd ed.). State College, PA: Venture Publishing, Inc.

Maryland-National Capital Park and Planning Commission, Prince George's County, Department of Parks and Recreation Inclusion Services Staff. (2000). *Inclusion resource manual*. Prince George's County, MD: Author.

Shank, J., & Coyle, C. (2002). *Therapeutic recreation in health promotion and rehabilitation*. State College, PA: Venture Publishing, Inc.

Application of the APIE Process

Therapeutic Recreation in the Community
Inclusive Recreation Case Study

Registration

Mrs. Smith has two children, ages six and eight. The six year old has autism. She would like her children to attend day camp together at the community center in her neighborhood. Mrs. Smith contacts the community center to inquire about the summer day camp program and the registration process. While talking with the staff member from the community center, Mrs. Smith mentions her younger son, Jack, and asks if the program accepts children with disabilities. The community center staff replies "yes of course, do you think he may need additional assistance to participate?" Somewhat surprised by this response, Mrs. Smith says "I'm not sure". At this point the community center staff suggests they call the Therapeutic Division and set up a meeting to help determine the necessary accommodations. Later that week, Jane from the Therapeutic Division meets with Mrs. Smith and the community center staff to discuss the program and any additional assistance or arrangements that might be necessary. The Assessment-Accommodation Request document is used to facilitate this process.

Assessment

       Assessment / Accommodation Request (Part A and B)
       Teacher Questionnaire (release of information form required)

Mrs. Smith completed "Part A" of the Assessment / Accommodation Request document, providing very helpful background information on Jack. She agreed to allow Jane to contact Jack's school teacher to see if there was additional information that might help with the transition from school to the community center day camp program. The "Release of Information Form" was signed and sent to the school along with the "Teacher Questionnaire". Jack's teacher, Mrs. Thomas, was very helpful and happy to provide Jane with the information requested. The assessment information collected was compiled and used in developing the "Plan for Accommodation" (Part C).

Planning

       Assessment / Accommodation Document (Part C)
       Behavioral Observation Sheet
       Behavioral Support Plan

Implementation

       Inclusion Notes (observation form)
       Behavioral Support Plan (number 8, Progress Notes)

Evaluation

       Inclusion Notes

Cincinnati Recreation Commission
ASSESSMENT and ACCOMMODATION REQUEST

This form is intended to assist in identifying accommodations which may be necessary for successful participation. Please complete as thoroughly as possible. *Thank-you.*

Part A PARTICIPANT INFORMATION (to be completed by participant/parent/guardian)

Participant ___*Jack Smith*___ Date of Birth ___*2-12-97*___

Address _____ City _____ Zip _____ Phone _____

Parent/Guardian _____ Home Phone _____ Work Phone _____

Participants School/Workshop/Employer _____ Teacher/Supervisor's Name (Phone Number)
_____ _____

I. Disability Information
Place a check next to each that applies to the participant and/or write in any disabling condition not listed:

✔ Autism	___ Attention Deficit Disorder	___ Hearing Impaired
___ Down Syndrome	___ Psychiatric Disability	___ Vision Impaired
___ Severe Mental Retardation	___ Cerebral Palsy	✔ Speech Impaired
___ Moderate Mental Retardation	___ Spina Bifida	___ Other
___ Mild Mental Retardation	___ Head Injury	_____
___ Learning Disability	___ Behavior Disorder	_____

Does participant walk independently? Yes ✔ No _____ If no, please identify any mobility devices used or assistance needed (wheelchair, walker, etc.)
_____

Does participant have seizures? Yes_____ No ✔ If yes, please indicate type_____
Date of most recent seizure _____

Medications taken: (type, time, dosage, purpose)_____ *None at this time* _____
_____

Allergies (include food/medications/other), activity restrictions, special diets or other medical concerns:_____
none _____

II. Skill Assessment
Please check each statement that applies to the participant. Please use the comment section to identify additional skills needed and/or areas of difficulty.

Eating/Drink
✔ Drinks from a cup
✔ Able to use straw to drink
✔ Able to grasp; use spoon
✔ Able to unwrap, open containers
✔ Able to open drink containers

Bathrooming (toileting, washing)
___ Wears diaper (Attends/Depends)
___ Indicates need to use toilet
___ Uses toilet with physical assistance
✔ Uses toilet independently
✔ Washes hands independently

Comments/Areas of difficulty: ___*may require verbal prompts, reminders*___

Cincinnati Recreation Commission
ASSESSMENT and ACCOMMODATION REQUEST

Communication (please check all that apply)

__ Unable to communicate needs/wants
☑ Communicates with gestures, signs or non-verbal behavior
__ Communicates using basic sign language

☑ Uses one or two word statements
__ Uses a communication device to communicate
__ Uses partial or complete spoken sentences

Comments/Areas of difficulty: _*is beginning to use picture/symbols (Boardmaker)*_
at school

Receptive Language (please check all that apply)

☑ Recognizes own name when called
☑ Reacts or responds when spoken to
☑ Responds appropriately to one-step directions

☑ Responds appropriately to two or three step directions
__ Responds appropriately to directions when in a small group
__ Responds appropriately to directions when in a larger group

Comments/Areas of difficulty: _*You need to get his attention before giving directions*_

Motor Coordination (please check all that apply)

☑ Able to catch a ball rolled
☑ Able to catch a ball bounced
☑ Able to catch a ball tossed from a short distance
☑ Able to kick a stationary ball

☑ Able to kick a rolling ball
☑ Able to grasp small objects (beads, pencil, etc.)
☑ Able to grip/grasp larger objects (tennis ball, racquet, etc.)

Comments/Areas of difficulty: _*Jack has very good motor skills*_

Social/Behavioral (please check all that apply)

☑ Shows interest in others _- sometimes_
__ Will play/interact cooperatively with others
☑ Is tolerant of others, not easily agitated or annoyed
__ Is aware of safety concerns when out in the community (traffic, staying with group, etc.)

☑ Will sit quietly to watch a program, show, movie, etc.- _sometimes_
__ Can identify and take responsibility for personal belongings
__ Will play/interact cooperatively within a group

Comments/Areas of difficulty: _*Jack will wander away from group*_

Does your child swim independently _____ yes _☑_ no

If no, please explain? _*Jack loves the water but does not swim independently and does*_
not recognize safety concerns.

Please identify any activities, games, hobbies, etc. the participant enjoys or has expressed interest in:

*Jack likes pictures- story books, toy cars, puzzles, legos.*

Please explain any behavior management techniques used at home or school which eliminate or reduce negative behaviors:

*Jack may pinch others if he becomes anxious or if someone is crowding him: hold*
*his hands firmly and say "no pinch." He understands "time out" but has little*
*concept of time. Brief time outs using a timer work best.*

Cincinnati Recreation Commission
ASSESSMENT and ACCOMMODATION REQUEST

<u>**(This portion of the Assessment & Accommodation needs to be completed if the participant is under 18 years of age.)**</u>

Does your child have an aide/ personal assistant at school? ✔Yes ○ No

If so, how much time is the aide/ personal assistant with your child? _His aide splits her time with two other children._

Please describe your child's classroom? ○ Special Ed ○ Inclusive ✔Both

Please be specific regarding the structure of the classroom environment _Jack spends most of the school day in regular classroom, goes to resource room for part._

How many students are in your child's classroom? ____

Approximately 15

Additional comments, suggestions: _Jack will occasionally become over-stimulated in the classroom and his aide will take him for a walk or to get a drink._

RELEASE OF INFORMATION

I, _Carol Smith_ (Parent/Guardian Care Provider) hereby give my permission for you to release the information requested below for my child. I understand this information will be used to plan appropriate activities for my child. Please initial all methods you give permission for release of information.

____ ✔ IEP Information

____ ✔ Completion of Teacher Questionnaire

____ ✔ Inclusion Specialist Observation

____ ✔ Teacher / Inclusion Specialist Phone Conversation

Signature of Parent/Guardian _Carol Smith_ Date _May 20, 2003_

MULTI — MEDIA RELEASE FORM

I, undersigned, hereby authorize the Cincinnati Recreation Commission to utilize (including but not limited to) photographs, videotapes, and/or voice recordings, etc. of the participant listed to be used exclusively for promotion, advertising, and/or marketing of the Cincinnati Recreation Commission and its programs, facilities, and/or services. The images may be repeatedly used at any time and I will not seek recourse or payment for the use of the aforementioned materials from the Cincinnati Recreation Commission.

Signature of Participant/Parent/ Guardian _Carol Smith_ Date _May 20, 2003_

Cincinnati Recreation Commission
ASSESSMENT and ACCOMMODATION REQUEST

Name *Jack Smith*   Program/ Yr. *day camp, 2003*

Part B RECOMMENDATIONS for ACCOMMODATION (to be completed by Inclusion Specialist)

Identify potential areas of concern relating to program activities, program environment, staffing, and/or participant abilities:

Jack will be dropped off at camp around 8:00am. Approximately forty children are in the gymnasium with no structured/group activities until 9:00am/9:15am. The children are divided in three groups. (continued next page)

Supports/accommodations recommended for successful participation. **Including:** activities, interventions, skill training, adaptations, management strategies and communication techniques (include aspects of the program that could benefit the inclusion process).

Current staff to participant ratio is approximately 1-12.

Due to the amount of low organized time and the length of each activity period, it is recommended that an additional staff member be hired for Jack's group. An inservice on autism for all staff is recommended. Would be beneficial to develop pictures/symbols specific to the day camp program.

I have reviewed the recommended support(s) / accommodation(s) and agree with the stated plan for inclusion.

Carol Smith	*June 9, 2003*	*Jane*
Participant/Parent/Guardian	Date	Inclusion Specialist

I have reviewed the recommended support(s) / accommodation(s) and would like to **request** the following revision(s) / addition(s) to the plan for inclusion:

I would like Jack to have one to one assistance in the pool and for all field trips (Mrs. Smith).

(continued from pg. 4)

Usually a physical activity, followed by a craft activity. Both of these activity periods go way too long! The group goes to the pool for swimming from 11:00am-12:15. This is a "free swim" format with no instruction planned. After swimming, the children dress and eat lunch (picnic tables near playground). Lunch leads into "playground time" which lasts until 1:30pm (largely unsupervised). Afternoon activities vary from day to day and can include sports, games, relays, watching videos, etc. These activity times are inconsistant and are subject to change. This program will also go on a field trip once per week, going to the zoo, water park, roller skating, etc. Jack will be picked up around 5:15pm each day.

Cincinnati Recreation Commission
C. PLAN FOR ACCOMMODATION

Participant Name: _Jack Smith_   Plan Date _June 2, 2003_

Program/Center _day camp,_

Day(s)/Time(s) of Program _Mon. - Fri., 8:00am to 6:00pm_

Center Staff Name(s) and Phone Numbers _____

I. Summarize accommodations needed for successful participation:

Additional staff member for group, training on autism, develop communication tool; one to one attention at pool, on field trips *Work with Jack on swim skills.

II.   Resources needed? How provided?

T.R. Division will hire staff (paid through center).
T.R. Division will conduct in-service on autism
T.R. Division will (with Mrs. Smith) develop communication.
(*T.R. Aquatic staff to develop lesson plan, oversee)

III.   Inclusion Specialist's role, frequency and schedule of on-site support

T.R. Inclusion Specialist will spend first day of camp with Jack, assisting center staff in becoming familiar with him, communications, behaviors, etc.

IV.   Center Staff's role/responsibilities relating to Inclusion Plan:

Center will pay salary of additional staff member.
All camp staff will attend autism in-service.
All staff will review Assessment/Accommodation document and become familiar with Jack, communications, etc.

V.   Evaluation/Recommendations (Summary of Inclusion Support Plan at the conclusion of the on-site support stage)

Jack had a very difficult first day, too many kids, too noisy, etc. Staff spent alot of time with him away from group. Jack shows little interest in camp activities (except swimming). Additional strategies needed to keep him with group.

_____
Jane
Inclusion Specialist

Cincinnati Recreation Commission.

Dear Teacher:

Your student, _____Jack Smith_____, is currently participating in a recreational program through the Cincinnati Recreation Commission. We would appreciate any information you can give us concerning the child s behavior and skills at school to more effectively meet his/her needs during the recreational program. Please check below all areas that apply to this child.

I. **Language Skills**

    1. Does the child communicate verbally?   o Yes   ✔ No

    2. Can the child speak and be understood?   o Yes   ✔ No

    3. Can the child follow simple verbal directions?   ✔ Yes   o No
        If yes, which ones? _minimal speech, uses gestures_____

    4. Does the child have a speech or hearing difficulty?   ✔ Yes   o No *(sometimes)*
        If yes, please exlpain._____

    5. Does the child have receptive language?   ✔ Yes   o No

II   **Social Skills**

    1. Does the child seem to enjoy interacting with peers?   ✔ Yes   o No

    2. How does the child socially interact with people? (i.e. smile, initiate contact, etc.)
        _interacts regularly with one of his classmates_____

    3. Does the child relate well with groups? o Yes ✔ No   To one or two children? ✔ Yes o No
        _Jack tends to avoid group situations_____

    4. What are a few of the child's favorite indoor activities? ___Jack likes picture books, will sit with someone reading to him._____

        Outdoor Activities? _Jack likes to explore the outdoor environment, not much interest in games._____

III. **Cognitive**

    1. Can the child sort? ✔ Yes   o No

    2. Can the child match? ✔ Yes   o No

    3. Does the child know colors? ✔ Yes   o No *(some)*

    4. Can the child sequence?   o Yes   ✔ No

    5. Can the child identify body parts? ✔ Yes   o No

    6. Does the child understand dangerous situations (i.e. crossing the street)?   o Yes   ✔ No
        only with frequent verbal reminders

IV. Behavior

1. Does the child exhibit any behavior problem? ✔ Yes o No
   If yes, please explain. *will pinch when agitated, excited*

3. What type of behavior management does the child respond to best?

   ✔ Positive Reinforcement   ✔ Time Out

   o Withdrawal of reinforcers   o Token system

   Please specify other special methods used *Can usually get Jack to attend to less favored tasks with short term rewards*

V. Motor Skills

1. Does the child require any Therapy?

   Physical o Yes ✔ No   Occupational o Yes ✔ No   Speech ✔ Yes o No

2. What specific skills are being developed? (i.e. walking, head control, etc.) *speech therapist working with basic word usage.*

3. What therapeutic equipment does the child use? *none*

4. Is the child tactilely defensive?   o Yes ✔ No

5. Can the child work puzzles?   ✔ Yes o No
   What other fine motor skills does the child have? *Jack can assemble models, lego kits, string beads, etc.*

6. Can the child walk independently?   ✔ Yes o No

VI. Self-Help Skills

1. Dressing

   ✔ Dresses independently
   o Dresses with assistance
   o Needs total assistance

   If assistance is needed with dressing, please explain. *Likes to take shoes off, but can put them back on himself.*

2. Eating

   ✔ Feeds self   ✔ Drinks from a cup   ✔ Chews

   ✔ Swallows   o Chokes   o Finger Feeds

   What special utensils are used in feeding? *none*

3. Toileting

✔ Bladder Control   ✔ Bowel Control

How does he/she indicate need for toileting? *points, grabs, says "potty"*

Is he/she on schedule for toileting? o Yes   ✔ No
If yes, please explain. _____

VII.   Medical Considerations

1. Is the child on medication during school hours? o Yes ✔ No

   Does it seem to interfere with his/her activities? o Yes o No
   If yes, please explain._____

Are there any other special skills, goals, or activities that you would like to see this child work on during the recreation program?

continue to encourage speech. Boardmaker is being used. but ask for speech as well. Remind him to eat his own lunch, not others.

Additional Comments

Jack benefits from a predictable routine and schedule. he had some difficulty early in the school year with transitions. moving to different rooms, etc. Would fuss, not stay in his chair.

Thank you very much for your time and effort to help us learn more about this child. The information will help us better serve him/her in our programs.

_____
Mrs. Thomas
Teacher Signature

_____
Phone Number for contact

Center:

Region:

Program:

Visit:

Date:

Cincinnati Recreation Commission
Inclusion Notes

Time Arrived: ___8:30am___ Participants Name: ___Jack Smith___

Observations/Contact: _____

Jack was dropped off during "open gym" time. Kids playing basketball, jump rope and tag game. The extra staff assigned to Jack's group (Jason) greeted Jack, attempted to get him into tag game. Jack showed interest for about 5 minutes. Eventually settled into corner with his toy cars. Attempted to leave gym twice. First structured activity was dodge ball game. Jack was quickly "put out," but did not understand he was supposed to stay out. Staff attempted to get him to sit and watch, but Jack left the gym and headed outside before being returned. When reseated, he pinched girl seated next to him.

What intervention/ suggestions were discussed with center staff? (ie: Inclusion Plan, Behavior Support Plan, pamphlets, or any information discussed)_____

During "open gym" time, would help if an activity within Jack's skill range or an adaptation could be identified.

Jack is focused on the pool and swimming. A picture schedule for the day would help clarify swim time.

Be conscious of "spacing" especially when frustrated.

If dodgeball played, need an activity option when "out."

Other Comments: _____

At this time, the primary behavioral issue is Jack's leaving the group/gym. He is very quick to sneak away. Need to determine the motivation for this behavior, possibly develop a behavioral support plan.

Time Left Center: ___10:30am___

Scheduled Next Visit: _____

☐ See back side

05/24/02

Jane

Inclusion Specialist Signature

Cincinnati Recreation Commission
Therapeutic Recreation

BEHAVIORAL OBSERVATION SHEET

Participant *Jack Smith*   Program/Location_____

Target Behavior(s) *Leaving group, facility*   Date *June 16, 2003*

A. Situational Variables: **Observations**

Is there any circumstance under which the   *when swimming, eating lunch*
behavior does NOT occur?

Is there any circumstance under which the
behavior ALWAYS occurs?   *open gym, morning activities*

Does it occur at certain times of the day?   *more often in the A.M.*

Does the behavior occur only with certain   *no*
people?

B. Operant Variables   **Observations**

Does the participant engage in the behavior   *no, he would like to go unnoticed*
to gain attention? Is it peers or staff?

Does the participant engage in the behavior   *yes*
to escape the activity?

Does the participant engage in the behavior *possibly, he seems to be trying to go somewhere*
out of boredom or lack of challenging
activities?

Does the behavior occur prior to or along   *when returned, may pinch*
with any other behavior?

Could the behavior be related to any
social or activity skill deficit?   *yes*

C. Physiological Variables

Observations

Could the behavior be signalling some
emotional problem?

no

Could the behavior be a side-effect
of medication (tired, headache, upset
stomach, etc.)?

no

Does the participant engage in the behavior
as a self-stimulation activity?

no

Could the behavior be related to
environmental factors (noise levels,
heat/humidity, lighting, over stimulation, etc.)?

yes, noise, activity level

D. Other Considerations

Observations

Is the behavior dangerous to self or others?

possibly to Jack

Does the behavior disrupt activities?

yes, takes staff away

Does the behavior cause the participant
to be socially excluded by peers?

yes

Recommendations: *Jack is very good at finding the right moment to "escape." This is a major concern due to the business in/around center and upcoming field trips. Environmental factors will be difficult to address (see support plan).*

(This information is used in developing the Behavioral Support Plan)

Staff member completing this document: *Jane*

Adapted from Bailey and Pyles, 1989 in L. K. Koegel, R. L. Koegel & G. Dunlap (Eds.), Positive Behavioral Support, (1996, p. 212). Baltimore, MD: Paul H. Brookes Publishing Co.

CINCINNATI RECREATION COMMISSION
DIVISION OF THERAPEUTIC RECREATION

BEHAVIORAL SUPPORT PLAN

PLAN DEVELOPMENT DATE *June 20, 2003*

Participant *Jack Smith* _____ Program/Location _____

1. Description of Behavior: Describe specifically the behavior(s) to be addressed. If more than one area of concern, prioritize according to severity or frequency.

   Leaving his group, leaving the building to go outside. _____

   _____

   _____

   _____

2. Documentation of previous incidents (list or attach, include date)

   _____

   _____

   _____

   _____

3. Antecedents. (observations/recommendations from the Behavioral Observation Sheet)

   _____

   _____

   _____

   _____

4. Based on staff observations and parent/guardian input, what could be the cause of the behavior? What (do we think) participant is communicating or gaining through this behavior? What outcomes may be maintaining this behavior? *In some instances, it appears Jack is over stimulated and wanting to remove himself from setting. Other times it appears Jack is looking for a more rewarding activity - swimming, playground, etc.*

5. Positive Reinforcement. What activities or items are considered rewarding to the participant? *Reading with staff member, puzzles and legos are sometimes effective, responds very well to his older brother.*

6. Strategies: Identify strategies which may be effective in reducing the negative behavior(s). Include pro-active strategies intended to prevent behavior(s) from occurring as well as consequences to apply following behavior(s). (These strategies should incorporate parent/guardian suggestions as well as school based plans if available).

   • Look into possibility of using smaller craft room near gym for some quiet activities during the open gym time.

   • Work with picture schedule, develop more "breaks" and shorter time blocks for Jack, allowing him to go outside on a schedule.

   • (Jason) Work with Jack to use his communication tool, (picture cards) to express what he wants, as opposed to running off. Reward him for communication (i.e. take him outside or to see his brother when he communicates his wants.)

7. Timeline. Suggested time frame to review and evaluate plan.

   Is the target behavior considered to be a direct threat (aggressiveness towards others, potentially harmful to self or others)?

   Yes ✔ No_____ *Jack is not fully aware of personal safety issues.*

   If yes, please indicate the degree of threat as follows (circle number):

1	2	3	4	5	6	7	8	9	10
some potential for slight injury (scratch, bruise)		moderate potential for slight injury		slight potential for more serious injury		moderate potential for more serious injury			high potential for serious injury

What will be the time frame used in determining the effectiveness of the accommodation (number of program meetings, number of weeks, etc.)

Recommend we implement these strategies for two weeks. Meet to evaluate progress on _____ .

What will be the measurement (number of incidents per session, severity of incident, etc.) used in determining the effectiveness of the accommodation (behavior support plan)?

Staff determination that behavior reduced/under control.

8. Progress Notes: (attach additional notes, incident reports, as needed)

_____

_____

_____

_____

_____

If accommodation(s) are effective in eliminating or reducing "direct threat" behavior, and accommodation(s) remain in place, future incidents will be addressed in accordance with the CRC behavioral guidelines.

Signature of Parent/Guardian	Date	Signature of Parent/Guardian	Date

Center: Visit:

Region: Date:

Program:

Cincinnati Recreation Commission
Inclusion Notes

Time Arrived: __8:30am__ Participants Name: _____ Jack Smith

Observations/Contact: __Jack was greeted by Jason (staff) upon arrival in the gym.__ Jason had set up a bowling game in the corner. Jack enjoyed rolling the ball and knocking down the pins (many times!) Several other participants took turns as well. Jack did not show much interest in the ring toss game, used rings to knock bowling pins over! First organized game was kickball on the ballfield next to pool. Jack pointed to pool at which point Jason showed him his picture schedule. Jack played with the dirt on the ballfield during most of the game. When it was Jack's turn to kick he stepped right up and kicked the ball very well. Everyone cheered and Jack appeared pleased with this reaction.

What intervention/ suggestions were discussed with center staff? (ie: Inclusion Plan, Behavior Support Plan, pamphlets, or any information discussed) Jack showed marked improvement today, staying with the group, not overly fixated with pool. The picture schedule and daily routine has helped. Jason has learned Jack's tolerance levels and knows when he needs a break. I suggested shorter "break" times for Jack as the program progresses.

Other Comments: _Jack's participation in group activities remains limited, however, staff_ have learned to work him into games when opportunity develops. Jason has a ready supply of alternative activities which appear to interest Jack. Jack is starting to show some interest in other participants.

Time Left Center: ____10:00am____   Scheduled Next Visit: _____

                                                             ☐   See back side

                                                           Jane

05/24/02   Inclusion Specialist Signature

INDEX